Revisiting the Idea of Vocation

Revisiting the Idea of Vocation

Theological Explorations

edited by John C. Haughey, S.J.

The Catholic University of America Press

Washington, D.C.

The paper used in this publication meets the minimum requirements of American National Standards for Information Science—Permanence of Paper for Printed Library materials, ANSI z39.48-1984.

∞

Library of Congress Cataloging-in-Publication Data

Revisiting the idea of vocation: theological explorations / edited by John C. Haughey.—1st edition

    p. cm.

    Includes bibliographical references and index.

    ISBN 0-8132-1361-4 (pbk.: alk. Paper)

    1. Vocation, Ecclesiastical. 2. Vocation—Catholic Church.

I. Haughey, John C.   II. Title.

BX2380.R48 2003

248.8'0—dc21

2003007838

Contents

Acknowledgments

Books don't write themselves. The people who wrote this book were innocent when they started with me and guilty of excess by the time they had finished. The excess was of generosity, good will, and fidelity. Those who have been guilty were my colleagues at Loyola University Chicago, most of them members of the theology department that I have been happily part of these last twelve years. Three of our team were from other parts of Loyola, two from the Institute of Pastoral Services and one from the Jesuit First Studies Program. If these authors had not spent hours on their own working on the materials presented in these chapters, and then hours gathered together discussing each other's insights and checking each other's contributions, this volume would have been just a hodgepodge of juxtaposed pieces. The reason it is so much more coherent than that is the care each took hearing the others' efforts to name, insofar as that is possible, the mystery of personal callings. I believe the reader will see the learning that has gone into the chapters and the added sensitivity to the subject matter that is the result of our learning from one another.

But writing, of course, is just the beginning of the work, maybe the easiest part of it. The generosity, good will, and fidelity of the authors were replicated in the persons of Lourdes Morales and Barbara Hughett. Lourdes is "Miss Efficiency" here at Loyola in her running of the EVOKE office. (I will explain that acronym and office in a minute.) Barbara is an author and Lincoln scholar who in a moment of insanity agreed to do the copyediting or proofing of every inch of this work. To both of them we, the authors, are deeply indebted.

The idea for the book was inevitable because of the Lilly Endowment grant that Loyola University received in 1999. The endowment had entitled its initiative "Programs for the Theological Exploration of Vocation." I was the point man here at Loyola for creating the proposal that ended up being awarded the grant. It was obvious that the faculty would have to take ownership of the importance of the subject of calling, hence the invitation to our theologians to join me in this undertaking.

But, being an impractical sort, I immediately handed the whole responsibility for the implementation and management of the university's vocations project over to Lucien Roy. Lucien, who does everything well, and his team dreamed up a creative name for the program: EVOKE, i.e., Eliciting Vocation through Knowledge and Engagement. Without his continuing interest and encouragement, this publication would still be in manuscript form.

John C. Haughey, S.J.

Introduction

This volume is a collection of ten essays composed by theologians from Loyola University Chicago, members either of its theology department's graduate faculty or of the Institute of Pastoral Studies, with one happy exception, which I will mention shortly. The faculty members' contributions have been determined by their own areas of expertise or academic interest. They have taken seriously and critically the idea of call in their respective essays, primarily to stimulate faculty in other disciplines to reflect on their understanding of themselves as called (if that is how they experience their work in academe) or of the relationship of their own field of study to the idea of call.

Intentionally, definition of call was not determined ahead of time by the contributors to this volume. This left the authors free to determine what they meant by the term and how they were going to address the subject. As editor of this volume, I am the one responsible for this intentional indeterminacy about call since I judge it to be initially in the category of a notion before it arrives at the many contents it is able to attain. I take a notion to be something immanent in us that is prior to the conception we eventually develop of it. It doesn't do justice to it to freeze it in one or two concepts. In that sense I take call to be a heuristic notion, which can lure one into ever greater depths, rather than something one arrives at and lives happily ever after in possession of. Calls lie less in the area of knowledge and are more a matter intending a "more" that moves one in the direction of the self-transcending necessary to "go there." One conviction common to all of the authors of this volume is that every human is *capax Dei*, scripted with a capacity for nothing short of God. How one understands God and acts on that capacity is how one answers his or her call.

I was the person at Loyola University designated to respond to a generous offer from the Lilly Endowment, Inc. to "encourage young people to consider questions of faith and commitment when they choose their careers." In our grant proposal to Lilly, we said that we see students, faculty, staff, and administrators as "already responding to our respective calls by seeking to grow in knowledge and that knowledge is pursued within a faith horizon with a view toward living our lives for others." We went on to describe the fruitful tensions that this notion of call contains. "Vocations are a way of being and a particular mode of doing for and serving others; they are found and evolve in the combination of practice and practice reflected on; they are a way of coming to self-fulfillment while transcending the self that would be fulfilled; they are invited, yet one is responsible for discovering the invitation by probing one's deeper desires; they are utterly personal and discovered in the depth of one's interiority, but are socially confirmed." We completed this description by saying that "they are from God but need the people who are given them to say 'amen'; they are a commitment to a way of being for others, but external circumstances change the way that commitment evolves."

We appreciated the stimulus Lilly provided us for thinking about our university in terms of the calls of all of us who teach, work, study, and serve here. The more we thought about it, the more we realized that we were not importing something alien into our culture but teasing out something that has been intrinsic to the purposes of Loyola from the beginning. When one drives onto the campus today, one sees pole banners that read "Faith, Knowledge and Service." Faith is, of course, a call to live a life of religious commitment; knowledge is a call to emerge from the darkness of ignorance; and service is a call to define oneself in terms of meeting others' needs. Vocation is a welcome *superadditum* that combines these three things together and traces them to a Caller.

The authors of this volume bring rich backgrounds to the idea of vocation, and their essays prove the value of allowing call to be a notion. I should say also that, being good faculty members, they are not concerned to promote the idea of vocation but to examine it critically. Without denying that one's call might be to a "state of life" such as priesthood, or religious life or marriage or consecrated lay life, the essays verge far beyond these earlier confines.

In my opening essay, I have chosen to see call in terms of conversion and conversion as threefold, as that concept is understood by Bernard Lonergan, a twentieth-century Jesuit philosopher. Whatever one's particular call, we are all called to make responsible judgments about "what is so" and to act in light of those judgments. While we also have to make judgments about the accounts of the true and the good we have received from others, and therefore are in a dialectical relation to these traditions, we are not in a *tabula rasa* condition of being wholly self-determining in the matter of beliefs or moral norms. Hence conversion to community is part of the call in this essay. Finally, there is religious conversion, wherein one judges and makes one's choices and takes one's actions from within a condition of love that has God as its author.

The chapter by Camilla Burns, who since writing this piece has become Superior General of the Sisters of Notre Dame de Namur, takes call as primally and foundationally as possible. To be is to be called by the word of God into being, she asserts. She reflects on the implications of this "summons into being," which is peculiar to humans, and on their consequent, subsequent responsibilities. Her texts are all taken from the Hebrew Scriptures, a tradition all three major Western faiths have in common.

One of the values of call as notion rather than concept is that it excludes few if any from taking account of themselves as in some manner called. Here at Loyola we speak of ourselves as "a home of the faiths." This is not just a catchy slogan but a firm commitment shown in our hiring process. Two non-Christian scholars, therefore, enrich our volume with their reflections. Edward Breuer's essay takes the view of an Orthodox Jew to the idea of call *sans* the layers that generations of Christians tend to assign to it. Breuer, who teaches Jewish Studies in Loyola's department of theology, does not see an immediate correlate between the Christian notion of call and his understanding of his faith. But his essay allows that there have been "countless Judaisms"; and the more they have been affected by Western civilization, the less alien the notion of call has become to them.

Urban von Wahlde, a professor of the New Testament at Loyola, refreshes us with a picture of call as the Gospel of John unfolds Jesus' understanding of his own call. The author sees those who would follow Jesus as being confronted by the reality of Jesus, his claims, and his vocation. Each has to make a decision about him and therefore about themselves, given the Christology of this unique gospel portrait. If they affirm that Jesus is who he claims to be, a purchase is made on their own lives—meaning they are called into a relationship with him that will change everything about their self-understanding and their *raison d'être* in life. Marcia Hermansen, a Muslim and scholar of that faith, also marks the distance between the Christian idea of call and the texts of the Qur'an. But she also bridges some of this distance by examining the Sunna tradition of the prophet Muhammad and Islamic philosophy and mysticism, as well as some contemporary Muslim scholars on the subject.

I mentioned above that we have one happy exception to the rest of the authors. Paul Harman, a Jesuit priest here at Loyola, was recommended by a number of our team to cover the question of how vocation surfaces in the course of the spiritual exercises of Ignatius Loyola. He has been the guide for the Jesuit scholastics here on campus, who number forty at present, through the two- or three-year period of their post-novitiate formation. While attending to that duty, he has impressed many of us with his knowledge of Ignatius and his wisdom in leading the younger Jesuits into depths that have enriched all of us. His essay is on Ignatius's insights into the eliciting of call, as these are found in the Spiritual Exercises.

An intriguing insight into vocation is developed by Mark McIntosh, an Episcopal priest and associate professor of theology at Loyola, in his analysis of John Bunyan's *Pilgrim's Progress*. This Puritan allegory is a seventeenth-century classic that addresses in very specific ways the journey each one is called to take to avoid the imprisoning illusions to which flesh is commonly heir on the way to salvation. Here we have a great assist in understanding the features common to each person's vocation, coming at a moment in history when individuation was not as variegated as it is in modern and postmodern cultures.

Daniel Williams, who has moved on from Loyola to be professor of patristic and historical theology at Baylor University, uncovers an important piece of information that explains a strange lacuna in contemporary culture. The idea of a providential calling once fueled Protestant Christianity. It led to the founding of institutions of higher learning whose sense of call guided their desire to reform the social order through individuals formed for that task. What happened to this ubiquitous conviction? Williams uncovers the strong biases against tradition that gradually eroded the sense of calling and eventually made the values of these institutions indistinguishable from the general American culture, thereby de-legitimizing the idea of both institutional vocation and personal vocation as a result. This enlightening history is also a warning to Catholic institutions of higher learning that many of the biases that diluted their Protestant counterparts in an earlier age are resurfacing in the academic circles of Catholic institutions.

John Neafsey, whose training is in theology and whose credentials also enable him to function primarily as a psychologist, introduces ideas about the true and false self via psychoanalytic object-relations theory, as well as through Jungian insights into individuation, which require one to distinguish between the ego and the deeper self. As will be obvious, he is not unaware of the Rogers/Maslow understandings of self-actualization and the existential psychology tradition, which address the issue of an authentic inner truth. These psychological understandings are then discerned by introducing ideas from Ignatius Loyola and his understanding of how one goes about discerning call.

Mary Elsbernd, director of the Institute of Pastoral Studies at Loyola, started from the other end, so to speak—not from ideas but from the written personal statements of one hundred students who applied and were accepted in the Masters of Divinity program at the Institute. She classified the many ways in which these students saw themselves as called to a life the program would train them for. This gave her an empirical base from which to study their experiences of being called. She noticed the ways in which they tended to fumble with words to express the mysterious character of call, without shedding doubt on its reality. From her theological reflection on the responses of these students, she makes some explicit suggestions about how educators might educate in ways that abet and enhance the individual's sense of call.

John C. Haughey, S.J.

⟫ John C. Haughey, S.J.

The Three Conversions Embedded in Personal Calling

The more I looked at this idea of call, of being called, of
having a call, the more obscurities began to develop in my mind. I
decided to look at it under a different lens than has been previously
used to understand it. That lens is the notion of conversion. Not
conversion from no faith to faith or from one faith to another. The
conversion I have in mind is threefold. It is a conversion, first, from
the biases one brings to interpreting reality to accurately hearing the
ever-unfolding call that reality itself emits. Following Bernard Lonergan, I will call this an intellectual conversion. The second conversion is to hearing the call to live meaningfully, as this is construed
through the meaning-making communities of which one is a part.
In a derived way, Bernard Lonergan would refer to this as moral
conversion. The third conversion is from living a good life to living
a life that abides in love. With some further specification of my
own, I will refer to this as affective conversion—again inspired by
Lonergan.[1] Some of the obscurity about personal calling, I believe,
can be overcome by these three compenetrating conversions.

1. These three understandings of conversion come from his *Method in Theology*
(Herder and Herder, 1972).

I

All three conversions produce a condition of ongoing self-transcendence: the first to reality, the second to a tradition of meaning, the third to love and to the unique way one is to express it, which I will term charism. As I hope to explain in more detail, the first, ongoing call to which all human beings are invited is extended to them from no less a caller than reality itself. To hear it is to undergo a continual conversion out of a self-enclosed immanence. Intellectual conversion invites one to deepen one's grasp of the way things are, while refraining from imposing on reality what we would like it to be. Moral conversion, the focus of the second section of this essay, is a call to move away from self-satisfying, ignorant choices and self-interested perception of the good to authentic values and meaningful choices. Affective conversion, the focus of the third section, calls one to live a life of love for God and neighbor in the particular way in which the individual is called to love. These three conversions fold into one another, each pushing the others for completion.

I. Conversion to Reality

Of the three, intellectual conversion is the most universal way of awakening to call. But it is also the most crucial. Lonergan's profound analysis of how our minds work might be clarified somewhat if we were to unpack four of his preferred terms: intentionality, objectivity, meaning, and rational self-consciousness. About *intentionality:* he saw the human being as driven to self-transcendence by the desire to know everything. This insatiable eros to know manifests itself in a voracious seeking of answers to questions. In the process of arriving at answers, one transcends one's subjectivity and attains to the real to the extent that the process isn't diverted by prejudgments or self-interested feelings. About *objectivity:* he didn't see it as something that was over against the subject's subjectivity, but as attained by subjects being attentive to objects and allowing them to speak for themselves, so to speak. The dichotomy between objectivity and subjectivity is easily misconstrued. Lonergan makes a good case for seeing authentic subjectivity as able to attain to objectivity.

About *meaning:* it is arrived at by judgments about the truth or the lack of truth in one's intuitions, insights, and understandings, as these are derived from experience, and from our *prima facie* look at the data of sense and consciousness. And, finally, about *rational self-consciousness:* this refers to when we leap from what we have judged to be what is, what the reality is, what is true, to the decision to act on it as good. When the true is judged to be good, good for me/us, and therefore the right thing to do, we are in a volitional level of consciousness, which enables us to deliberate and choose who it is we will become.

Lonergan's ideas drive us all the way back to the primordial Aristotelian questions that humans have always asked and answered for themselves about concrete reality as it impinges on them. Their questions are: What is it? Is it so? Is it of value? Is it of value to me or us? Do I choose to act on this or that judgment of value? These seem to be the ever-present questions that face us as we continue on in the process of making ourselves into who we are in answer to the call being extended to us from reality in all its concreteness. Lonergan would describe this whole process, if done reflectively, as a conversion to authenticity. We are inauthentic insofar as we are inattentive to the data our senses can supply and the data of our conscious processes. We are also inauthentic if the process of apprehending the intelligible is sloppy, rushed, or lazy. Likewise, we can be inauthentic at the point of judgment about the apprehensions our reason proposes to us. And finally, we can be inauthentic if we choose other than what we know to be true and, therefore, good for us to be or do. In brief, we are obeying reality if we are attentive, intelligent, reasonable, and responsible. We are not if we come down on the opposite side of these "precepts."

Lonergan's analysis of intellectual conversion is a very useful foundation for discerning call. The unceasing and most universal level of call is to be authentic by living in reality, by judging what is and being responsive to it, by judging what is not real and naming it as such. This call comes into our consciousness through our senses and understandings. It is a call to live in reality and to make our choices accordingly. The student who cannot pass college biology courses has to deal with the reality that he is not called to be a doctor. Intellectual conversion is not a matter of IQ but of refusing to act from fantasies or fears, biases or ideologies, or any other merely subjective state. Intellectual conversion is a conversion to knowledge. As Lonergan pithily puts it: "Knowledge, in the proper sense, is knowledge of reality; knowledge is intrinsically objective; knowledge is the intrinsic relation of knowing to being; being and reality are identical."[2]

Since Lonergan's spirituality was Ignatian, he sought to find God in all things. But he wanted to make sure that the things were really there in the first place. Lonergan's epistemology, therefore, is technically that of a critical realist. The critical part comes from the intending subject, and the realism part comes from the inbreaking object. Critical realism is the mean between two extremes. Naïve realism, the one extreme, is too obeisant to and uncritical about the object. And the other extreme consists of all the forms of idealism, in the philosophical sense of that term, that settled on knowing reality through alleged categories immanent in the subject. These fail to do justice to the object as it is in itself and wherein God can be found to be actively present.

II. Conversion to Meaning

So far, I have said that people are being true to their calls by seeking to know the truth in the myriad daily little and big ways it continually addresses them. The second way to understand call is as a conversion to the ever-unfolding good, to the ways of being and doing that are seen as the right and valuable way of choosing to be. Moral conversion is the movement of the subject from impulsive, self-regarding acts to the choice of values that are self-transcending. Like intellectual conversion, moral conversion is moving toward authenticity—but now the emphasis is on the good and a life constituted by meaning.

2. Mark Morelli, ed., *Collected Works of B. Lonergan,* 4:211.

But where does this knowledge of meaning and the good come from? We don't make knowledge of what is good out of whole cloth. It would seem that it comes from the experiences of the self in the several communities within which we operate. Accounts of the good and of meaning are socially received. We are not open to all possibilities but only to those valorized by our norming communities. We learn from others whom we take to be trustworthy about what counts as good and what to value in our life and career choices. These norming communities, in turn, convey their particular versions of the good by what their members value or by the narratives they tell and seek to embody. These models and their choices shape the horizon of meaning in those who identify with them. Trusted figures who embody traditions convey a sense of the meaningful, of what is a meaningful way to live and what would be a meaningful purpose for which to give one's life. The possibilities to be sorted out about personal call come from such figures and, in turn, from the meaning-making communities of which they are members.

A call would have to include a conversion of one's moral conduct from living to meet one's own wants to living with a larger agenda. Of course, it would be superficial and hardly merit the description of a conversion if it simply left the judgment about right acts to an inherited moral code or a career choice to a tradition, neither of which one has made one's own. This misunderstanding of a conversion would invite one into a psychological condition of heteronomy.

The genesis of a personal call frequently comes from a religious faith's account of what would constitute a purposeful life, as that faith tradition understands it. These understandings are conveyed horizontally before they are explained vertically. So, whether we are talking about the good as moral conduct or as a valuable life commitment, one must make one's own what has been socially mediated. One's choices must be one's own to be moral. Being influenced by a respected tradition is not the same as being determined by it, as if from without. That would be tantamount to a conversion to a fundamentalism whereby one hands over the role of judgment to an authority extrinsic to oneself. We make ourselves who we are by internalized judgments of fact and judgments of value for which we are beholden to others. What we inherit as social beings must be appropriated by our own interiority.

⌐⊃

A moral or religious tradition is always incomplete. It is a never-finished argument between the members of the community who have been shaped by its past renderings about meaning and values and the shape of the good. Members' life choices are made in the light of these and, at the same time, these choices take sides about the ongoing arguments that these accounts of meaning, value, and the good foment.

III. Affective Conversion

An affective conversion is a conversion to love. It affects and heightens the energy that goes into all of one's choices. Before elaborating further on this kind of conversion I want to mention friendship, since that phenomenon has its foot in both the already described moral conversion and in the affective one I will develop in this section. Friendships are the smallest norming communities we freely enter into. A freely chosen friendship is entered into because the friend is valued, at least initially. To enter into a friendship is to enter a world of values, which may or may not confirm and reinforce my own. Friendships, therefore, confirm, enlarge, or challenge one's version of the good. They can also entail diversion from my deepest values and moral norms. Friendship is the stuff of both moral and affective conversion.

Most comments on friendship are mere footnotes on the ideas Plato and Aristotle had about the subject twenty-five centuries ago. Plato's experience was that he heard a call to wisdom and beauty coming through the relationships he had with his friends. His friends sound at times like they were being made means to the end of his contemplating the archetypal ideas of the eternal realm. For

Aristotle, true friendship was a way of coming to know the good in greater depth and committing to it. Through good friends one is called to a deeper grasp of the good, which is always moving us into a greater degree of self-transcendence. That happens because we learn to desire their good for their sakes rather than our own. In other words, a true friendship is a call to authenticity that assists one in the self-transcending that a conversion requires. An inauthentic "friendship," by contrast, will be an occasion for deepening one's confusion about the good, the valuable, and the meaningful.

An affective conversion is multilayered. It is always catalyzed by love, but at its zenith point it becomes a love that is initiated by God for God. This experience of God loving one admits of many degrees. It is seldom a sudden experience and it is one that usually ebbs and flows. The measure of the depth of this level of conversion is whether one abides in love and whether one's choices express that love. St. Paul names the Spirit as the source of this conversion. "The love of God has been poured out into our hearts through the Holy Spirit" (Rom. 5:5). This Spirit gift, for Catholic Christians, is experienced as the completion or flowering of what began in them at their sacramental baptism with the conferral on them of the theological virtue of *caritas*. The experience of abiding in God's love completes all that goes on in intellectual and moral conversion, and in fact may come before either of them.

Lonergan includes a whole range of loves under this rubric of affective/religious, self-transcending conversion. There is the self-transcendence of true friendship, the love of one's spouse, one's child, one's family, church, community, nation, God. Love is indivisible! "Where love is, God is, for God is love" (1 John 4:8). Therefore, there are many levels to abiding in love that, if it is love, all have their source in God, without those experiencing their love as necessarily coming from God or as love of God. Abiding in God's love is the fullness of affective conversion. With human loves there is almost always an unevenness, with enough self-regard admixed with other-regarding until the relationship matures into real love or backslides into all the other forms of relating that fall short of love.

There is more mystery than clarity about this outpouring of the spirit of love in the heart of a person that ultimately is the best explanation of an affective conversion. Some of the questions that beg for light are: Why has *caritas* flowered into an abiding love in this one rather than that one? When does this occur? Under what conditions does this happen? If it happens, how is it experienced? What are the effects? Are there degrees of it? What does it have to do with call, with being called? What does personal vocation have to do with this outpoured love that is religious conversion? I know that most of us do not know very much about these questions, so I will expound on the little I know.

I believe that considerable insight into these questions can be gained by having recourse to a singular event in the New Testament. That event is Pentecost, the descent of the Spirit of Christ on Jesus' followers fifty days after his resurrection from the dead. This event is the opening curtain on the character and consequence of the Holy Spirit's outpouring of love into humans' hearts.

The Pentecost event, as it is described in Acts 2:1–12, is a Spirit theophany that can reveal many of the dimensions of the affective conversion, which is always a call to love. When the spirit of love was outpoured into hearts, what did the recipients do? They ceased being over against one another and became one body, one in the Spirit of Christ. "Tongues as of fire" first came to rest on each of them, but then apparently disappeared into their hearts, which burned with love. Immediately this love translated into deeds—the deeds of words. They were no sooner loved than they were missioned, on mission. Their mission was to make God's love, which had made them one, known to others who were puzzled about what their experience meant. The call of each of these followers of Jesus was simply to love. The energy of the Spirit they received enabled them to love. The commandment Jesus left them with (i.e., to love one another) is now their collective and individual vocation. Their vocation is to walk in the way of the Lord, in the light of the Spirit, with a love for one another. They understood this vocation as coming from Christ who had loved them to his death and would now love them to the end with the gift of his Spirit.

The text is vividly eloquent about how immediately missionary this energy of love is. The disciples are on mission from the start. This mission takes the form of each "making bold proclamation as the Spirit prompted them" (Acts 2:6). What is unique to this essay is the contention that it was with the charisms that their mission of love was to be enacted. Here, the Spirit conferred on the disciples charisms of speech that enabled each language group in Jerusalem at the time to hear and understand as its own language. The charisms of tongues and bold speech bore such eloquent witness to God in their midst that, as the story goes, "some 3,000 were added their number that day" (Acts 2:41). Luke's account testifies both to the outpouring of the Spirit and to its distinctiveness in each of those receiving it.

The purpose of the charisms (to make manifest the love of God to those who have ears to hear and eyes to see) has not differed from that day to this, although the Church's understanding of its mission has become more universal and worldly than it was on the initial evangelization of Pentecost. By worldly, I mean the Church now understands her mission as assisting all "to uncover, cherish and ennoble all that is true, good, and beautiful in the human community" (#76 *Gaudium et Spes*).

IV. Charism

We need to look more deeply into this matter of charisms, since I want to claim that they are key to one's understanding his or her personal call. One of the more clarifying texts about the particular forms these charisms take is 1 Cor. 12:4–6: "There are different *gifts* but the same Spirit; there are different *ministries* but the same Lord; there are different *works* but the same God who accomplishes all of them in everyone." I would prefer to characterize these different gifts, ministries, works *(charismata, diakoniai, energemata)* with one term rather than three. But which one? Each one enlightens the other two. Charisms are ministries as well as works. Works require charisms to make them ministry. Ministry is a work done with the assistance of a charism. Their slightly different connotations notwithstanding, I prefer to use charism to gather the three because it is explicit about its origin in the same charism, or favor of God, as its originating source. Further, the purpose of these differently termed conferrals is the same, namely, to make evident to communities of believers and to society at large God's reaching out and favoring them in love through the members of the Body of his Son: "To each person a [distinct] manifestation of the Spirit is given for the common good" (1 Cor. 12:7). So each of these gifts is God's way of ministering to the vast variety of human needs through those who are being charismed or gifted. (I will use the terms *gifts* and *charisms* interchangeably in the rest of this piece.) These gifts/charisms are as distinctive as each person is and they are given to the individual so that each can be "a manifestation of the Spirit" in two worlds, that of the church and that of society. Each charismed or gifted-by-the-Spirit person is a favor of God to the world; each adds a distinctively new note to the symphony of God's love that all are meant to hear in the course of their lives on earth. "In exercising spiritual gifts we are involved in the restoration (the bringing together again) of God's perfect work of creation. An activity can only be characterized as a spiritual gift when it assists in the restoration of creation and contributes towards the healing of a sick world."[3]

Religious conversion that is initiated by God is both a call to love and an empowerment to abide in love. For most contemporary Christian denominations, while this outpouring is associated with the individual's baptism, it is often not experienced at that time. Love is shown by one's actions, so the evidence of the conversion will be in the love shown by deeds of a given individual. Generically, love is shown by the many qualities spelled out by Paul in his first letter to the Corinthians: "Love is patient; love is kind; love does

3. Arnold Bittlinger, *Gifts and Graces* (Grand Rapids: Eerdmans, 1967), 25.

not put on airs . . ." (1 Cor. 13:4ff). But specifically, the call to love is shown by the deeds done from the particular matrix of gifts/charisms that individuals receive. In Paul's experience these charisms were as varied as the members of the Body; nonetheless it is "one and the same Spirit who produces all these gifts, distributing to each of them as he wills" (1 Cor. 12:11). Paul lists a number of charisms in his letters: Rom. 12:5–8; 1 Cor. 12:8–10 and 14:26; Eph. 4:11. But these lists are not uniform, nor should they be read as exhaustive. They are merely suggestive of the distinct ways he found God ministering to people through the distinctive charisms of those in the earliest Christian communities.

Interestingly, the term charism itself appears infrequently in the New Testament. The study of charism, however, should not be confined to a word hunt—i.e., to a hunt for the term charism, since it is never used in the Gospels. Even Paul, its main witness, only used it when he wanted to correct an abuse. These are several of the reasons why the word is rarely used in the ordinary circles of contemporary mainline churchgoers. Most Christians would not speak of themselves as having a charism. The infrequency of the use of the term and all that is implied by it is, I believe, the main reason why the idea of ministry in the churches has unnecessarily been reserved to what is done by professional ministers.

What is needed is a reawakening to the rich variety of ways in which God chooses to grace human beings through human beings. Where God's *charis* (favor) is, there *charisms* will be! Catholic theology has traditionally distinguished charisms from graces, charisms being understood to mean for the good of the community within which the charismed person operates. "Graces," by contrast, were to heighten the recipients' own way of being made pleasing to God. Technically, the former (bestowed because of God's gratuitous love for "the world") were *gratiae gratis datae* and the latter (because of God's personal love for the person) were *gratiae gratum faciens.*

So it is not the word charism that uncovers this central concept. Rather, it is the realization that where the *charis* of God is *received,* there the *charismata* should be in evidence. So many New Testament metaphors carry this simple connection. The parables teem with it. Think of the parable of the sown seeds and their thirty-, sixty-, and hundred-fold productivity. For whom was the abundance intended? Think of the talents and the yield expected from those who have been given them in order to produce an increment. For whom? Think, further, of the vine and the passion of the vine dresser for the branches to produce fruit that will last. Then there is the one commandment, underscored by Jesus at the Last Supper, that was to guide his followers: Love one another. Generic descriptors for the ways in which love should be shown cannot do justice to or exhaust its character. Jesus' commandment was not and is not meant to have a uniform, undifferentiated effect. The gift of the Spirit is given so that each recipient will be a distinct and unique manifestation of the presence of God's caring in the human order. Neither a theology of charism nor one of ministry will be satisfactorily articulated in the Church as long as theologians and church leaders bypass this particular category, the unpacking of which would clarify both theologies.

⚯

A further observation about charisms is appropriate here. They make their recipients original. But their originality is seldom if ever reducible to a single type of action. A charismed person, it would seem, is rather a matrix of gifts, with virtues mixed with graces, with character traits, with genes, with talents—all sublated by the Spirit, which bundles these together into a giftedness that is *sui generis.* And observation would have me conclude that suffering has to be thrown into what makes the mix unique, since it is so often this experience that helps to produce such original qualities in people. The concept of sublation needs to be unpacked for this paragraph to be clear. It refers to carrying something upward to a whole new level of significance and value without eradicating the reality of that which has been carried upward. In the Eucharist, for example, bread and wine are sublated by God into the body and blood of Christ without their ceasing to be bread and wine. Thus a natural talent and all that has gone into the natural nurturing of that talent can be sublated by the Spirit into a charism of the Spirit without what was natural being lost with the sublation. Although the sublating is enacted by the Spirit, the cooperation of faith, hope, and love in the one whose talent is being sublated is indispensable for "the natural" to become a charism of the Spirit. I suppose charisms can develop independently of human cooperation, but that condition would be the undesirable exception rather than the rule.

One thing that has been misleading in this matter of charisms is that in the few explicit texts we have, they usually refer to a charism as enabling a particular act, like healing, or as giving the carrier a particular role, like prophet. Just as we should not confine the idea of charism to a word, neither should we confine it to a specific act or role. Just as a charism is a matrix of sublated gifts or energies, so the manifestations of Spirit that we experience are more the people themselves than a particular action of theirs—but either way, one can be led to see God as the explanation of their originality. It seems that the matrix of sublated giftedness, if received and nurtured after the manner of the talents or the seeds or the yeast as the Gospels speak of them, makes the whole person into a gift for those who interact with him or her. They are an upbuilding gift to the community and its "common good" (1 Cor. 12:7).

I want to comment here about this matter of naming a person's charism. I personally am uncertain about naming my own sense of being charismed with any one term. And when I ask others whom I have experienced as charismed, they too are unsure what name they would give to their particular giftedness. Conclusion: a single descriptor is not essential to the validity of this doctrine. What is essential is that over time a particular spiritual efficacy develops through a life of union with God and a growing realization that one has been dependent on God for his or her giftedness. The branch, to use one of the images in John's Gospel, is not exhorted to focus on and name the specific kind of fruit it is to produce. Rather, "abide in me and I in you" (John 15:4) is the exhortation. It is from its union with the vine that the life and fruit of the branch come. It is as if the character of the charism will take care of itself if the branch concerns itself with being one with the vine and with the *wholly unmerited favor* that has had the branch joined to it. I think of the way the author of the Gospel of John, whose charism was that of evangelist, names himself, not by his charism as evangelist, but as "the disciple whom Jesus loved."

A charism, in brief, is a constitutive part of one's call. It is the specific way one concerns oneself with another's or the community's good. It is the specific way one loves others. For those who have eyes to see, God or the Spirit will be considered the explanation for the distinctiveness that results. For those who don't, they and the community still benefit from the charism. Though the training of persons for professions or careers will probably be the same for charismed and non-charismed alike, in the execution of their similar duties the charismed will contribute something original, as suggested by the explanation of the relationship of the natural to the sublated. This originality can raise the minds and hearts of those who benefit from the charism's exercise to God if they sense that its origin cannot be humanly accounted for. The originality, of course, may be left without such an explanation but it is not likely to go unnoticed.

V. The Charisms Historically

There is an early history of enthusiasm about charisms, which was then followed by a virtual silence that descended upon them that suggested to many their virtual disappearance. I will not elaborate on this early history here, since I have done that elsewhere.[4] The effect of this history of initial ebullience followed by suspicion and silence was a general lack of expectation that has continued to the present time, even in those who consider themselves devoted followers of Christ. One of the cultural consequences of this complex history has been a theologically unwarranted centering of ministry in the clergy and hierarchy of the church and, consequently, a

4. Doris Donnelly, *Charisms: An Ecclesiological Exploration: Retrieving the Charisms for the 21st Century* (Collegeville, Minn.: Liturgical Press, 1999), chap. 1.

widespread passivity in the laity. Another consequence—especially since the twentieth century—has been a professionalization of the many specialized forms of service in the world of work that have tended to leave God out of the picture. For a secularized mind, sublation by the Spirit of the giftedness one brings to the workplace makes no sense.

Over the centuries, charism talk and therefore charism expectation have been infrequent. We have already commented that a major reason for this is that exegetical reasoning seems not to have noticed the many ways that God is described as working to minister to the needs of the human race, which I believe can be aptly summed up in charism terms. But another reason for the infrequency of their expectation is the Church's practice of canonization. In failing to see charisms as ubiquitous, the church has preferred to see a few as the *virtuosi* who have made the Spirit manifest for the common good of the church and society. The saints canonized by the church (or acclaimed as saints by the faithful) have been Catholic Christianity's preferred way of seeing God's faithfulness through the specially gifted. This selectivity ignores Paul's important contention that "*to each* a manifestation of the Spirit is given for the common good" (1 Cor. 12:7). What intrigued Paul about the charisms was not only their distinctiveness but also their ubiquity. So, one charism to this person, and a completely different one to that. "They are apportioned to each one individually as the Spirit wills" (1 Cor. 12:11). And what does the Spirit will? "God so loved the world that he sent his Son [and then the Spirit] into the world" (John 3:16) not to condemn it but to heal and open it up to love.

There are several other reasons why the notion of the charisms has not been congenial or attractive, especially to Catholic Christians. Traditionally, call has been referred to as one's vocation. These vocations have ordinarily (and I believe, superficially) been understood as calls to states of life such as marriage, religious life, priesthood, consecrated lay life, or the single life. I have no doubt that people are called to these states, but the emphasis on these, as if they exhausted the meaning of call, has diverted attention from the even more particular calls within these states of life—or even independently of them—that each is given to follow. This has been a serious deficiency in the vocational catechesis of the churches, since these more specific calls are intrinsic to a full and correct understanding of discipleship as the New Testament elaborates it. So the need is to differentiate the call—which is always to love—from the particular way of loving each is given to manifest that love from their particular state of life and their particular matrix of giftedness, which we are calling charisms of the Spirit.

It was not until Vatican Council II that the largely overlooked charisms were rediscovered. Although the term charism had not even appeared in the documents that had been prepared ahead of time for the Council's deliberations, it did manage to make its way into the discussions and into the final documents some fourteen times, having been introduced from the floor. Even the broaching of the subject created tension in the aula. One of the weightier Council figures, Cardinal Ruffini, seeing the attraction a number of the bishops had to this ancient yet now somewhat novel notion, assured the two-thousand-plus hierarchs that charisms were only meant for the early years of the church, so that there would be striking evidence to unbelievers in those early centuries that the Church was divine in origin. Furthermore, he assured them, if these were to resurface now, an instability would develop in the Church because the laity would make more of their giftedness than they should be encouraged to. Fortunately, the rest of the bishops deemed this tack nonsense.[5]

The Council's advertence notwithstanding, because of their long neglect in the Church and in theology, the Vatican II documents reveal a diffuse and at times confusing understanding of the meaning of charism. They are insufficiently differentiated from the more generic categories of graces, or the gifts of the Spirit, or the fruits of the Spirit. Furthermore, they also tend to be construed almost al-

5. I covered these details in "Connecting Vatican II's Call to Holiness with Public Life," in *The Proceedings of the 55th Annual Convention of Catholic Theological Society of America*, ed. Michael Downey, 1–19, Washington. D.C.

ways in an ecclesiocentric way. For example, in the Constitution on the Church document #12, the Spirit is described as distributing "special graces among the faithful of every rank" and by these gifts the faithful are expected to be "fit and ready to undertake the various tasks and offices advantageous for the renewal and up building of the Church." The text then proceeds to specify these "special graces" as "charismatic gifts [which are] exceedingly suitable and useful for the needs of the Church." In only one of the Council documents, the Decree on the Laity #3, is there an acknowledgment that the common good the charisms were meant to effect was society's good, and not simply the intra-ecclesial good of the church. "From the reception of these charisms or gifts, there arise for each believer the right and duty to use them in the Church and in the world for the good of mankind [sic] and the up-building of the Church."

Karl Rahner lamented the Council's reluctance to make charisms intrinsic to the very constitution of the Church. He saw profoundly into the implications of their "ultimate incalculability," as he described it. For him, the charisms were the usual way the Spirit "ushers the Church as an open system into a future, which God alone and no one else arranged."[6] He saw the institutional Church as too closed a system, even though it was "encompassed by the charismatic movement of the Spirit." This kept the Church functioning in a way that was too prearranged and closed off from the Spirit, which must be free to blow where it will. Rahner describes the charisms as "divinely inspired individual impulses" that "the hierarchy has the duty to accept from those quarters in which they originally strike the Church in the providence of God." These charisms are "antennae of the individual divine imperatives given to the Church."

The new attention to charisms did not stop with the Council. They were the objects of considerable inquiry at the International Synod on the Laity in 1987 and in the subsequent Apostolic Exhortation, *Christifideles Laici* (1989), Pope John Paul II's reflection on that

6. Karl Rahner, "Observations on the Factor of the Charismatic in the Church," in *Theological Investigations* (New York: Seabury Press, 1974), 12:86.

synod. The synod's message, for example, commented, "We know that God acts in all Christians, and we are aware of the benefits which flow from charisms both for individuals and for the whole Christian community" (Prop. 9).[7] In his reflection on the synod, Pope John Paul was even more open to the ubiquity and importance of the charisms in the church's mission than many of the synod's bishops had been. The ecclesiology he appealed to in calling forth charisms was that of the Church as a communion. The pope described the charisms of the Spirit, which are given in abundance to the baptized "according to his [the Spirit's] own richness and the necessities of the Church's life and apostolate," as needing to "exist in communion and on behalf of communion" (CL #20). Because of the outpouring of both "hierarchical and charismatic gifts," all the baptized are called to take an "active and co-responsible part" in the church's life and mission (CL #21). John Paul II sees the Spirit as the source of the efficacy of the charisms because it is the Spirit that makes the charismed "fit and ready" for their work for the common good (CL #24). He comments enthusiastically on both the varieties of charisms and their abundance and calls for their manifest presence to be received with gratitude by the entire people of God (CL #24).

The pope judges that the charisms are "an immense treasure" that must be brought to fruition by wise pastors, who are to see themselves as serving this initiative of the Spirit rather than by overdetermining how things should operate. He comments that ordination to the priesthood should not be looked on as an increase in dignity, but as an increase in a capacity for service of the gifted (CL #20). This pontiff has not ceased speaking about the subject of charisms since this Apostolic Exhortation. He is always careful to point out that their exercise must be done in the spirit of mutuality. That is why he suggests that a communion ecclesiology is the best framework for understanding charisms: because it enables members of the body of Christ to see themselves as functioning in a way that *en bloc* upbuilds the common good.

7. This material is well covered by Robert Oliver in *The Vocation of the Laity to Evangelization*, Serie teologia 26 (Rome: Pontifica Universitá Gregoriana, 1997).

This papal emphasis on charisms as needing to steep us in mutuality and communion must be underscored precisely because charisms, as treated in this essay, heighten a sense of one's individuation, but they must not prolong or deepen the cultural blight of individualism. If call as conversion to charism is individualistically construed, it is being misconstrued.

I should add here several other reasons for the disfavor in which charism is held. One of these is the narrowing of the term to only some of the faithful (i.e., the charismatics). Has the so-called charismatic renewal been a positive influence in this matter of charism? I believe that it has not, but I would not blame that particular phenomenon or movement for this. Its leaders did not intend to have the term charism confined to that movement's members. Nonetheless, many have been turned off by the very idea of charism because they felt discomfort with the piety or the ecclesiology of the "charismatics." Its members were judged too "Pentecostal" or "emotional" or "sectarian" or "fundamentalist" in the judgment of the onlookers. The fault is not with these "charismatics," it seems to me, but with those who judge charisms to be alien even though they were constitutive of the mission of the Church at one time in its life.

Second, in light of the pervasive misunderstanding of the relation between nature and grace in the minds of many Christians, charisms were bound to incur neglect. Although grace is not nature, a separation of the two does not help the Church's mission. Related to the subject of charism, the dichotomy would imagine the Spirit's action as infrequent and adventitious, as coming out of the blue and down from above despite what was coming up from below (i.e., from nature) by way of talents, interests, aptitude, education, opportunity, even genes. Charism, then, caught in this misunderstanding, would be seen to be wholly apart from nature. Hence their oddity and rarity, rather than their being coterminous with those who are open to being led by God to serve their neighbors by their particular giftedness.

A final misunderstanding, which has led charisms to be ignored or even dismissed unfavorably in church circles, even in theological or pastoral circles, is their takeover by a cognate form—*charisma*—by social scientists, notably Max Weber. While there is no reason for complaint or blame in this, the conflation of charisma with charism has given rise to the misconception that a person must shine like a star in a dark firmament of lackluster individuals in order to be seen to possess this rare quality. One way to test the inappropriateness of the conflation of charism with charisma is to ask oneself how often in our own experience "little folk" who supposedly lack all charisma have given evidence of being led by the Spirit, or have been manifestations of the Spirit to us.

VI. Social Impact of Charisms

Maybe the best way to determine what has its origin in the Spirit is to inquire whether a charism's effect is social, or communal, with the common good upbuilt in some way by its exercise. Let us examine three examples.

Think of the charism of earth care, if I might coin a term inspired by Rachel Carson, Thomas Berry, Brian Swimm, Jane Goodall, Jacques Cousteau, John Muir, John Haught . . . the list is long and getting longer. The few have invited the many into an intellectual conversion to reality, in the sense that they have enabled the many to see, as if for the first time, the deep interconnection we humans have with earth and sky, with planets and microbes, coyote and coral reef, with the worms that will eat our corpses, and the sun that melts the ice floes. We are now hearing a much clearer call from the material universe, one that our forebears, notably Native Americans, heard long ago. We are also learning that the inability to hear this call, or the refusal to listen, carries a higher and higher price. The individuation of those with the charism of earth love has affected a conversion to reality in many.

A second example, this one of moral conversion, can also be seen in terms of the charism experienced by individuals whose fidelity affected the conversion of many to a new perception of value. I have in mind the profound conversion that the Church underwent, especially in the course of Vatican Council II, about the subject of religious freedom as a human right. What prepared the Council for this radical change? Charismed individuals, I would suggest, such as the Dominicans de las Casas and de Vitoria; philosophers such as John Locke and Thomas Paine; Church figures such as Pope John XXIII and John Courtney Murray; the framers of the UN Declaration of Universal Human Rights such as Eleanor Roosevelt and Jacques Maritain. The sacred value that the Church had sought to preserve in its pre-rights epoch was the inviolability of the revealed truth entrusted to her. This real value, however, was ecclesiocentrically construed for centuries. Hence, since "error had no rights," those who were in any error about the sacred truth should not be accorded even a sliver of freedom to search for God in their own way and at their own pace. As these narrow views were subjected to alternatives—from philosophy, constitutional theory, the experience of democratic regimes, and especially a new appreciation for the historical nature of church doctrine—they began to change under the persuasion of the charismed. Human rights surfaced in a universal way with the 1948 Universal Declaration of Human Rights. The new value was the human person, and his or her dignity—especially in the matter of freedom with respect to belief. This value, expressed in terms of the right to religious freedom, trumped, in a sense, the other value of preserving sacred truth. We have the charismed to thank for this enormously important contribution to the common good.

A third example of affective/religious conversion is always near to hand. Who would deny that there is nothing quite so contagious as love? Where love is, there community in its smallest and in all its wider forms develops. Presumably we have been in many social contexts in which there has been an experience of abiding in love. I can think of a parish where the love of parishioners for one another was tangible, communities of religious where I have had the same experience, not to mention families. The common note here, once again, is that communal relationships flower where love abides and holds individuals together in its thrall. I think of the Truth and Reconciliation Commission in South Africa, where love found a way through the charisms of Bishop Desmond Tutu and Nelson Mandela, et al. This love prevented untold quantities of blood from spilling. I think of General George Marshall and the architects of the Marshall Plan, which brought a devastated Europe into viability decades before a loveless, retaliatory response would have done. I think of the effect of the love Sister Helen Prejean had for her friends on death row and the effect of her love on thousands' attitude toward the death penalty. We are still early in the process of a conversion about this, but the call has been heard and a large-scale conversion is underway communally.

VII. Lonergan *Redivivus*

In this article I have commented on the three understandings of conversion in Lonergan as being susceptible to interpretation in the light of personal call. Although these three conversions are distinguishable, they are not separable. The order of their emergence in a person can vary, but each will eventually have to include the other two for a person to be fully called forth. This is also how the called become whole and able to respond fully to their call. So a call is already being responded to, at least initially, by those who are formally pursuing knowledge in an effort to overcome their ignorance. A call is being responded to, at least initially, by those who are living in a self-transcending manner by their moral choices, their friendships, and their attention to the needs of others. A call is being responded to, at least initially, by those whose faith has brought them to the experience of God loving them, thereby orienting them to their ultimate purpose.

Bernard Lonergan himself did not have much to say about one's calling or vocation as such, or about charisms either. The way he connected his work to these *desiderata*, as I take them to be, was by assisting people to come to authenticity through a process he called self-appropriation. He supplied a method for doing so. By means of this method people had to be, first of all, fully attentive to their feelings and their experiences; then experience themselves understanding by their acts of understanding and as having insight into these; then arriving at a judgment about the insight and understanding that was the most cogent; and finally making their decisions and choices on the basis of their judgments. For Lonergan, meaning comes from true knowing and true knowing about oneself or anything else is achieved by making right judgments. Conversely, by inattention, or by sloppy, unintelligent response to data, or by immature judgment or indecisiveness or impetuous decisions, people drift further and further away from their calling or, as he would prefer, their authenticity.

Lonergan did not expect that one's call comes from some deep lair within the self. He believed, rather, that the more one's subjectivity can become authentic by means of this method of achieving objectivity, the more likely the person is to be self-authoring in a way that is of God. The usual ways of falling short of the conversions elaborated in this essay are by being blocked or deranged by biases. Biases keep one from dealing with reality. Biases can come from several sites: an unconscious motivation, an individual egoism, a group egoism, or the presumption that my own common sense is in touch with whatever I think is necessary to know in order to do and become what I am meant to do and become (*Method in Theology*, 231).

Knowing what is of value usually has its start in feelings or intuition, before the feelings mature into judgments that beckon one to commit to the value. It is from the resulting judgments of what is of value that one can determine "what it would be worthwhile for one to make of oneself, and what it would be worthwhile for one to do for one's fellow man. One works out an ideal of human reality and achievement, and to that ideal one dedicates oneself. As one's knowledge increases, as one's experience is enriched, as one's reach is strengthened or weakened, one's ideal may be revised and the revision may recur many times" (*Method in Theology*, 40). This is as good a description of a calling as I think one will get from Lonergan.

≈ Camilla Burns

The Call of Creation

We exist. The fact of our existence is laden with a biblical importance that gives direction and meaning to our entire unfolding life. According to the first story of the Bible, everything created is "called" into being by the word of God. The phrase, "God said let there be . . ." precedes each day of the creation story. On the sixth day, God calls the human person into being. "God said: let us make humankind." To be is to be called. Foundational to biblical understanding is the common summons of all creation into being by the word of God. At the same time that human beings share a common origin, each of us contributes a unique way of being and a particular mode of doing as an expression of our being.

The concern of this chapter is to reflect on the implications of our summons into being, with particular interest in the pattern of humanity as the "image of God," "God's likeness," and the subsequent responsibilities of fertility and dominion. Both of these lifelong tasks involve fecundity, righteousness, and peace in all the relationships of our lives. Since the creation story directs the fulfillment of our call in terms of relationship, it will be instructive to turn to wisdom—whose association with creation offers insight about living our relationships.

Since we are all called into being, our concern is to reflect on a biblical notion of vocation as an invitation to a particular way of being and mode of acting. "Call" in the Bible is understood as the communication of God. There are marvelous accounts of individuals—such as Abraham (Gen. 12:1–4), Moses (Exod. 3:1–11), and the prophets (Isa. 6:1–13; Jer. 1:4–10; Amos 7:14–15; Ezek. 1–3)—who are called to new positions of leadership. In the New Testament, the call is to the following of Jesus (Mark 1:17; Matt. 4:19; Luke 5:10). The importance of these accounts notwithstanding, the interest of this study is the call to the "whole people of God" in the creation story.

The primary call to all of God's people begins in the first creation story (Gen. 1:1–2, 4a). Elements in the story that reveal the meaning of our call involve the word of God, chaos and order, being made in the image of God, the directive to bear fruit and multiply, God's blessing, the Sabbath, and Wisdom. We will examine these aspects of the call of creation and seek its meaning for our life.

The Word

The first action of God in this story is speech. The phrase "God said" begins the account of each of the first six days of creation, the days of drawing into being the heavens and the earth. Earth and heaven are a merism, an inclusive idiom meaning "everything" or "everywhere." There is a calmness and purpose about God's speech, with everything deriving its life from God's word. This is the deepest meaning of the creation account. To interpret this story as a scientific statement is to misconstrue its most profound meaning as a statement of faith. To understand what it means to be "called" into being is to understand that we are a response to the word of God. The poetic rendering of creation in the Psalms does not lose sight of the primacy of the word of God. "By the word of the Lord the heavens were made, and all their host by the breath of his mouth" (Ps. 33:6).

Beyond the creation story, there is a strong biblical tradition for the life-giving power of the word of God. "One does not live by bread alone, but by every word that comes from the mouth of the

Lord" (Deut. 8:3). In the Valley of Dry Bones, Ezekiel is told to re-store life to the bones with the command, "O dry bones, hear the word of the Lord" (Ezek. 37:4). What is important about this un-derstanding of the continuing power of the word of God is that cre-ation is not a temporal account of what happened at one moment in time but a statement about a permanent relationship with God. Creation is not only an event in the past that brought us into exis-tence, but an ongoing occurrence that sustains us in existence.

The Psalms are replete with examples of God's continuous pres-ence in our lives, and God's word is sought in times of trouble. "My soul clings to the dust; revive me according to your word. . . . My soul melts away for sorrow; strengthen me according to your word" (Ps. 115: 25, 28). "He sent out his word and healed them, and deliv-ered them from destruction" (Ps. 107:20). It is also a source of great support: "Your word is a lamp to my feet and a light to my path" (Ps. 119:105), and of hope, "You are my hiding place and my shield; I hope in your word" (Ps. 119:114).

The words of God are brimming with energy. "He sends out his command to the earth; his word runs swiftly" (Ps. 147:15). The word creates and re-creates, "For as the rain and the snow come down from heaven, and do not return there until they have watered the earth, making it bring forth and sprout, giving seed to the sower and bread to the eater, so shall my word be that goes out from my mouth; it shall not return to me empty, but it shall accomplish that which I purpose, and succeed in the thing for which I sent it" (Isa. 55:10–11).

We human beings are not the only part of creation in relation-ship with the word of God. The earth, the sea, the sky, the plants and animals are also called into existence by the word of God. We are in relationship with all that has existence precisely because we have a common rootedness in the word. The whole ecological movement, which reminds us of our responsibility and relationship to all of creation, honors the deep roots of the first creation story. When we live all of our relationships with integrity, we are living our vocation: being aware that all of creation has been called into existence by the word of God. Furthermore, we understand that we all are held in existence by God's continuously creative word.

Chaos and Order

The story of creation begins with "When the earth was wild and waste, darkness over the face of Ocean, rushing-spirit of God hovering over the face of the waters" (Gen. 1:2). The chaos of the opening scene is subdued and ordered by the word of God. The divine activity proceeds in two distinct phases. The first three days involve the process of separation, and the last three days are occupied with filling the universe. On the first day, God separates light from darkness. Then God calls forth a dome that separates the waters above from the waters below. Finally, God separates the earth from the seas and then begins the activity of filling the earth with sprouting growth and fruit trees. At the end of the first three days, the chaos has been subdued by the work of separation, and ordered harmony exists.

The following three days of creation involve filling the universe. The fourth day parallels the first day, when light replaces darkness. The sources of light appear, the sun, moon, and stars marking the festal calendar and the passage of time. On the fifth day, the waters bring forth swarms of living creatures and birds fill the sky. On the sixth day, animals of every kind come forth. Finally, humankind, male and female, come at the peak of creation with a special vocation.

In light of recent chaos theory, we must be reminded that the process of transforming chaos into order is not a scientific statement, but a religious one. Ancient wisdom conceived of the initial wildness and darkness as the polar opposite of creation. Without God, the world is disordered chaos, dark and watery. The ordered universe is the sign of God's activity and God's presence.

The mythic language of cosmic disorder as the absence of God is used frequently in the Psalms. Jonah sang a psalm describing his distance from God in the whale's belly: "You cast me into the deep, into the heart of the seas, and the flood surrounded me; all your waves and your billows passed over me. . . . The waters closed in over me; the deep surrounded me; weeds were wrapped around my head at the roots of the mountains" (Jon. 2:3, 5–6). The chaos describes Jonah's loss of God: "I am driven away from your sight" (Jon. 2:4). Several phrases describing the loss of God's presence in Psalm 88 appeal to the images of confusion and darkness. "You have put me in the depths of the Pit, in the regions dark and deep . . . you overwhelm me with all your waves. . . . They [dread assaults of God] surround me like a flood all day long; from all sides they close in on me (Ps. 88: 6, 7, 17).

Since the creation story frames all existence as a call, we can look for the account to tell us something about the nature of our call to human existence. Living our existence with an awareness of God can be understood to bring a harmony to our lives. It does not imply that there will not be confusion and chaos as part of our human experience. However, on a very deep level, below the billows and waves of the surface, there is a deep experience of union with the one who spoke us into being.

Image of God

The origin of humankind as the final and ultimate act of creation puts humans, male and female, at the peak of creation with a special vocation. God's decision to "make humankind in our image, according to our likeness" (Gen. 1:26) gives us a clue about the being and doing of our existence—our special role.

The Hebrews were forbidden to make images of God. "You shall not make for yourself an idol, whether in the form of anything that is in heaven above, or that is on the earth beneath, or that is in the water under the earth" (Exod. 20:4; cf. Deut. 5:8). The problem with images is rehearsed frequently by the prophets and the Psalmists. "The idols of the nations are silver and gold, the work of human hands. They have mouths, but they do not speak; they have eyes, but they do not see; they have ears, but they do not hear, and there is no breath in their mouths (Ps. 135:15–17).[1] All of the polemics charge the idols with ineffectiveness. They are lifeless and a poor substitute for the living God. The God of Israel can only be imaged by living beings, and that role is given to humankind.

Two responsibilities come with the honor of imaging God. The first has to do with our being, and the second with our doing. To be an image is to recognize that we are deeply related to the living God in such a way that we are not the primary source of our own life, but a reflection of the life of God. We are intimately involved in a relationship that acknowledges our creaturehood and dependency on the One who created us. All that came into being in the universe is a gift from God. Humans have the call to image that giftedness by acknowledging our complete dependency on God.[2]

We are given two specific directions on how to "do" our imagehood. "Bear fruit and be many and fill the earth and subdue it! Have dominion over the fish of the sea, the fowl of the heavens, and all living things that crawl about upon the earth!" (Gen. 1:28).

Bear Fruit, Multiply, and Have Dominion

To bear fruit and multiply is precisely what God did in creating the universe. We are to imitate the generosity and fruitfulness by being a life-giving source. This imitation surely includes procreation. It also encompasses whatever we do that is life-giving for others and ourselves. It includes the quality of our relationships with God and other humans, and with all of creation. The creation story respectfully enumerates each aspect of creation, and asks no less of us.

The second directive is to subdue, to have dominion. This is a problematic issue in that it has sometimes been misinterpreted as a license to ravage the earth. Some ecologists spurn and condemn this creation account because they believe it has supported control and

1. See also Jer. 10:1–11; Isa. 44:18–20, 9–20.
2. Michael D. Guinan, *To Be Human before God: Insights from Biblical Spirituality* (Collegeville, Minn.: Liturgical Press, 1994), 17–18. See also Guinan, *The Pentateuch, Message of Biblical Spirituality* (Collegeville, Minn.: Liturgical Press, 1990), 21–26.

wanton destruction of nature. The solution to this misinterpretation is to give the text a fair hearing, not to abandon it.

Having dominion is a royal activity. God's creating activity is a role of kingship. "The Lord is king, he is robed in majesty; the Lord is robed, he is girded with strength. He has established the world; it shall never be moved; your throne is established from of old; you are from everlasting" (Ps. 93:1–2). "Say among the nations, 'The Lord is king! The world is firmly established; it shall never be moved'" (Ps. 96:10). The terms righteousness *(tsedaqa)* and peace *(shalom)* best describe the responsibilities of royalty. "In his days may *righteousness* flourish and *peace* abound, until the moon is no more. May he have *dominion* from sea to sea, and from the River to the ends of the earth" (Ps. 72:7–8). Having dominion implies a royal responsibility for righteousness and peace.

Justice and righteousness are often used as parallel concepts. "Let justice [*mishpat*] roll down like waters, and righteousness [*tsedeqah*] like an everflowing stream" (Amos 5:24). They have similarities, but they are not identical. *Mishpat* has to do with the actual doing of justice, which can involve public law. Hence it has a more forensic meaning. The legitimacy of the execution of *mishpat* comes from the community's understanding of what is right, *tsedeqah*. It deals with the rights that belong to each person in the community, and the safeguarding of these rights. Furthermore, it deals with the vision of what is right. These words are often used in parallel because our biblical ancestors understood that action and vision are intimately related. In other words, our view of life motivates our actions.

The critical issue for us is the understanding of righteousness, as it is presented in the Hebrew Scripture. Because of our particular culture, we have absorbed a vision of human life that often stresses the value of control and having possessions. In this cultural context, biblical righteousness is frequently misunderstood as a legalistic, impartial giving of what is due. We interpret the biblical text with our modern, Western vision of life. It is difficult to enter into a new vision of human life when we already wear glasses that mediate a vision for us. The key to the solution is our imagination; because our vision is rooted in imagination, it is there that the transformation happens.

The Bible is a work of imagination and requires imagination to yield fresh interpretations and new visions. Only the imagination can uncover the revolutionary power of the text. "Once we focus upon the Bible as essentially a work of the imagination, a work discovering new possibilities in the present moment, then we have perceived this truly subversive character."[3] The poet David Rosenberg makes an even stronger statement about the ravages of the failure of imagination:

The Bible, arguably the most important work of art in the Western literary canon, is an uneasy subject in the classroom. Why are our great poetic stories taught in the dullest of ways? I believe the fault can be traced to a failure of imagination in academic life. Imagination can be stifled by dogma, but it can also be flattened by theories that handle merely the skeletons of texts. The Bible is a luminous guidebook to our past yet it is put out of reach by colorless professors. And the broad range of poets who gave voice to the original words has been rendered voiceless by prosaic translations. Once, the poets lent us what one critic has called, in the context of soul music, the "spiritual magnitude of the individual voice." It is time to rediscover the original text.[4]

Opening us to a broader, more imaginative understanding, Elizabeth Achtemeier surveys the many manifestations of righteousness

---

3. Mark Coleridge, "The Necessary Angel: Imagination and the Bible," *Pacifica* 1 (1988): 180. See also Walter Brueggemann, "Imagination as a Mode of Fidelity," in *Understanding the Word: Essays in Honor of Bernhard W. Anderson*, ed. James T. Butler, Edgar W. Conrad, and Ben C. Ollenburger; *Journal for the Study of the Old Testament*, supp. 37 (1985): 15–36.

4. David Rosenberg, *A Poet's Bible: Rediscovering the Voices of the Original Text* (New York: Hyperion, 1991), xi. See also Sandra M. Schneiders, *The Revelatory Text: Interpreting the New Testament as Sacred Scripture* (New York: Harper San Francisco, 1991), 102–8, who views the New Testament text as the product of the "paschal imagination"; Michael L. Cook, "Revelation as Metaphoric Process," *Theological Studies* 47 (1986): 388–411; and Gerald J. Bednar, *Faith as Imagination: The Contributions of William F. Lynch, S.J.* (Kansas City: Sheed & Ward, 1996), 58.

in the Old Testament (OT) and concludes that it is neither behavior, nor an action, nor an impartial ministry, nor giving everyone what is due.

Rather, righteousness is in the OT the *fulfillment of the demands of a relationship* (my emphasis), whether that relationship be with men [*sic*] or with God. Each man is set within a multitude of relationships: king with people, judge with complainants, priest with worshippers, common man with family, tribesman with community, community with resident alien and poor, all with God. And each of these relationships brings with it specific demands, the fulfillment of which constitutes righteousness. The demands may differ from relationship to relationship; righteousness in one situation may be unrighteousness in another. Further, there is no norm of righteousness outside the relationship itself. When God or man fulfills the conditions imposed upon him by a relationship, he is—in OT terms—righteous.[5]

The concrete manifestations of this relationship are described in the Wisdom books of Job and Proverbs. The righteous person is one who preserves the peace and wholeness of the community. Like Job, the person is a blessing to the community—one who cares for the poor, the fatherless, and the widow (Job 29:12–15, 31:16–19; Prov. 29:7) and defends their cause in court (Job 29:16, 31:21; Prov. 31:9). The righteous person gives liberally (Prov. 21:26), provides for the wayfarer and guest (Job 31:31–32), and counts righteousness better than wealth (Job 31:24–25; Prov. 16:8). Although a good steward of the land (Job 31:38–40), the righteous person treats the animals with care (Prov. 12:10) and the servants humanely (Job 31:29–30). Whenever the righteous person makes a decision that restores the community, that decision is a righteous judgment (Prov. 17:15, 26, 18:5, 24:24).

The righteous person preserves the peace and prosperity of the community by fulfilling the demands of communal and covenantal

5. E. R. Achtemeier, "Righteousness in the OT," in *Interpreter's Dictionary of the Bible*, vol. 4 (Nashville: Abingdon Press, 1962), 80.

relationships. For this reason, righteousness can stand parallel with peace. "I will appoint Peace as your overseer and Righteousness as your taskmaster" (Isa. 60:17). The biblical concept of peace *(shalom)* is not the absence of conflict but a very broad and deep concept of a sense of fullness. The notions of wholeness, health, and completeness inform all the variants of the word. A greeting of *shalom* implies a wish of wholeness or health or completeness that includes the physical and spiritual resources sufficient to one's needs.

Both directives—to be fruitful and multiply, and to have dominion—imply something about our relationships. The first stresses the fecundity or life-giving quality of relationships. The second focuses on the obligations involved in a particular relationship. The latter responsibility of having dominion is a call to effect righteousness and peace.

God Blessed Them

After the creation of humankind as male and female, God blessed them before assigning the responsibilities of fecundity and dominion. Blessing, in the Old Testament, is a profound rite that imparts a vital power. According to Johannes Pedersen, a presupposition for understanding blessing is recognition of soul.[6] A person's total state of being alive is expressed by the Hebrew *nephesh,* translated as soul. The soul is the totality of a person that is filled with power, allowing the soul to grow and prosper and do its work in the world. This vital power, which the Israelites called blessing *(berākhāh),* is a constitutive dimension of the existence of every living being. Like the two aspects of vocation, blessing also has an energy of being and an energy of doing. The inner power of the soul realizes itself in the growth of the soul, which impels an expression of itself within the world as a vital presence. Vital power is a fundamental dimension of the exis-

6. Johannes Pedersen, *Israel: Its Life and Culture,* vols. 1–2 (London: Oxford University Press, 1926), 162–212. See also Claus Westermann, *Blessings in the Bible and the Life of the Church: Overtures to Biblical Theology,* trans. Keith Crim (Philadelphia: Fortress Press, 1978).

tence of every living being and is at the same time the presence of the blessing of vitality.

Biblical blessing manifests itself in many ways, but its primary expression is that which we find in the creation account, the power of fertility. When God blesses, it is the Creator who blesses. Blessing implies creation, and is effective as the work of the Creator. The command to be fruitful and multiply often occurs in the context of blessing. "By his blessing they multiply greatly, and he does not let their cattle decrease" (Ps. 107:38).[7] Blessing is fruitfulness in family, farming, and the raising of sheep and goats. Most important, however, blessing *is* fertility. It is life itself, and includes all phases of life. When humankind receives the commission to be fruitful and multiply, the blessing of God gives them the power to accomplish the task of fertility. The act of blessing means imparting vital power to another person.

In our previous discussion, we looked at the centrality of relationship in the dual charge of fertility and dominion. Interpersonal relationships in the biblical tradition are not possible without blessing. In Israel, meeting another was acknowledged by a blessing. Giving a blessing imparts vital power to another person. The deep reality of the exchange of blessing was an establishment or confirmation of a spiritual community, a necessity for establishing a relationship. Large gatherings were always concluded with a blessing, so that each individual might take with him or her the power of the community.

The blessing at the time of our creation imparts a vitality that has the potential of developing many vital relationships. The oldest blessing of the Hebrew tradition includes the gift of peace *(shalom)*, which is also part of the responsibility of dominion. "The Lord bless you and keep you; the Lord make his face to shine upon you, and be gracious to you; the Lord lift up his countenance upon you, and give you peace" (Num. 6:24–26). The blessing of a relationship brings with it the gift of peace.

7. See also Ps. 128:3 and Deut. 30:16.

Sabbath

"God had finished, on the seventh day, from all his work that he had made, and then he ceased, on the seventh day, from all his work that he had made. God gave the seventh day his blessing, and he hallowed it, for on it he ceased from all his work, that by creating, God had made." (Gen. 2:2–3)

God "rested" (Hebrew: *shabath*) from all the work of creation. God claims this one day as holy, endowing all time with ultimate meaning. The day itself is blessed, receiving the gift of vitality, which it shares with all who participate in the Sabbath.

As we have seen in the creation story, the individual exists only in relationship, so that Sabbath rest has an effect on all relationships—those of "you, or your son or your daughter, or your male and or female slaves, or your animals, or the alien who lives with you" (Exod. 20:10).[8] All share the Sabbath rest. It expresses our awareness of the gift of existence and the interconnectedness of our lives with other people, with the animals, and with the natural world itself. We live because of God's creating activity, and we continue to fulfill the vocation of our existence when we participate in keeping holy the day that has been blessed.

In the images of the creation story, Sabbath rest allows us a time to repair the disorder and chaos that has crept back into ourselves and our relationships. Our creation is an ongoing process that allows us an opportunity for re-creation. Re-creation is an opportunity to renew the call that started "In the beginning . . ."

In the Beginning

Most Bible translations present the opening of the Bible as, "In the beginning God created the heavens and the earth." The question, which has been debated for centuries, is whether this means

---

8. See also Exod. 23:21 and Deut. 5:14.

the *very* beginning of all creation or whether God had done some work previous to the creation of heaven and the earth. The translation used at the beginning of this essay allows for the latter interpretation ("At the beginning of God's creating of the heavens and the earth"). A passage from Proverbs buoys this argument: "The Lord created me at the beginning of his work, the first of his acts of long ago. Ages ago I was set up, at the first, before the beginning of the earth" (Prov. 8:22–23). These words clearly indicate that God had created wisdom prior to the rest of creation, and many ancient interpreters concur. "Before the ages, in the beginning, he created me (wisdom)" (Sir. 24:9).[9]

An interpretation frequently given to wisdom's creation before all things is that it had a role to play in creation. "Oh Lord, how great are your works, with wisdom you have made them all" (Ps. 104:24).[10] Wisdom was especially associated with the creation of humanity on the sixth day, when the singular person of the creation account changes to the plural, "Let *us* make humankind" (Gen. 1:26). "And on the sixth day I commanded my wisdom to create man" (2 Enoch 30:8).[11]

In an attempt to understand the apparent omission of wisdom in the Genesis creation account, ancient interpreters connected "In the *beginning* God created . . ." (Gen. 1:1) with "The Lord created me at the *beginning* of his work" (Prov. 8:22). The word *beginning* became an allusion to wisdom, and hence the Genesis account could be interpreted as "In [or with] wisdom God created the heavens and the earth." "With wisdom did God create and perfect the heavens and the earth" (*Fragment Targum* Gen. 1:1).[12]

Whether one is convinced by these ancient interpreters or not, it is beyond dispute that wisdom is associated with creation. At the very least, she was an observer.

---

9. See also Aristobulus, Fragment 5 (cited in Eusebius, *Praeparatio Evangelica*) and Philo, *On the Virtues* 62; *Targum Neophyti*, Gen. 3:24.

10. See also Jer. 10:10, 12, and Prov. 3:19.

11. See also Hellenistic Synagogal Prayer, *Apostolic Constitutions* 7.34.6.

12. See also *Targum Neophyti*, Gen. 1:1 and Philo, *Allegorical Interpretations* 1:1.

The Lord created me at the beginning of his work, the first of his acts of long ago. Ages ago I was set up, at the first, before the beginning of the earth. When there were no depths I was brought forth, when there were no springs abounding with water. Before the mountains had been shaped, before the hills, I was brought forth—when there were no springs abounding with water. Before the mountains had been shaped, before the hills, I was brought forth—when God had not yet made earth and fields, or the world's first bits of soil. When he established the heavens, I was there, when he drew a circle on the face of the deep, when he made firm the skies above, when he established the fountains of the deep, when he assigned to the sea its limit, so that the waters might not transgress his command, when he marked out the foundations of the earth, then I was beside him, like a confidante; and I was daily his delight, rejoicing before him always, rejoicing in his inhabited world and delighting in the human race. (Prov. 8:22–31)

Understanding wisdom's intimate involvement with creation, we can seek further insights into the meaning of the vocation of our human existence.

The Wisdom Tradition

In the Old Testament, wisdom is a body of literature representing a tradition throughout Israel's history. The literature includes Proverbs, Job, Ecclesiastes, Sirach, and Wisdom of Solomon. The concept of wisdom in this literature has a very broad meaning. It can refer to a skill of ability or expertness, an attitude toward life, or a search for self-understanding. Because of its concern with relationships, and the skills and attitudes surrounding them, the Wisdom Tradition returns to the call of creation, which concerns our relationships.

No details in living out our relationships are insignificant for wisdom. "Better is a dinner of herbs where love is than a fatted ox and hatred with it" (Prov. 15:16). The quality of relationships includes sensitivity to the timing of human interaction. "Whoever blesses a neighbor with a loud voice, rising early in the morning, will be counted as cursing" (Prov. 27:14).

The skills and abilities involved in daily living are matters of wisdom. Mourners (Jer. 9:16), weavers (Exod. 35:25), goldsmiths (Jer. 10:9), sailors (Ezek. 27:8; Ps. 107:27), or administrators of state (Isa. 10, 13, 29:14; Jer. 49:7) are all expressions of wisdom. Multiple examples of the understanding of wisdom as a skill occur in Exodus 35, when Moses calls on the Israelites to prepare a worship space. All who were skillful (wise-hearted, Exod. 35:10) were invited. "All the skillful [wise-hearted] women spun with their hands. . . . [Bezalel and Oholiab were] filled with skill [wise-hearted] to do every kind of work done by an artisan" (Exod 35:25, 35).

In addition to the practical arts of living, wisdom also includes the arts of poetry and music, both vocal and instrumental. Song in ancient Israel was coextensive with life itself. Harvest and vintage, worship, courtship, and marriage were all accompanied by song and dance. Sometimes no distinction was made between poetry and music. Evidence of Solomon's wisdom was his ability to compose "three thousand proverbs, and his songs numbered a thousand and five" (1 Kings 4:32). The composer and poet, instrumentalist and singer, were all part of wisdom. "My mouth shall speak wisdom; the meditation of my heart shall be understanding. I will incline my ear to a proverb; I will solve my music to the riddle of the harp" (Ps. 49:3–4).

As evidence of his wisdom, Solomon also spoke "of trees, from the cedar that is in Lebanon to the hyssop that grows in the wall"; he would speak "of animals, and birds, and reptiles and fish" (1 Kings 4:33). The call of wisdom is not only to the practical arts of living but also to the pursuit of knowledge and the fine arts. The practical aspects of our lives, as well as our academic pursuits, are honored in wisdom's call to full human existence.

Wisdom also calls for a skill in living in equilibrium within the moral order of the world. It calls for good sense, sound judgment, moral understanding, and the capacity to consider profound problems of life. Solomon exemplifies this level of wisdom when he prays before ascending the throne. "Give your servant a *listening* [Hebrew: wisdom] *heart* to govern your people, able to discern between good and evil" (1 Kings 3:9). Wisdom includes the gift of discernment, which is demonstrated in Solomon's ability to resolve the court case of the two prostitutes who claimed the same living child (1 Kings 3:16–28).

At its deepest, wisdom is the search for self-understanding in relation to others, nature, and God. It is deeply immersed in the meaning of the relationships inherited at our call into human existence, and in the relationships experienced as we continue to know the sustaining call of creation in our lives.

Wisdom is personified as a woman in the book of Proverbs, and her opening words are a call: "Does not wisdom call, does not understanding raise her voice" (Prov. 8:1).[13] The call of Wisdom summons us to attentiveness to our relationships with God, others, and nature. Attentiveness yields an awakening. At the center of our being there is an inner sound that we learn to listen to, and be attentive to amidst the other noise that usually fills our mind. It is a hard discipline of daily effort, and of daily forgetting and remembering. The search for self-understanding in relation to God, nature, and others is a life-long process of a listening heart. "From your youth up, choose instruction, and until you are old you will keep finding wisdom" (Sir. 6:18).

Conclusion

According to the first creation account in Genesis, God spoke all creation, including humankind, into being. We have been summoned into being. The "image of God, God's likeness," is the pattern of our humanity. The subsequent responsibilities are fertility and dominion. Both of these life-long tasks involve fecundity, righteousness, and peace in all the relationships of our lives.

Wisdom's association with creation gives us some clues about living our relationships. Nothing is too insignificant for attention, from the practical arts of living to the timing of our words, or the

---

13. See also Prov. 1:20–21.

quality of our relationships with God, others, and nature. Our vocation as a human person is about the art of living that requires a listening heart and being attentive to all facets of our life. It can be
summed up in a disarmingly simple example from Proverbs: "I
passed by the field of one who was lazy, by the vineyard of a person
lacking sense; and see, it was all overgrown with thorns, the ground
was covered with nettles, and its stone wall was broken down. Then
I saw and considered it; I looked and received instruction" (Prov.
24:30–32).

What the observer learned is not as important as the process of
seeing and considering, looking and receiving instruction.[14] Wisdom calls us to a thoughtful, contemplative attitude toward all aspects of living. Insight and understanding reside in the experiences
of our relationships. We contact this wisdom with a listening heart.
The call of creation into human existence invites us into relationships in which we are fruitful and have dominion. Wisdom guides
us in this call by summoning us to live attentively, with a listening
heart.

In the context of Loyola University, the search for knowledge,
pursued within a faith horizon and with a view toward living our
lives for others, is a primary way to mature in our call into personhood at creation.

Like the gift of life itself, the wisdom to respond to the call is also
a gift. "I perceived that I would not possess wisdom unless God gave
her to me . . . so I appealed to the Lord and implored him, and with
my whole heart I said:

"O God of my ancestors and Lord of mercy, who have made all things by
your word, and by your wisdom have formed humankind to have dominion over the creatures you have made, and rule the world in holiness and
righteousness, and pronounce judgment in uprightness of soul, give me the
wisdom that sits by your throne." (Wisd. of Sol. 8:21–9:4)

---

14. *The Tanakh: A New Translation of the Holy Scriptures According to the Traditional Hebrew Test* (Philadelphia: Jewish Publication Society, 1985) offers an interesting
translation. "I observed and took it to heart; I saw it and learned a lesson."

Edward Breuer

Vocation and Call as Individual and Communal Imperatives

Some Reflections on Judaism

The very exercise of writing an essay exploring Jewish perspectives on religious vocation and call, I will admit, seems somewhat unnatural and contrived. My initial reaction to this project, in fact, was one of incomprehension, tinged with a touch of exasperation: incomprehension because the notion of vocation does not appear to be significantly operative in Jewish teachings, and exasperation because the very question thereby appeared to ask one religious tradition to speak—conceptually, if not literally—in the language of another.

It is generally unwise, of course, to speak of any tradition as a monolithic, historically homogeneous entity, especially one with as variegated a past as Judaism; three millennia of exposure to the major religious and cultural upheavals of Western civilization and a good measure of internal restlessness have, in effect, produced countless Judaisms. In the discussion that follows, however, we shall attempt to take in a broad sweep of Jewish history and literature in light of its dominant, normative expressions, in an attempt to shed light on the question of what role, if any, the concepts of vocation and call have played in Judaism.

Biblical and Rabbinic Perspectives

At first glance, the Hebrew Bible would appear to serve as the historical basis for the Christian ideas that we are exploring in these essays. The very nature of biblical prophecy is predicated upon the notion of a divine call that humans discern and that subsequently redirects their lives. The call received by Abraham, Moses, Isaiah, and others was surely extraordinary, but the values of responsiveness and devotion function as a paradigm or model not only for ancient Israelites, but all humanity. In its biblical context, however, the singular role played by these prophets was eclipsed by the broader and more biblically fundamental notion of the covenant and the explicit assertions that this covenant was ultimately a tribal and communal pact. The early narratives of the Pentateuch, within which the individual prophetic calls were articulated, are constructed in anticipation or explication of the covenantal relationship with God, while the later narratives, those of the classical books of prophecy, are incessantly preoccupied with calling the community back to the covenant.

As such, to the extent to which the Hebrew Bible embraces a notion of call or vocation, it is fundamentally subsumed into the life of the ancient Israelites not as individuals, but *qua* community.

"Now then, if you will obey me faithfully and keep my covenant, you shall be my treasured possession among all the peoples; indeed all the earth is mine. And you shall be to me a kingdom of priests and a holy nation . . ." (Exod. 19:5–6)

After this juncture, individuals certainly continued to hear the prophetic call and to serve in distinct and unique ways; indeed, the biblical narrative is fleshed out and compellingly driven by the lives of its assorted *dramatis personae*, as they sought to respond to the divine imperative that they heard. But even the prophetic call received by many of these biblical figures was circumscribed by broader communal imperatives. If one considers for a moment the artistically gifted Bezalel, or the zealously indignant Phineas, it is evident that they serve the community with their talent and leadership, only to vanish into the greater body of Israel and the narrative flow of its communal history. The point may also be made with reference to the "communal priesthood" in the citation from Exodus above. The invocation of priesthood is significant here, and not only for rhetorical purposes, for what began as Aaron's unique role and vocation as a priest in the book of Exodus evolved, at the hands of the priestly traditions of Leviticus, into a set of hereditary positions with defined roles, responsibilities, and privileges. Individual priests may have thought of their station in life as a calling or vocation, but it was a role determined by birth, defined by their clan, and circumscribed by their function within the larger Israelite community. By referring to the Israelites as a kingdom of priests, the text was doing more than simply iterating the holiness of Israel—it was underscoring the sense in which all Jews shared a vocation by dint of their communal commitments.

The Judaism of the past two millennia, however, is fundamentally that of its rabbinic custodians and interpreters. As such, it is telling that from the perspective of post-biblical traditions, Scriptural prophecy and call narratives were regarded as belonging to another, unattainable reality. The rabbinic insistence that prophecy had ended with Malachi in the fifth century B.C.E. was intended to preclude the possibility of any direct access to the word of God, including any kind of divine call. The Sages, significantly, did not replace this extraordinary call to prophecy with a call to a ministry or to some particular path to holiness. The cadre of rabbinic scholars, as Maimonides would later explain in the twelfth century, certainly assumed the mantle of religious authority left behind by this prophetic vacuum, but this transference was mainly that of functional authority. Even with the loss of prophecy, however, the Pharisees and their rabbinic descendants were able to effect one crucial transposition from the biblical age—the notion of a covenantal relationship with God. These Sages identified their oral traditions *(torah she-be-ʿal peh)* and legal strictures *(halakhah)* as the substance of the covenant, and as such, insisted that these teachings were applicable to *all* Jews by dint of their covenantal inheritance. With the ascendance of rabbinic traditions as the reigning worldview of Judaism, these norms were taken to define and shape the lives of Jews *qua* members of a larger religious community, and this remained the case down to the nineteenth century.

The point is significant because this covenantal inheritance and the traditions of Rabbinic and medieval Judaism that followed in its wake insistently spoke in the language of *mitzvot* (commandments) and *halakhah*, thereby reinforcing the centrality of duty and obligation in defining the religious vocation of the Jew. Ritual and civic imperatives constituted only one portion of the biblical corpus, but the Deuteronomic view of the observance of *mitzvot* as the heart of one's relationship with God came to dominate the rabbinic worldview. To be a Jew meant to live according to *halakhah*, and this served as both a temporal standard as well as a means by which to effect the ultimate personal and communal redemption that stood at the pinnacle of all religious yearnings.

At a fundamental level, moreover, classical Judaism knew no notion of adult initiation or confirmation, nor, for that matter, personal choice with regard to a life of Torah. With the obvious exception of conversion, a Jew became a *bar* or *bat mitzvah* automatically, and the passage marked by this event was that from an age of apprenticeship, if you will, to that of full membership in the community of others encumbered by the law. I use the language of "encumbered" deliberately; although biblical and rabbinic traditions are replete with calls to embrace God with a full heart, to perform the *mitzvot* with passion and meaningfulness and love, the bottom line was still that of responsibility and obligation—including, of course, the obligation to embrace God with a full heart.

The fusion of notions of covenantal community with the language of duty and responsibility has many profound and far-reaching implications. At the most basic level, the way in which Jews were to live their lives, the way in which they were to "be in the world," was fully transparent. One's entire being, and the very purpose of one's existence, was to live the life of *halakhah*. And the life of *halakhah* was intended to be all-consuming. The texts and traditions of classical Judaism do not demarcate an area of life that we can call religious (note that biblical and rabbinic Hebrew have no word for religion), nor, in essence, do they treat the donning of *tephillin* (phylacteries), the regulation of financial transactions, the strictures concerning the onset of menstruation, or the preparation of tea on the Sabbath as wholly different aspects of life. Given the transparency of these covenantal obligations and the fact that no area of daily existence was left untouched by biblical and rabbinic traditions, individually generated and applied notions of vocation or call had little room to take root or flourish.

These points can be usefully illustrated by briefly noting aspects of the post-biblical development of the rabbinate. To begin with, the rabbis that appear in the formative Jewish literatures of late antiquity are not distinguished from other Jews in terms of *mitzvot*, nor did they have a particular role in communal prayer or ritual. By their own world-view, rabbis were no more, and no less, bound by the same *halakhic* traditions as every other Jew. What distinguished rabbis from others was superior learning and erudition, from which their role as judges and teachers emanated. These sages, certainly, were lionized and greatly respected, and even occasionally endowed with supernatural powers. But in other ways, there was something almost prosaic and functionalist about their roles; those who mastered the Torah were expected to share that knowledge, and the teachings of those who were truly exceptional were granted the authority to shape the teachings of subsequent generations. Although these sages and their Pharisaic predecessors fashioned themselves as an elite fellowship of learning and purity, they also insisted that the study of Torah (read: rabbinic traditions) was the highest pursuit of each and every male Jew. As such, the many tomes that make up the corpus of rabbinic literature do not speak of rabbis in what we could recognize as the language of vocation or call.

Contextualizing the Individual Quest for Spirituality

A natural question that emerges from the discussion above concerns the life of the individual. Simply put, the notions of covenantal community and obligation would appear to discourage or even squelch individuality, especially in post-biblical Jewish traditions. The life of a Jew is so laden with minutely prescribed obligations and responsibilities that we have gone beyond pointing out an absence of the language of vocation to shutting out the possibility of a Jew finding his or her own spiritual path. Implicitly and explicitly, this problem is one that Jewish thinkers recognized and grappled with long ago and, in many ways, the full answer (mercifully omitted here) is synonymous with the history of medieval and modern Jewish thought. A briefer answer, one that will also underscore our argument regarding vocation and call, may be gleaned by pointing somewhat anecdotally to the medieval Jews of the mountainous Provençal region of southeastern France.

The Jewish communities of thirteenth-century Provence were vibrant places of learning and scholarship. Provençal Jews were steeped in rabbinic traditions, but much of their intellectual liveliness stemmed from the fact that this small geographical region served as home to the two most stimulating and repercussive developments in medieval Judaism, namely, the emergence of Jewish philosophy and Jewish mysticism. Leaving aside the story of how this came to be, it is sufficient for our purposes to note that within the confines of relatively small communities, sometimes numbering no more than a few hundred Jewish souls, we had individual men with radically different notions of the world, of God, and of their lives as Jews. On the one hand, philosophically minded Jews, embracing the example, image, and teachings of Maimonides, espoused an Aristotelian interpretation of Scripture that cast God as an unmovable First Cause that acted on the world in a series of fixed causal relationships. The ability of this God to act providentially in history, or even to respond to prayer, was seriously circumscribed; prophecy was a matter of intellectual perspicacity. In this religious worldview, the *mitzvot* were performed to create the requisite physical, moral, and intellectual perfections necessary to attain the highest goal of religious life, that being the love of God, a biblical notion here taken to mean knowledge of God.

This heavily intellectualized interpretation of Judaism stood in contrast, on the other hand, to the mythologized views articulated by thirteenth-century Provençal mystics, standing at the beginnings of what would become a rich tradition of medieval Jewish Kabbalah. Here, the language and conceptualizing of God was utterly different; instead of a concern with the laws of nature and natural law, these mystics focused upon the mystico-theological process of divine emanation that *preceded* the account of creation in Genesis 1. In place of a language dominated by logical inferences and proofs, these early kabbalists read and spoke in a language of rich and dynamic symbols that constituted the system of the *sephirot*, the ten emanations that represented forces within the Godhead, within the world, and within ourselves. The performance of the *mitzvot* was not reducible to the attainment of various human perfections; rather, observing all the prescribed duties and obligations punctiliously enabled the individual to partake in the essence of the divine world, effecting changes in the dynamics operative within the Godhead.

Although we have suggested that classical Judaism does not incorporate notions of vocation and call, might the pursuit of philosophy or mysticism or other such coherent systems not include those notions in other forms? These worldviews found expression in the intense and esoteric discussions of small circles of enthusiasts, in which the participants themselves understood that such reflections were intended for a select few. Their ability to peer into the deepest secrets of the Torah, as they would put it, was an extraordinary voyage that could be embarked upon by dint of the native talent, preparation, and discipline.

The teachings of these circles, moreover, were not only socially limited and small, but they espoused a spirituality wherein the emphasis was necessarily placed on the transformative journey of the individual; only the refined soul, nurtured and cultivated in the ways prescribed by these schools, could possibly undertake the kind of journey that could lead to this encounter with God.

Still, the language of vocation and call did not manifest itself among Provençal Jews or their philosophical or mystical heirs. There was an ever-present tension between this private, intensely reflective activity, and the overt public life of Jewish observance. This tension, tellingly, did not result in any serious antinomian manifestations, but in the reaffirmation of the primacy of the *mitzvot*. Philosophically and mystically oriented individuals lived virtually indistinguishable lives as Jews. They not only performed the same *mitzvot* with identical attention to the smallest *halakhic* detail, but could—and almost certainly did—share ritual objects and even pray together. The last comment should not be taken lightly, because for all intents and purposes, the Gods they invoked in identical language were utterly incompatible. Philosophers and kabbalists certainly took the elitist view that they alone understood the Torah, that they had the keys to an attic that allowed them to see what others could not; but they remained keenly aware of the building within which the attic rested. This structure was not only the egress through which they passed; it was the home from which they departed every morning and to which they returned every evening. Their speculations, visions, and interpretations were theirs to cultivate, but they were never allowed to subsume their daily existence as Jews. At the end of the day, philosophical and mystical reflections served as a channel for individual expression, but such reflections were well grounded in the life of *halakhah* and hence no more open to notions of vocation or call.

Modernity

As with so much in the history of Judaism, everything began to change in the late eighteenth and early nineteenth centuries. Until this point, the mandated corporate existence of medieval Jewry had supported the ancient self-identification as *ʿam yisraʾel* (the nation of Israel) and the even earlier tribal self-identification as *bnei yisra'el* (the children of Israel/Jacob). With the advent of the modern nation-state, equal citizenship, and universal rights, Jewish corporate citizenship ceased to exist. Jews were now legally—and eventually socially and politically—Frenchmen, Germans, and Americans. For Jews, identity became more than just a private and voluntaristic affair to be mediated over and against the dominant cultural and social values of the majority. For the first time, Jews needed to grapple with the inextricable national-religious character of their tradition in ways that didn't afford easy answers: were Jews primarily a people, dispossessed of land and language, for whom traditional Judaism was but one form of spiritual expression; or did Jews constitute a religious community, defined essentially by its beliefs and rituals, that was molded into national form only in the crucible of an unfortunate diaspora existence?

The implications of these questions were as serious as they were intractable, and out of them have come a wide variety of religious responses (Reform, Conservative, Reconstructionist, and Orthodox, with their multiple permutations), nationalist/Zionist movements (with their differing political, cultural, and religious values), and secularist expressions of various cultural and political hues. Many Jews, of course, have taken what seemed to be a more natural path commensurate with their newfound civil equality, and have chosen to assimilate fully and cease identifying as Jews in any way. On the other hand, the various strains of traditional Judaism, also buffeted by modernity, continued to cling to the language and notions of rabbinic and medieval Judaism. But for those Jews who sought to remain Jewish and wished to "modernize" Judaism in tandem with contemporary needs, the notion of covenantal community, and the imperatives of duty and obligation, became problematic—ideas to be reinterpreted, diluted, or simply ignored.

The insistent individualism of the modern age has, therefore, challenged the covenantal and communitarian qualities of Jewish traditions, and has had a profound impact on Jewish theological ruminations. This is true of thinkers who abandoned traditional Jewish practices as much as it is true of philosophers who remained committed to *mitzvot* and *halakhah*. Martin Buber, for example, developed an abiding interest in Hasidic literature, a mix of folktales, biblical commentaries, and mystical teachings spawned by a group of late-eighteenth-century Eastern European charismatic figures. Despite early fears to the contrary, the Hasidic sects of Poland and the Ukraine continued to uphold the normative practices of rabbinic Judaism, injecting a reinvigorated sense of community and personal passion into the life of Torah. For Buber, who resolutely embraced religiosity *(religiosität)* while rejecting all commitments to normative religion, the attraction of Hasidism lay in what he perceived as the perfect embodiment of the I-Thou relationship, a relationship to the divine that was all presentness, devoid of all the problematic assertions of objectified God-language. In his retelling of these Hasidic tales, then, Buber wrenched them from their social and communal contexts, and in a dramatic fashion shifted notions of a national-tribal relationship with God to the individual existential plane.

Something of the same impulse informed even the normatively inclined and thoroughly rabbinic thinking of Rabbi Joseph Baer Soloveitchik, the preeminent Lithuanian Talmudist who was widely viewed as the spiritual leader of the progressive wing of American Orthodoxy. Even though Soloveitchik remained fully committed to notions of the covenant, *halakhah*, and the *mitzvot*, he spoke of the intimately personal quality of an individual's relationship with God, stressing the solitary and even lonely nature of that spirituality. Soloveitchik's writing, in fact, was fraught with tensions between the externally oriented, socially active nature of communal faith and the introspective, highly personal existential religiosity that was overwhelmed with the magnitude of the All. For Soloveitchik, as for Buber, the individual encounter with God was not the esoteric, highly elitist endeavor that had informed their philosophical and mystical predecessors; this encounter, rather, was the very imperative that gave universal shape to, and defined, our humanity. As such, although one can detect something of the notion of call in these modern articulations of the human-divine relationship, they are purposefully universalized in ways intended to go beyond notions of vocation and in order to allow for that which modernity has rendered so problematic—the very possibility of an encounter with God.

In the less rarified social milieu of contemporary American Jewry, it is not altogether rare to hear the language of vocation and call, particularly among Jews who have chosen to serve in the rabbinate. American Judaism has come to mirror the suburbanized civic religion of its neighboring Christian churches. In this setting, Jews took up synagogue membership and attended on important holidays, but for a vast majority, such participation was circumscribed and clearly overshadowed by other familial, social, or economic commitments. Jews successfully aspired to a wide variety of careers and professions—but the rabbinate was not among them. When a young man or woman expressed an interest in the rabbinate, it came not as a culmination of years of study and a mastery of traditional texts. In recent decades, the majority of Jews seeking ordination are not products of the Jewish parochial school system, and often have limited knowledge of Hebrew or Jewish traditions. As such, those choosing to work in the rabbinate are often doing so as a means of reconnecting with Judaism, but this choice is also expressed as a means of serving other Jews, an opportunity to minister to the spiritual, emotional, and psychological needs of their co-religionists. It is here, in this contemporary rabbinate, that one hears the language and conceptual notions of vocation and call.

Because this contemporary development is born of the intimate Jewish encounter with modernity, I suspect that expressions of vocation and call among many Jews would have much in common with other such expressions at the hands of Catholics and Protestants. At the same time, one must bear in mind the varieties of Judaism extant today, and the fact that different Jewish communities have accommodated themselves to modern realities in dissimilar ways, some admitting notions of vocation and call much more readily than others. For some Jews, our discussion of vocation and call might be most illuminating, an important articulation of the life of faith that can serve to deepen religious commitments and under-standings. But we must also bear in mind that there are contemporary Jews for whom such language remains foreign and awkward, for whom a life of *mitzvot* will always subsume, if not obviate, the very idea of vocation and call.

⌒∂ Urban C. von Wahlde

"My food is to do the will of the one who sent me" (John 4:34)

Jesus as Model of Vocation in the Gospel of John

What Sort of Vocation?

For many people, to speak of a "vocation" in a religious context, particularly the Roman Catholic context, is to speak of a call to the priesthood, or life in a religious order. When it is used in a purely secular sense, the term can be used as a synonym for "career." Here the term will be understood in a sense slightly different from either of these but related to both, for "vocation" can also refer to the conviction that one's life, in whatever specific form, can be lived in such a way as to cooperate, or be in touch, with God's plan for the world. In this sense, the notion of "vocation" is born of the conviction that one's life task can be chosen and lived out in some sort of response to a divine invitation. It is a combination of recognition of one's own talents as God-given with the conviction that such talents, if used well, can contribute to the betterment of the world. In this sense, of course, vocation is being understood in a religious context. It is the purpose of this essay to explore this notion of vocation as set forth in the Gospel of John.[1]

The Vocation of the Believer or the Vocation of Jesus?

From the very beginning of the Gospel of John, Jesus invites others to follow him. In 1:19 and the following verses, when Andrew and another disciple approach Jesus, he invites them to "Come and see." In 4:4 and the following verses, Jesus meets a Samaritan woman at the well in Sychar and offers her "living water." After a prolonged discussion, she goes into the town to tell others about Jesus and they come out, meet him, and take him into their village for two days. As a result, many come to believe in him. In chapter 9, Jesus heals a man born blind and, soon after, invites him to believe "in the Son of Man."

Yet what are these people called to? Essentially they are called to meet Jesus and to make a decision for or against him. In the language of theology, their call is directly and exclusively connected with "Christology." They are invited to recognize and affirm that Jesus is who he claims to be, and, therefore, to follow him.

The acceptance of Jesus is at the heart of Christian theology, but in the Gospel of John it assumes a unique and all-encompassing focus.[2] When we look closely at the Gospel, we find that it does not give us as much insight as we might hope into the Johannine perception of Christian vocation, except as a response to Jesus.

---

1. In this sense, "vocation" is closely related to the notion of "mission." If we focus on etymology, we see that the first relates to being "called" while the second views one's life from the point of view of being "sent." Of course, these are two aspects of a single whole, just as the original followers of Jesus were called both "disciples" (learners, Lat. *disco*) as well as "apostles" (ones sent, Gk *apostello*). To understand "vocation" in the Gospel only as being called would diminish the term, as vocation is very closely related to mission.

2. There are two primary reasons for the focus on the Christology in John. First, in the Gospel of John, the primary gift offered by Jesus is not the "kingdom of God" or "salvation," but "life." This life is "eternal" life, that is, the life that is the principle of God's own life and that he will share through the gift of his Spirit. But the great "eschatological" gift of the Spirit will be made only to those who believe the promise of it

Yet, as we read the Gospel, it becomes clear that if there is relatively little detail about the vocation of the believer, there is a remarkable amount of detail about the response of Jesus himself to the call of the Father. Much more so than in the other Gospels, we are given an in-depth view of the interiority and intentionality of Jesus. Because of this, we are able to examine the way Jesus' response is portrayed and then ask whether Jesus' own understanding of his ministry can serve as a means of learning about the response appropriate for the believer.

Following this lead, we will attempt to become familiar with the way the Gospel portrays the response of Jesus. We will begin with a brief "reading" of the Gospel, allowing the evangelist to work his art as he gradually reveals what it is that leads Jesus to live out his life in the way he does. We will then take up several of the themes that emerge in this reading and reflect on these to see what they may tell us about dedicating one's resources to the work of God.

A Reading of John's Gospel

The Gospel of John begins with a prologue in which the entire ministry of Jesus is placed in cosmic perspective. It ends with the appearance of Jesus to his disciples along the shore of the Sea of Galilee. Between these two "bookends," the Gospel presents a unique portrayal of Jesus' ministry and a unique insight not only into the depths of Jesus' identity but also into the depths of his interiority.

---

made by Jesus. Much hinges on the ability and authority of Jesus to make such promises: who is this person who offers such a gift?

Second, at one stage in the community's history, there seems to have arisen a division about the relation of Jesus ("Son of God") to the believer who has received the Spirit and has been born again and so is a "child of God." How is Jesus, who also received the Spirit, different from the believer? It is in this context that other dimensions of the identity of Jesus become clearer: his status as "unique" *(monogenês)* Son of God, his pre-existence, etc. As a result of these two impulses, there is a focus on delineating the full dimensions of the identity of Jesus that is not found anywhere else in the New Testament.

Jesus' public ministry begins in Galilee, where he performs a number of miracles. At a wedding feast he transforms a lack of wine into abundance, and his disciples, seeing his identity reflected in this act, come to believe in him. The meeting with the woman from Samaria leads to her conversion and that of many others. But not only does Jesus have a ministry in Galilee; he also regularly comes to Judea and Jerusalem, particularly for the major Jewish feasts (i.e., Passover; Tabernacles; Dedication; and Passover). During these visits, Jesus enters into dialogue with a variety of persons; but between chapters 5 and 12, he speaks and debates primarily with "the Jews" (John's special designation for the authoritative representatives of Judaism).[3]

His public ministry comes to an end in chapter 12, with his third trip to Jerusalem and his final celebration of Passover there. Knowing that his arrest, trial, and death are imminent, Jesus celebrates a final meal with his disciples and then instructs them on what they are to do after his death. After going forth to the garden, he is arrested and brought to Annas, Caiaphas, and finally to Pilate. He is crucified, dies, and is buried before sunset. But on the first day of the week he appears to his disciples, gives them final instructions, and fills them with the Holy Spirit. Finally, he appears on the shore of the Sea of Galilee and, after a miraculous catch of fish and a meal with his disciples, appoints Peter to be the leader of the community. Throughout the course of this remarkable ministry the reader is given repeated descriptions of the interior state of Jesus, descriptions that reveal numerous facets of his response to the Father.

---

3. John has been accused of anti-Semitism in his use of the term "Jews." In fact, John uses the term in a variety of ways: to identify customs or feasts as being "of the Jews"; to refer to the inhabitants of Judea (the same Greek word identifies groups which in English would be called "Judeans" and "Jews"); and, some thirty-six times, to refer to Jewish religious authorities. Of course, Judaism in the first century was hardly monolithic, so it is best to say that the "official Judaism" John portrays is that with which his community was in contact and conflict. For more detail, see U. C. von Wahlde, "The Gospel of John and the Presentation of Jews and Judaism," in *Within Context: Essays on Jews and Judaism in the New Testament*, ed. Leon Klenicki, David Efroymson, Eugene Fisher (Collegeville, Minn.: Liturgical Press, 1993), 67–84.

The Gospel's Ways of Presenting Jesus' Response to God

In what follows we will examine the nature of Jesus' response to the Father as variously presented in the Gospel of John.[4]

The Hour of Jesus

The first theme to appear in the Gospel requires the most discussion for a full appreciation.[5] At the wedding in Cana, Mary informs Jesus that the wine is running out. Jesus replies, "What is this to you and to me? My hour has not yet come." With this puzzling response—more puzzling still because although Jesus distances himself from the request, in the end he does precisely what his mother has asked—Jesus sets in motion a questioning on the part of the reader that continues as his ministry unfolds.

In John the term "hour" is used in two different but related senses. In one sense, the entire ministry of Jesus can be said to indicate the arrival of the eschatological "hour." This is the historical moment when, according to hopes of the Jews, God would intervene to bring about a restoration of his people and pronounce ultimate judgment on evil. When Jesus speaks with the Samaritan woman, then (4:23), he says, "the hour is coming *and is now here* when those who worship will worship in Spirit and in truth." In 5:25, Jesus again says that "the hour is coming *and is now here*" when those who are spiritually dead will hear the voice of the Son and will live. Thus it is the ministry of Jesus itself that marks the advent of this special hour.

But there is another sense in which Jesus speaks of his hour and it

4. The order in which these themes are discussed will help to show the relation between them, but it should be noted that this sequence is our own and is not the Gospel's. It may be that not all of them even derive from the same period of the community's theology, but the way they nevertheless cohere illustrates the coherence of Johannine theology, in spite of its complex history.

5. For a brief discussion of the theme of the "hour" of Jesus, see Raymond E. Brown, *The Gospel According to John* (Garden City, N.J.: Doubleday, 1966–70), 517–18. Although written thirty-five years ago, Brown's commentary remains one of the best in terms of scholarly insight and clarity.

is this that we encounter in chapter 2 and that is our focus here. This is precisely an hour that has *not* yet come. It is an hour that the reader will not understand until later. One might call it "an hour within the hour," in the sense that it is a special time within Jesus' ministry, although the ministry itself constitutes a special time within history. But that Jesus will not act before relating his actions to "the hour" creates a tension and expectation that carry the reader on.

It is not until chapter 7 that the theme of the hour appears again. It is now time for the feast of Tabernacles, and Jesus' brothers urge him to go up to Jerusalem for the feast so the crowds may see his miracles. But, as at Cana, he refuses at first, saying that the time is not right; yet, in the end, he goes up. During Tabernacles, he runs into conflict with the religious authorities. When they see Jesus' popular following, they attempt to "seize" him (7:30), but they are unsuccessful. Why? The evangelist gives us two reasons. In one set of texts, we hear that the temple police who have been sent to arrest him are so impressed with his words that they do not arrest him. But in 7:30, we hear that the arrest attempt is unsuccessful because "his hour had not come." This scene takes the reader's knowledge a step further. The first two mentions of "the hour" have to do with miracles, but this one has to do with imminent danger. Like the proper time for the performance of miracles, so also the reality of danger will not touch him until the "proper" time—until his hour has come. The exchanges between Jesus and the religious authorities, which begin at Tabernacles, continue in chapter 8, when again the authorities attempt to arrest Jesus, but they cannot do it because his hour has not yet come (8:20).[6]

In chapter 9, we find the narrative of the healing of the man born blind. Before the miracle proper, we witness a brief exchange be-

6. It is not completely clear to commentators whether the discussions and debates of chapter 8 are meant to be understood as a continuation of the exchanges at Tabernacles or whether they took place at a later meeting. For our purposes, the ambiguity will not be significant.

tween Jesus and his disciples. When the disciples ask whose sin is responsible for the man's blindness, Jesus responds that it is not a result of sin but "so that the works of God might be manifest in him." Although the wording of this statement may sound almost offensive to the modern ear, it serves to focus the reader on the glory of God that will be manifest in the man's healing.[7] Jesus then puts this event into the larger context of his ministry and explains that he has been sent to do the works of God "while it is day"; that "night" is coming when no one will be able to work; and that while he is in the world, Jesus is the "light of the world."[8] Although the hour is not mentioned, it is clear that Jesus is now interpreting the set time of his ministry in a context larger than just "the hour." Not only is his ministry leading to an hour, his ministry has a certain urgency to it, for it is to do the works of God that he has been sent; and while he does this, his presence is like the sun and he is "the light of the world." When night comes, such deeds will not be possible. The coming of the hour and the onset of night appear to be closely related. Having explained the larger context and meaning of what is about to happen, Jesus proceeds to heal the man born blind.

The next mention of the hour occurs in chapter 11. Jesus hears of the sickness of his friend Lazarus and the disciples express surprise that Jesus would consider journeying again to Judea since there is a clear danger there. Once again, Jesus tries to explain to his disciples, in ever more explicit language, that his ministry is guided by a divine plan. Returning to the notion of "day," Jesus develops the image further. Are there not twelve hours in the day and is it not true

---

7. The text here has been edited and this has caused some of the difficulty. The point is not that God blinded the man from birth *so that* there would be an occasion for a miracle, but that the man's blindness allowed the demonstration of God's ability and desire to heal.

8. That Jesus is the light of the world is a theme that has been present since the beginning of the Gospel. In the prologue, Jesus' presence in the world is described by the narrator as light coming into darkness. In 8:12 Jesus proclaims himself the light of the world. This continues to be a theme for the remainder of the ministry. In 12:36 Jesus urges his listeners to believe in the light so that they might become "children of light" (so also 12:50).

that if one walks in the day, one will not fall, "because the light of this world is shining"? Likewise, "If one walks in the night, one will stumble; for there is no light in the person." Combining the description of himself as the "light of the world" with the notion of twelve hours in the day—and also playing on the image of the sun as the light of the world, which makes walking possible—Jesus explains that no one is able to walk without the presence of Jesus, who is the "light of the world."

What had started out as the image of the hour has now grown to include the image of "the sun," "the day," "the night," and a period of "twelve hours." By the sheer amount of attention given to the theme and its development, it becomes clear that this sense of a divinely appointed time for Jesus' ministry is an important one. But the questions remain: How long is the day? When will the hour come? When will the night come?

Shortly after the raising of Lazarus and a few days before Passover, Jesus enters Jerusalem to great public acclaim (12:12–15). There is a crowd with him, which is coming from Bethany. There is another crowd that comes out from Jerusalem because they have heard of the miracle. Together they welcome Jesus in a public procession that alarms the religious authorities. Clearly, things are approaching a climax. Soon after this, we are told that "some Greeks" wish to see Jesus. In its context, this coming of the Greeks fulfills the words of the prophet Zechariah (14:16) who promised that in the end times the Gentiles would come to Jerusalem seeking the Lord. When he hears of the advent of the Greeks, Jesus is obviously moved and declares in a solemn and profound way that now his hour has come! It is the hour in which "the Son of Man will be glorified" (12:23). If there had been hints earlier of the hour being a period of danger and suffering, this now becomes clear. It is in this hour that Jesus will be put to the test, but he does not ask to have the hour taken from him, for he knows that it is for this hour that he came into the world (12:27). If he describes the hour as a "glorification" of the Son of Man, it is clear that it involves suffering and death. Although it is an hour of death, he does not ask for it to be taken away. Instead, he asks the Father to glorify his (the Father's) name. Soon afterward, Jesus sits down to his final meal with his disciples. After the meal and after Jesus' example of foot washing, Judas is revealed as the betrayer and departs. The evangelist then explains: "It was night." Jesus' hour has now truly arrived.

We can see clearly how Jesus' entire ministry was conducted under the aegis of the hour. What it tells us theologically is that in John's view, when Jesus acted, he was governed not by human motivation but by a timetable set for him by the Father. For everything he did there was a proper time, and each action of his ministry was entirely in accord with that hour given him. The concept of "the hour" provides a framework within which the entirety of the ministry transpires.

The One Sent by the Father

If the notion of the hour provides an overarching framework for Jesus' ministry, the second theme we will review is nevertheless the most frequently invoked by Jesus to describe his purpose: he is one "sent by the Father."[9] More than forty times Jesus speaks of himself this way.

When scholars attempt to understand what such a notion would have meant to the Gospel's first-century readers, they often point to the way this expression parallels the description of a king's emissary, whose sole function is to deliver the message he has been given, to repeat what he has been told. In this sense, Jesus is indeed the emissary of God, for he seeks to do what he has been told to do by the Father.[10] The close association between Jesus' understanding of the

9. The Gospel uses two verbs for this sending. Some twenty times it uses the verb *pempô;* and another eighteen times it uses *apostellô.* Although the question has been raised whether a distinction is intended between the two verbs, most biblical scholars think not. As is sometimes the case in Greek, *pempô* seems to be preferred when a participle is called for, and *apostellô* when a finite verb is called for.

10. A helpful discussion of this can be found in B. Witherington III, *John's Wisdom: A Commentary on the Fourth Gospel* (Louisville: Westminster/John Knox, 1995), 140–41. For a more detailed discussion, see Peder Borgen, "God's Agent in the Fourth Gospel," in *Religions in Antiquity, Essays in Memory of Erwin Ramsdell Goodenough,* ed.

Father and his self-understanding as one "sent" is mirrored in his frequent reference to "the Father who sent me," which occurs as a refrain throughout the Gospel. However, while Jesus is indeed an emissary, it is also clear that Jesus is much more than that, for he is also the Son. And so the Johannine emissary is a unique one: the Son sent by the Father.

Not only is the Johannine Jesus the Son of the Father, who is sent by the Father; he regularly claims the prerogatives of God himself! In 5:17–18, for example, when he is challenged for working on the Sabbath, Jesus explains that just as the Father works on the Sabbath, so does "the son."[11] Not only does Jesus claim the privilege of working on the Sabbath, but also, just as the Father has the power to give life and to judge, so does Jesus (5:19–22). In this respect, the person and function of Jesus, as John describes him, is a profound mystery; for although Jesus claims to possess the powers of God himself, he is at the same time totally self-effacing in his claim to possess none of those powers in himself, but only as a gift from the Father.

Jesus' description of himself as "being sent" clearly indicates that his whole purpose and aim is determined by the Father. If the hour speaks of the plan of the ministry, his being sent speaks about the "why" behind it.

One Who Does Nothing "On His Own"

Closely connected with Jesus' description of his being sent is his repeated insistence that he does not act "on his own." It would seem to go without saying that an emissary would not take it upon himself to act on his own. But we have seen that Jesus is much more than an emissary; he is the Son who has been given the powers of the Father. There is, in fact, a complex of terms through which Jesus

---

Jacob Neusner, vol. 14 of *Studies in the History of Religion* (Leiden: E. J. Brill, 1968), 137–48.

11. This prerogative of God to work on the Sabbath was explicitly stated in Jewish law, but it was a prerogative reserved exclusively for God. The Jews therefore saw Jesus' claim to the privilege as blasphemy. See Brown, *The Gospel According to John*, 216–17.

denies that anything he does is a result of action "on his own": he has not *come* "on his own"; he does not *act* "on his own"; he does not *speak* "on his own." Nor does he witness "to himself."

Some examples may help us appreciate what Jesus means by these statements. In chapter 5, immediately after he claims for himself the two unique powers of the Father, he states that "the Son is not able to do anything of himself but only what he sees the Father doing" (5:19). He repeats this—almost word for word—eleven verses later (5:30). In 8:28 he says again that he does not do anything "of himself," but only what the Father taught him.

In 5:30–40, immediately after explaining the paradox of having the powers of God the Father but not of having them on his own, Jesus goes on to talk about the ways one is able to "prove" his claims; and here again he is entirely self-effacing. The Gospel's language is that of "witness." Jesus does not "witness" to himself; but there are other witnesses to him: John the Baptist; Jesus' works; the word of Jesus given by the Father; and finally, Scripture.[12]

If chapter 5 sets forth the most detailed exposition of both Jesus' exalted claims and the origin of all of them in the Father, the following chapters pick up these themes again and again. In 7:17, 12:49, and 14:10, Jesus says that he does not speak of his own accord ("of himself"), but speaks only what he hears from the Father. In 7:28 and 8:42 he has not come "of himself"; in 8:14 and 8:18 he does not act "of himself." If this repetition creates a monotony, it is a monotony that reflects the strong and single-minded focus of Jesus: his total self-emptying in the service of the Father.

---

12. As many commentators have observed, this notion of witness, which pervades the public ministry, gives the ministry in John the aura of a forensic dispute. Such witnesses are generally associated with judicial trials and many readers have observed that the trial, which is contained in the Passion in the other Gospels, is extended through the ministry in John. See James M. Boice, *Witness and Revelation in the Gospel of John* (Grand Rapids: Eerdmans, 1970). The most extensive treatment of this theme is found in Johannes Beutler, *Martyria: Traditionsgeschichtliche Untersuchungen zum Zeugnis thema bei Johannes,* vol. 10 of *Frankfurter theologische Studien* (1972).

The One Who Does the Will of the Father

A fourth expression that clearly reflects the interior attitude of Jesus is his repeated assertion that he has come to do the will of the Father (4:34; 5:30; 6:38–40; 7:17; 8:39–47; 9:31). For Jesus, his time on earth is a matter of doing the Father's will, pure and simple. He is sent, and he is sent *to do the Father's will.* In a sense, this is the positive counterpart to the statement that he has not come "of himself." Twice he makes explicit that he does the will of the one who sent him *and not his own will* (5:30; 6:38–40). The contrast is clear; he is dedicated solely to the will of the Father. But it is perhaps significant that Jesus identifies the one whose will he seeks to follow not as "Father" but as "the one who sent him." Thus it is because he is sent that he must do the will of the sender. He has come with a mission, and because he has been sent, he wishes to do only the will of the one who sent him.

In chapter 8 we see another aspect of the concept of doing another's will. Although it does not describe Jesus as doing the will of the Father, it is a passage that puts the concept of doing someone's will in a larger framework and the steadfast faithfulness of Jesus in clearer perspective. In 8:38–47, a passage that is often misunderstood because of its apocalyptic rhetoric, Jesus explains that children naturally "do their father's wishes."[13] He adds that if God were their father, they would love him (8:42) because he himself has come from God. But instead they do the wishes of their father, the devil, who was a liar and a murderer from the beginning. And they show

---

13. A complicating factor in chapter 8 is the fact that in 8:39, 41, the author uses the expression "to do the works of" someone to mean "doing the will of" the person. This is not the "works," which I address in the next section, but rather an idiomatic expression found regularly in apocalyptic writing where one's actions are understood to be done under the direction of either God or Belial (Satan). In this sense, "to do the works of someone" has the more general meaning of "to do the will of someone." This usage has been recognized and explained in, for example, Roland Bergmeier, "Glaube als Werk? Die 'Werke Gottes' in Damaskusschrift II, 14–15 und Johannes 6, 28–29," *Revue deQumran* 6 (1967): 253–60, and Urban C. von Wahlde, "Faith and Works in Jn vi 28–29: Exegesis or Eisegesis?" *Novum Testamentum* 22 (1980): 304–15.

this by not accepting Jesus, who speaks the truth.[14] Thus he argues that his opponents fail to do the will of God. In this strong polemical exchange, which reflects the choices of "fathers" open to all individuals, the steadfastness of Jesus' choice to do only the will of God becomes that much clearer.

The "Work" Given Jesus by the Father

In the Gospel of John the notion of "work" is perhaps the most important conceptualization of *what* Jesus is sent to do. We hear Jesus speak of his work for the first time in what appears to be a trivial incident. In chapter 4, as he returns to Galilee, Jesus has to pass through Samaria and stops at Jacob's well to rest. The focus of this episode is the exchange with the Samaritan woman, a powerful conversation that transforms the woman. And so, when the disciples return with food for him, we do not expect what happens next. Rather than simply accept it, Jesus startles his disciples by contrasting the food they have brought him with another kind of food that they know not of: to do the will of the Father and to bring his work to completion.

When the Gospel speaks of the "work" (and "works") of Jesus, it always associates this work with the work of the Father. What the Son does is done in close communion with the Father. The full revelation of the nature of this work takes place gradually and, like the development of the concept of the hour, culminates in the Passion. In chapter 4, as we have seen, Jesus makes his initial assertion that his food is to bring the work of the Father to completion. But what

---

14. Because his listeners are referred to in the wider context as "the Jews," many have taken this text to say that the father of all the Jews is the devil, but this is an error. Apocalyptic exhortation was dualistic, that is, it gave the individual only two choices, to follow God or to follow the devil. Such exhortation was used elsewhere in ancient literature by Jews against fellow Jews, as well as by Christians against fellow Christians. Although such exhortation is harsh and calls for a radical decision, it is not, and should not be taken as, anti-Semitic. For an excellent study of the rhetorical use of language in the ancient world, particularly among Jews, see Luke T. Johnson, "The New Testament's Anti-Jewish Slander and the Conventions of Ancient Polemic," *Journal of Biblical Literature* 108 (1989): 419–41.

precisely that food might be is not completely clear. In chapter 5 Jesus argues that the work he does can be done even on the Sabbath because, like God the Father, who must work in order for creation to be sustained, Jesus also must work even on the Sabbath. In chapter 5 we learn not only that his work involves the Sabbath prerogatives of the Father but that the work itself is a sharing in the two actions most characteristic of God—the giving of life and the passing of judgment. Jesus' work is both a response to the Father and also a sharing in the Father's work. Beginning in chapter 5 Jesus also regularly refers to his miracles as his "works."[15] These miracles, then, in the eyes of Jesus, are not conceived of primarily as stupendous or powerful, but rather as part of the work of the Father (5:36; cf. 17:4, 19:30).

But it is clear that the use of "work" in John should be understood against the background of its use in the Old Testament. "Work" is the term used to describe creation in Genesis 2:2. It is also used to refer to the miraculous events preceding and accompanying the Exodus (Exod. 34:10; Ps. 56:5, 77:12; Deut. 3:24). So it is clear that the Gospel uses this term in a very Jewish way—associating the activity of Jesus not only with the activity of his Father, but also with the creative and salvific events of Jewish history.

While these works have their primary meaning in the context of salvation history, they also function in a more legalistic sense as "witnesses" to him. Several times in the Gospel of John, but most clearly in 5:31–40, Jesus refers to the various witnesses given him by the Father to confirm that he is truly from God. Alongside the witness of John the Baptist, the witness of the words that Jesus speaks, and the witness of Scripture, there is also the witness of his works. The most extensive discussion of the witness value of the works of Jesus occurs in John 10:22–38. Jesus repeatedly says that if his listeners do not believe him, they should at least believe the works themselves (10:37–38, 14:11). For those who would see, all his works show that Jesus has been sent by God.

15. 5:20, 36; 7:21; 9:4; 10:25, 32, 33, 37, 38; 14:10, 11, 12.

There is one important final aspect of John's use of the word "work." As we have seen, "work" is regularly associated with the verb *teleioô*, which can mean both to bring to completion and to bring to perfection.[16] Both meanings are relevant in the context of Jesus' ministry. In his last discourses with his disciples, Jesus speaks of his having brought the work of the Father to completion (17:4); so it is no surprise that the actual completion of the work of the Father will take place in Jesus' death. And so, in John's Gospel, the final words of Jesus (19:30) from the cross are "It is finished."[17] The death of Jesus marks the attainment of his goal: a life poured out in completion of and in cooperation with the work of the Father.[18]

Seeking the Glory of the Father

In our exploration of the various ways in which the Gospel reflects Jesus' attitude toward his ministry, Jesus' repeated references to seeking the "glory" of the Father rank among the best known. For many people, "glory" is one of the terms most characteristic of the Gospel of John. Although it seldom appears in the synoptic Gospels, it is a central theme of John; but it is not always easy to understand.

In its most general meaning, "glory" is the external *manifestation* of a person's identity. But it can also refer to the *recognition* of that identity by others. It is generally used to refer to the recognition and acknowledgment of one's identity in a positive way, and so English-speaking translators often render it as "praise" or "honor." But the term means more than this, since glory is much more intimately connected with a person's deepest identity.

"Glory" too is best understood against the background of its use in the Old Testament. In Job 19:9, Proverbs 16:31 and 20:29, and Isaiah 8:7, it is used to refer to the glory (or "importance") of humans. More significant is the fact that the glory of the Lord is associated

16. 4:34; 5:36; 17:4, 23; 19:28.

17. Although the verb used here is *teleô* rather than *teleioô*, the meaning is quite similar: to reach one's goal.

18. For further reading, see Brown, *The Gospel According to John*, 525–31.

with his epiphany at Sinai and with the Tabernacles and then the Temple (Exod. 40:34; Num. 20:6; Ps. 24:7–10). It is also revealed in Ezekiel's visions (Ezek. 10:4, 28:22). The proper response to the recognition of glory on the part of humans is to *give* glory to God (Ps. 22:23, 29:2, 86:9; Isa. 66:5). All of these uses are reflected in John's Gospel and help clarify its use of the term.

But the use of "glory" in the gospel is complex, more so than is at first apparent. In John we read of both the glory of Jesus (which he does not seek) and the glory of the Father (which he does seek). During his ministry, Jesus is glorified in two ways. In his public ministry, his words and deeds glorify him. That is, Jesus' inner reality, his true identity, becomes manifest in his actions. Thus his glory is manifest in the power of his deeds and words. For example, it is said that when Jesus turned water into wine at the wedding in Cana of Galilee, the disciples saw his glory and believed in him (2:11).

But Jesus is also glorified by his Passion. It is this sense of glory that was the scandal and the paradox of early Christianity. At the end of the public ministry, the Father addresses Jesus, saying, "I have glorified my name and I will glorify it" (12:28). At the beginning of his final supper with his disciples, Jesus himself says, "Now the Son of Man has been glorified and God has been glorified in him. And God will glorify him and will glorify him very soon" (13:31–32). Thus both Jesus and the Father affirm that the true glory of God is manifest in Jesus' passion and death no less than in the miracles and powerful words. If the Passion was scandalous for the synoptic Gospels, for John it is seen as yet another manifestation of the true identity of Jesus.

But John reveals yet another dimension of the glory of Jesus, one that transcends his earthly ministry. In his so-called high priestly prayer in chapter 17, Jesus prays to the Father, recalling that he has glorified the Father by bringing to completion the work of the Father (17:4), and now he prays that the Father will glorify Jesus with the glory Jesus shared with the Father before the world existed (17:5). Here, as Jesus is about to enter into the most difficult part of his earthly glorification, his prayer recalls that beyond this suffering and ignominy is a glory with the Father from before time began. Clearly, his glory is divine and eternal, and far exceeds all aspects of human existence. His glory is, as the prologue says, "the glory of a unique[19] son from the Father, full of grace and truth" (1:14).

Up to this point, we have seen the various aspects of the true glory of Jesus. But in spite of this most exalted glory, there are two kinds of glory that Jesus does not seek. First, he does not accept any glory "on the human level." By this, Jesus rejects any recognition that would attribute his words and deeds to something that he possesses in himself. The clearest expression of this comes in John 5:41–47. As Jesus says in 5:41–43, if someone comes "in his own name," people are more ready to accept the person. Thus Jesus laments the fact that many who encountered him during his ministry looked for a glory, a self-understanding and self-presentation, that made sense only in human terms and within the sphere of earthly existence. Because they were looking for the wrong thing, they could not see Jesus' true glory (5:44).

This passage is prelude to the "true" glory of Jesus, the glory that attributes all of Jesus' accomplishments and power to the Father. As Jesus says in 5:43, he has come in the name of his Father, and people are therefore not ready to accept him. In this pronouncement Jesus is at his most self-effacing. Not only does the Johannine Jesus see his own life in terms of obedience to the will of the Father, he hopes that those who witness his ministry would also recognize that all Jesus possessed had come from the Father and that Jesus made no claims on behalf of himself.

The Gospel tells us that it is this glory that the disciples see (2:11), even though they need to learn still more from his resurrection. But "the world" does not see this glory. And at the end of Jesus' public ministry, the evangelist laments that so many failed to see Jesus' true glory. But he adds that this was not something unforeseen by God,

---

19. Although *monogenes* is generally translated as "only begotten," its actual meaning is "unique," from *mono* (one) plus *genos* (type). This was recognized first by Dwight Moody, "God's Only Son: The Translation of John 3:16 in the Revised Standard Version," *Journal of Biblical Literature* 72 (1953): 213–19.

for even the Hebrew prophet Isaiah miraculously foresaw both the glory of Jesus and the fact that so many would reject him (12:38–43).

The "Commandments" Given Jesus by the Father

Up to this point, we have seen six elements of the Gospel that seek to describe the reality of Jesus' response to the Father. But this is not all, for we now see that Jesus also speaks of his ministry in an even more compelling way. In two places in the Gospel, we read that what Jesus does in his ministry is a response to "commandments" given him by the Father. These commandments are to love his own to the point of dying for them (10:18), and to speak the words that he has heard from the Father (12:49, 50).[20]

In the context of the Gospel of John, this theology of commandment evokes the covenantal relation of Israel with Yahweh in the Old Testament, especially in the Book of Deuteronomy. The commandments given to Israel are an expression of the divine will for the people and are a result of both their election by God and his covenant with them. Keeping the commandments is to be the expression of the people's love for God (Deut. 5:10, 10:12, 19:9, 28:69). A person cannot be said to love God if the person does not keep the commandments (Deut. 7:9–10). In the Deuteronomic theology of commandment, a contingency is always expressed with regard to God's love and the commandments: failure to keep the commandments results in punishment (Deut. 8:11–20, 28:15–69), and observance brings rewards (Deut. 4:40, 5:16, 32, 6:2, 24, 28:1–14). The Johannine portrayal of commandment echoes this Deuteronomic theology throughout, even in the way Jesus speaks of his own being loved by God as contingent upon his own obedience.

If the concept of Jesus' being "commanded" by the Father seems harsh when compared with the utter self-effacement evident in all the other ways of expressing his relation to the Father, there may be a reason. The Gospel of John underwent several stages of editing be-

---

20. I have written at length on this in *The Johannine Commandments: 1 John and the Struggle for the Johannine Tradition* (New York: Paulist Press, 1990).

fore reaching its final form. These various editions reflected the specific circumstances of the Christian community during its formative years. One of these was a struggle within the Johannine community itself over the understanding and interpretation of the tradition as it had been handed down to them. In response to this, the author of 1 John and also the author of the final edition of the Gospel both included Jesus' references to commandments given to the disciples by Jesus.[21] These commandments, which were related to disputed points of the tradition, were understood to be correlated with similar commandments given to Jesus by the Father. Thus the disciples were commanded to keep the word of Jesus and to love one another, just as Jesus had been commanded to speak the words of God and to love the disciples. In light of the doctrinal disputes, the rigor of the notion of commandment as applied to the ministry of Jesus becomes understandable.

We saw above that the commandments are twofold, comprising the commands to speak what he has heard from the Father and to love his own in the world. Although it is not at first evident, these two commandments encapsulate the entirety of Jesus' ministry. All that he teaches, he has received from the Father. This is simply another way of saying what has been heard above: Jesus does nothing on his own; his words are the words of the Father. Likewise, the commandment of love is meant to summarize all aspects of his behavior in the world: it is to be motivated by and be an expression of love for others. The commandments are thus meant to summarize all aspects of Jesus' ministry.

The Gospel speaks of the necessity that Jesus himself obey the commandment of the Father in order to remain in the Father's love

---

21. It will be noted that there are relatively few references to this theology of commandment in the Gospel and that, where it does appear, the focus is more on the commandments given to the disciples than on the commandments given to Jesus. This is another indication that the real focus here is on the disciples. Moreover, in the first and second Epistles, this theology becomes more dominant. This is another indication that this commandment theology was first articulated in the context of the Epistles and later incorporated into the Gospel of John.

(15:10). While of course this conditional element is a necessary part of the covenantal relation, it is inconceivable that Jesus, especially the Jesus that John portrays, would disobey the commandments given to him. But in the context of the community for which the commandment tradition is articulated, the way Jesus models such obedience is of special importance. The selflessness of his commitment to the Father is nevertheless as clear here as anywhere else.

A Life of Love

In the previous seven sections we have seen the "what" and the "how" of Jesus' mission. When we examine the presentation of love in the Gospel, we see the "why," the basic motivation for Jesus' actions.

The Gospel and Epistles of John are known for their magnificent treatment of divine love, as we have already noticed. One of the most famous statements of the New Testament is John 3:16 ("God so loved the world that he gave his unique son so that everyone believing in him might not perish but have eternal life"). Although the frequent quotation of this verse tends to dull its impact, the text does indeed summarize the divine intention well and puts the ministry of Jesus within a context of all-embracing divine love. Equally well known is a second aspect of love as expressed in the Gospel, the commandment Jesus gives to his own "to love one another" (13:34, 15:12, 17). But it is the third aspect of this love that is of interest to us here: the love of Jesus both for the Father and for his own, which motivates his work.

From one point of view, the notion of Jesus' love for the Father is less developed than the other notions. In only one text is it said explicitly that Jesus' going to his death is a demonstration of his love for the Father (14:31). Yet this does not mean that love as a motive is any less important. From a number of other texts it is clear how much Jesus moves in an environment of total love. He speaks of his awareness of how much the Father loves him (15:9) and even says that the Father loves the disciples as much as he loves Jesus (17:23), and that the Father loved Jesus before the creation of the world

(17:24) and that it is this love that he has given to his disciples (17:26).

But the love of Jesus for his own is clear. In 13:1, at the beginning of the Last Supper, John says: "Having loved his own in the world, he loved them *eis telos*." The Greek phrase *eis telos* can mean both "to the end" and "perfectly." *Telos* is derived from the verb *teleioô*, the verb that, as we have seen, was associated with Jesus' performance of his "work." There it was a matter of both completing the Father's work and also bringing it to perfection. As a result, it is clear that the love of Jesus for both his Father and his own is the root motive for all he does.

Can Jesus Be a Model?

We have now reviewed a total of eight features of the Gospel that bear on and illuminate various aspects of Jesus' response to the Father. We set out to examine the "vocation" of Jesus in the Gospel, but what we found has been, I think, more than we anticipated. When one reads the Gospel of John straight through, it is perhaps easy to overlook the extent to which it concentrates on this aspect of Jesus' inner attitude. But when the various themes are gathered together, it becomes clear that the Gospel's reflection on the inner dispositions of Jesus with regard to the will of the Father is immensely deep and wide-ranging. Moreover, each of these eight themes can be said to be truly substantial, and indeed in many cases *central*, to the understanding of Jesus as he is presented in the Gospel.[22] Like no other work in the New Testament, the Gospel of John is at pains to show the extent to which the ministry of Jesus was a response to the will and desires of the Father.

Jesus is the one sent by the Father and he dedicates himself totally to doing the will of the Father. In that sense, he does nothing on his own, but only what the Father wishes. His entire ministry is

22. If the notion of "commandment" is less central to the Gospel, there is, as we have seen, a reason for this. But its role in the tradition as a whole is not diminished.

arranged as a response to the hour set for him by the Father. Although he himself is the unique, co-eternal Son, who has been given the prerogatives of the Father, he seeks not his own glory but only the glory of the Father. During his ministry he seeks to bring the work of the Father to completion, even though this means laying down his own life. He sees his life as a response to commandments given by the Father, but he responds to them all in total love. What this reveals is a Jesus who is at once the most exalted and the most self-effacing of the New Testament.

But can such a perfect model be a realistic model for the Christian? If this is a question for the modern reader, it clearly was not one for the community that wrote the Gospel. For the Johannine community, Jesus was not someone whose status was so exalted that he was beyond imitation. In fact, the Gospel presents such a thoroughgoing correlation between what Jesus thought and did and what his disciples were to think and do that it is abundantly clear that the Johannine community took Jesus as a model for their own response to both Jesus and the Father. The disciples are to do what Jesus did; they will encounter the same adversity Jesus did; and they will reap the same rewards.

⮰

Scattered throughout the Gospel of John are statements that show how the disciple is to imitate Jesus. The two most specific concern the Johannine commandments. Just as Jesus obeyed the commandment of God about speaking only the word that he had received from the Father, so were the disciples to keep that word. Just as Jesus loved his own to the end, so were the disciples to love one another as Jesus loved them.

But the relation extends beyond the notion of commandment to other aspects of their ministry. Just as Jesus performed works in the world that no one else had done, the disciples would also perform those works—and even greater ones (14:12). But the most all-encompassing statement of the parallel between Jesus and the disciples is the statement of 17:18, that just as the Father sent Jesus into the world, so Jesus sends the disciples! In this single statement, the reader is to understand that the disciple is to stand in the same relation to Jesus as Jesus did to the Father. Although it is stated in a single verse, this linking of the disciples to Jesus is abundantly clear. If the concept is not elaborated at any length, this is only because the focus of the Gospel is on Jesus the model, not on how the disciples were to imitate the model.

It is also evident that Jesus is to be seen as model for the Johannine believer in the statements that, if the disciples are to imitate Jesus, they should also expect the same rejection by the world that he experienced. Not only are the disciples sent as Jesus is sent, but, Jesus makes it clear, if the world hates them, they should know that it hated Jesus first (15:18–20). Thus Jesus will be their model not only in ministry but also in suffering and rejection.

A third way that Jesus serves as a model for the disciples is in the final reward, which accompanies his response to the Father. Several times in his ministry, Jesus refers to the intimacy of his relationship with the Father and to the nature of his relationship as the result of the faithfulness of his response. In John 10:17 Jesus explains, "this is why the Father loves me, because I lay down my life in order to take it up again." Jesus kept the commandments and remained in the Father's love. If the disciples keep Jesus' commandments, they will remain in his love (15:10).

The totality of this intimacy between Jesus and the Father is stated clearly and succinctly in 10:38: "The Father and I are one"! In 15:32 we read, "but I am not alone because the Father is with me." This unity between Father and Son is also extended to the disciples. Just as Jesus and the Father are one, so the disciples are to be one with one another (17:11). In 17:21 Jesus prays that, just as he and the Father are one, they (the disciples) may also be one ("I do not pray for these alone, but also for those believing in me through their word, so that all might be one, just as you, Father, are in me and I am in you, so that they also might be in us"). Jesus promises to the believer the same unity with the Father that he experiences. Later he says, "And I have given them the glory which you have given me, so that they might be one as we are one" (17:22). Thus the Johannine

Jesus promises to those who follow him the same intimacy with the Father that he himself experiences.

Jesus was not only a model for the disciples but the example of what they could hope to achieve and experience as reward. And so we come full circle in discovering the vocation of the believer. It was—and is—to respond to the Father as Jesus did.

In the synoptic Gospels, the instructions to the disciples are specific and the role of the disciple is much more concrete. If we look for this level of specificity in the Gospel of John, we are disappointed. The Gospel of John lays down abstract principles (doing the will of God, seeking his glory, obeying his commandments, seeking to cooperate in God's work, and so on). Yet, if these principles are general, they are all the more applicable. The Johannine portrait does not call for a specific *form* of response but for a particular *kind* of response. And it is in this that the unique contribution of Johannine theology lies.

⟍⟋⟍ Marcia Hermansen

Islamic Concepts of Vocation

> *"Come, Come whoever you are,*
> *Wanderer, worshipper, lover of leaving,*
> *It doesn't matter.*
> *Ours is not a caravan of despair.*
> *Come, even if you have broken your vow*
> *a thousand times.*
> *Come, yet again, come, come."*
>
> —Rumi (d. 1273)

The following essay will explore Islamic reflections on vocation. Christian approaches to the idea of vocation have included the concept of a specific calling to some form of the religious life, as well as broader constructions of the dignity and meaningfulness of all types of work. The sources for these various Christian articulations of vocation have included the Hebrew Bible, the New Testament, the Neoplatonic tradition, and the writings of theologians, such as Thomas Aquinas and Martin Luther.

"Vocation" *per se*—in other words, some Arabic equivalent of the concept of "calling"—has not been strongly marked in Islamic theological reflection. At the same time, it is clear that questions of human purposiveness and labors in this world must have been addressed in numerous contexts. I will therefore undertake a broad review of Islamic positions relevant to the concept of vocation. The main areas that I will cover are vocation according to the Qur'an and the tradition *(sunna)* of the Prophet Muhammad; the idea of vocation in Islamic philosophy, theology, and mysticism; and vocation in the works of contemporary Muslim thinkers.

Qur'an

A search for resonances with the "vocation" concept in the Qur'an includes its broader reflections on guidance, destiny, discernment, recognition, remembrance, gratitude, and intentionality.

Although one must be cautious about forcing theologically simplified identifications across traditions, Arabic words with a meaning similar to "call" are indeed present in the Qur'an. For example the word *nada* (to call) is used, most often in connection with humans calling upon God, but occasionally in terms of the divine summons. For example, the Lord is said to have "called" Moses (19:52, 26:10, 79:16) and Abraham (37:104). Derived from the same Arabic root (n-d-y) is the noun *munadi* (a caller) mentioned in Qur'an 3:193. "We heard a caller calling us to faith, 'Believe in your Lord' and so we believed."[1] This would be an example of "calling" in the general sense that is also present in Judeo-Christian Scripture.

Two other Arabic terms, *istafa* (being singled out or elected) and *da'wa* (call), are used for concepts of religious calling.[2] One of the titles given to the Prophet Muhammad is "al-Mustafa," the elected one, a derivation from the same root (s-f-a) as the noun *istafa* (election). A Christian theologian has defined election as the "deliberate act of God in choosing someone to share his saving purpose."[3] I be-

---

1. The "caller" is generally interpreted as being the Prophet Muhammad. Translations of the Qur'an are derived from Marmaduke Pickthall, *The Meaning of the Glorious Koran* (New York: Mentor, 1970).

2. As in Qur'an 14:44: "So that we might respond to Your call *(da'wa)* and follow the Prophets."

3. Gary D. Babcock, *The Way of Life* (Grand Rapids: Eerdmans, 1998), 3.

lieve that this characterization of "election" would fit quite well with the Islamic idea of *istafa,* except that in Islam the concept of salvation is not emphasized, as, in Muslim theology, heeding divine guidance is the antidote to the Fall.

Although beyond the scope of this essay, I should note that, while the Qur'an does recount the story of Adam and his consort and their disobedience of God, the point of the story, Islamically speaking, is that Adam turns to God and asks for forgiveness. He is then forgiven and receives words of guidance (2:37). Thus it is the idea of turning back to God and remembering one's connection with him that is stressed (7:172). Following the divine guidance is what is required in order for humans to fulfill their original sound nature, as Qur'an 95:4 states: "Indeed We created humans according to the best stature."

The episode of Adam's transgression and repentance is given as follows:

"And We said: O Adam! Dwell thou and thy wife in the Garden, and eat freely whereof what you will; but do not approach this tree lest you become wrongdoers. But Satan caused them to deflect and expelled them from the (happy) state in which they were; and We said: Fall down one of you a foe to the other! There shall be for you on earth a habitation and provision for a time.

Then Adam received from his Lord words (of guidance) and He relented towards him. Lo! He is the Relenting the Merciful.

We said: Go down, all of you from here, but indeed there will come to you from me a guidance, and whosoever follows that guidance, no fear shall come upon them neither shall they grieve." (2:30–38)

The Qur'an indicates that God has repeatedly sent prophets to humanity to remind persons of this bond of faith and guidance and to encourage them obey the divine commands. Hence, in Islam, emphasis is given to fulfilling the specifics of the divine law as brought by the final messenger, Muhammad.

The Arabic term *da'wa* (calling) also means inviting a person to accept Islam.[4] The *Kitab al-Luma* (Book of Brightness) of the tenth-

4. As in 2:186: "Let them hear My call *(da'wa),* and let them trust in Me."

century Sufi al-Sarraj discusses the distinction between the two terms, *da'wa* (calling) and *istafa* (election) in some detail.

Sahl [al-Tustari, a ninth-century mystic] said, "The call *(da'wa)* is general, while guidance *(hidayah)* is specific [to the person]." Here he was referring to God's statement, "Allah calls to the Abode of Peace, and guides whoever He wills to the straight path" (10:25).

Since the call is general and the guidance is particular to the one who is graced by it, he reflects the divine will in whatever he is guided towards. Those whom God chose and loved and elected are other than those whom He called.

Allah has also referred to "being elected" in certain places in His book. In one instance He said, "Say, praise be to Allah and peace upon His worshippers whom He has elected. Allah is better than those whom you associated with Him" (27:59). He referred by "peace upon" to the worshippers whom He had elected and loved and He did not explain who or how they were. He did not leave it at that and said in another verse: "Allah has *elected* messengers from among the angels and human beings" (22:75).[5]

Al-Sarraj goes on to explain that the Qur'anic verse (35:32) that speaks of the "Inheritors of the Book" broadens the scope of the "elected ones" from prophets alone to believers more generally. It is also recognized that within this elective process there are variations in activities and capabilities, for "We made for each one of you a different law *(shar')* and a way of life *(minhaj)* (5:48), and, "If Allah had so willed He could have made you all follow one single community *(umma)* but He wanted to test you by what He gave to you, so compete with one another in doing good" (5:48).[6] While the Sufi al-Sarraj focuses on the implications of this verse for individual vocations, it should also be noted that some commentators understand its meaning as explaining ethnic diversity and encouraging interreligious harmony.[7]

A broad notion of call is that of human deputyship *(khilafat)*:

5. Al-Sarraj, *Kitab al-Luma* (Cairo: Dar al-Kutub al-Hadithiyya, 1960), 108.

6. Ibid., 109.

7. Fazlur Rahman discusses this verse and its implications for religious pluralism: *Major Themes of the Qur'an* (Minneapolis: Bibliotheca Islamica, 1989), 167.

Man has been granted by Allah what has been described in the Qur'an as the vicegerency, and it is his moral duty to be appreciative of this his high calling, and to strive to attain to those qualities of character that are recognized in the attributes of Allah himself. Man was made vicegerent *(khalifa)* on the face of the earth (2:30–3), and this trust *(amanat)* of vicegerency, refused by the heavens and the earth and the mountains, 'man alone undertook to bear.' (33:72)[8]

Closely related to the idea of vocation in Islamic theology is the concept of divine Providence, in Arabic, *rizq.* The Qur'an states, "It is Allah who created you, then provided for you, then made you die, then brought you back to life" (30:40). Another verse states: "We divided up your means of livelihood in the life of the world and raised some of you above others by degrees so that they could avail themselves of one another's help—and your Lord's mercy is better than whatever (wealth) they amass" (43:32).[9] Therefore the Islamic perspective is that ultimately all guidance and provision are divine. Diversity in talents, inclinations, and abilities is part of God's plan. After all, the idea of one's profession or career as a "vocation" is relatively recent even in European Christianity. Finding one's calling in life is now a broad concept that includes individual fulfillment and the performance of valuable roles in society. It is no longer limited in Western Christianity to specifically religious roles. This reconfiguring of vocation emerged with the diversification and secularization of society at the beginning of the modern period.[10]

In Islamic tradition as in Judaism, the detailed provisions of a divine law regulating all human activities led to sacralizing all aspects of life. This nuanced concept of vocation, which hallows work or gives it a higher dignity, is present in Islam in the sense that one per-

8. Dwight M. Donaldson, *Muslim Ethics* (London: Society for Promoting Christian Knowledge, 1953). Donaldson translates al-Dawwani's preamble to *Akhlaq al-Jalali.* The contents are also summarized in English in Majid Fakhri, *Ethical Theories in Islam* (Leiden: E. J. Brill, 1994).

9. Qur'an 29:60 addresses the same theme.

10. Shirley J. Roels, *Organization Man, Organization Woman: Calling, Leadership, and Culture* (Nashville: Abingdon Press, 1997).

forms these actions of earning sustenance according to the provisions laid out by the Creator. Therefore, a preoccupation of early Islamic texts concerning work is "obtaining one's livelihood in a religiously lawful or sanctioned way."

Although earning a livelihood is encouraged as necessary in Islam, it is to be done primarily for the good of society and should never overwhelm one's sense of God consciousness *(taqwa)*.[11] It is a saying of the Prophet that "The best thing a believer can eat is that which he himself has earned."[12] At the same time, the Qur'an cautions that one should not be distracted from the remembrance of God by buying and selling (24:37).

The Qur'an contains rich commercial imagery that reflects the urban environment of Mecca.[13] There are references to honesty in trading, for example, and to giving proper weights and measures.[14] The Prophet was scorned by those opponents who said that he walked in the marketplace.[15] But the Qur'an defends Muhammad's involvement with everyday activities, affirming that all prophets were mortals who consumed earthly food and went about worldly business (25:20). In terms of scriptural references to labor, the Qur'an speaks of gardening and other agricultural occupations, as well as trade and sailing, indicating a range of work possibilities for humans. The phrase "How excellent is the wage of those who labor" is used repeatedly in the Qur'an in connection with the idea of rewards in the next life.[16] Hence there is a metaphorical connection between the rewards of labor in this life and the eternal rewards of the next.

Balance is a key concept in Islamic theology and moral philoso-

11. On *Taqwa* in Muslim theology, see Fazlur Rahman, "Some Key Ethical Concepts in the Quran," *Journal of Religious Ethics* 11 (fall 1983): 170–85.

12. Reported in *Ibn Majah* and *Ibn Hanbal*. Cited by al-Muhasibi, *al-Rizq al-halal wa haqiqat al-tawakkul 'ala Allah* (Cairo: Maktaba al-qur'an, 1984), 44.

13. Charles C. Torrey, *The Commercial-Theological Terms in the Koran* (Leiden: E. J. Brill, 1983).

14. Qur'an 11:84–5, 55:9.

15. Qur'an 25:7.

16. 3:136, 29:58, 39:74. *"Ni'ma 'ajr-u-l-'amilin"*.

phy. There is in human nature a balance of the conjoined aspects of the angelic or heavenly, symbolized by the divine spirit that is blown into the human being by Allah (15:29, 23:72, 32:9), and the earthly side, as seen in the many Qur'anic references to humans' creation from earth, mud, or a blood clot. The clear statement of Qur'an 3:195—"I [God] suffer not the work of any worker, male or female, to be lost"—affirms not only the value of human labor but also the potential of both sexes as workers.

A further idea of discerning one's vocation in life can be extrapolated from the Qur'anic concept of discernment. The Qur'an repeatedly states that God has placed signs upon the horizons and in human beings themselves, which they should attempt to read and reflect upon.[17] The key concepts of recognition *(ma'rifa)* and remembrance *(dhikr)* exhort to self-knowledge, both as an end in itself and as a means to greater effectiveness in outward activity. A divine plan is certainly in place, but we must discern it in order to fulfill our role or vocation within it.

The Qur'anic story of the "primordial covenant" (7:171) elaborated in Islamic theology is relevant. All souls are believed to have stood before Allah in a primordial experience of being called to witness and to have been asked, "Am I not your Lord?" To which each individual replied, "Indeed You are." Our human "forgetfulness" of this innate recognition is one reason why God sends reminders in the form of his books and messengers.

Sunna, Law, and Theology

The *sunna,* or practice, of the Prophet Muhammad, is another source for deriving a Muslim theology of vocation. As Islam is the most recent of the major religions to emerge, the Prophet having lived 570–632 C.E., and as Muhammad was recognized as a successful religious and political leader during his lifetime, many details of

17. These signs are known as *anfusi* (of the self) and *afaqi* (of the horizons) after a Qur'anic verse, "We shall show them our signs in the horizons and in themselves" (41:53).

his life have been preserved through his sayings, the *hadith*. In terms of vocation as "work," for example, Muhammad was employed in the caravan trade for a time, and his daily routine included mundane chores such as mending his own sandals.

There is an interesting saying of the Prophet: "God never sent a prophet except that he had tended flocks." A follower asked, "Even you, O Prophet of Allah?" "Even I," he replied. "I tended them for the people of Mecca."[18] Al-Muhasibi (d. 857), an early Muslim mystic, commenting on these reports, observes that the Qur'an also refers to Moses' working as a shepherd, and even to his use of his staff to knock down leaves for his flocks (20: 17–18). The dignity and worth of work is so great that King Solomon is portrayed in one Sufi narrative as imploring God to teach him a useful trade; thus he becomes the first to weave a certain type of basket.[19] Another important saying of the Prophet explains how each individual—man, woman, or child—of whatever status is entrusted with a responsibility, literally "a flock" to watch over.[20] The sayings of the Prophet, the *hadith*, contain extensive regulations regarding the realms of both commerce and agriculture. These include stipulations regarding proper kinds of contracts and regulations ensuring equity in water rights. There are also references to roles such as that of the doctor *(tabib)* and the one who pronounces legal judgments *(faqih)*.

A further Islamic concept related to "vocation" is the idea of intentionality *(niyya)*. The idea of intention is central both theologically and legally to the Islamic tradition. Legally speaking, Islamic ritual actions such as prayer and fasting need to be preceded by an intentional commitment to the act on the part of the person. This is usually accompanied by a particular statement of intention, and it is this formal act that renders the subsequent action valid in fulfilling

18. Ahadith found in al-Bukhari and other collections. See al-Muhasibi, *al-Rizq al-halal.*

19. Abd al-Qadir Jilani, *Sufficient Provision for Seekers of the Path of Truth*, vol. 1, trans. Muhtar Holland (Hollywood, Fla.: al-Baz, 1997), 78.

20. Cited in al-Muhasibi, *al-Rizq al-halal,* 51.

one's ritual duty. More broadly construed theologically, the intention is what underlies actions, and it is based upon the intention that the actions will be credited by God.[21] Thus, for example, one who becomes a physician with the intention of making money is not judged the same as one who does this out of commitment to human service.

A further way of understanding religious configurations of human activities is according to the categories of the *shari'a* rulings on all human actions. These activities might be ranked anywhere from obligatory to forbidden by Islamic law. Yet another dimension of individual duty regulated by the *shari'a* was that embodied in distinctions made between actions that were *fard 'ayn,* incumbent on all individuals (for example, prayer), and *fard kifaya,* duties that would be fulfilled for the entire community even if only undertaken by certain eligible members. Examples of *fard kifaya* duties included military service or higher religious education.

Thus a doctrine of work was part of the social and moral understanding of an Islamic community. Social self-sufficiency became the responsibility of the entire society to provide the necessary skills to fulfill social needs. If a society lacked an essential skill, whether out of simple absence or because those who possessed it refused to exercise it, then the entire society was to blame.[22] "In this light, Ibn Taymiyya (1328) stresses a person's obligation to utilize a skill as a serious requirement, by virtue of possessing such a skill, and as necessitated by social need."[23]

In Islamic thought, vocation and Providence need to be understood in the light of destiny *(qadr).* A well-known *hadith* states:

Abdullah ibn Ma'sud said, The Messenger of Allah, peace be upon him, narrated to us, "The creation of each of you is brought together in his mother's belly for forty days in the form of a seed, then he is a clot of blood

21. *Hadith Inna al-'amal bi-l niyya.* Actions are judged by their intentions. Related by Bukhari, Muslim, and others.

22. Victor E. Makari, *Ibn Taymiyyah's Ethics: The Social Factor* (Chico, Calif.: Scholar's Press, 1983), 165.

23. Ibid., 165–66.

for a like period, then a morsel of flesh for a like period, then there is sent to him the angel who blows the breath of life into him and who is commanded about four matters: to write down his means of livelihood, his life span, his actions, and whether he will be happy or unhappy. By Allah, other than whom there is no God, one of you may behave as the people of Paradise until there is but an arm's length between him and it, then that which is written overtakes him and he behaves like the people of hell fire and thus he enters it; while one may behave as one of the people of Hell until there is but an arm's length between him and it, and that which has been written overtakes him, then he behaves like the people of Paradise and enters it."

According to this *hadith* Providence has been measured and determined beforehand. The word in Arabic for this measuring out, *taqdir*, is related to the idea of *qadr* or destiny.[24] Since a person's sustenance or Providence has already been determined, a balancing concept is required to explain the apparent contradiction in making vocational choices or, for that matter, any efforts at all. Here there is a need to understand the interrelationship of ideas such as *kasb* (human acquisition through earning or acquiring), *rizq* (divine Providence), and *tawakkul* (complete trust in God). Muslim theologians, such as al-Ash'ari (935), formulated the idea of *kasb* "acquisition" as that which associates or connects a person with their actions. The unity and omnipotence of God, however, entailed that no act could be carried out beyond His will, choice, and power. Despite this apparent predestinarianism, staunch Asharites such as al-Ghazzali clearly maintained that individual choices had consequences—for example, in the development of character through repeated actions that would become permanent dispositions and habits.[25]

---

24. See William Chittick and Sachiko Murata, *The Vision of Islam* (New York: Paragon, 1994), 104ff.

25. Al-Ghazzali, *On Disciplining the Soul,* book 21 of *Ihya 'Ulum al-Din,* trans. T. J. Winter (Cambridge: Islamic Texts Society, 1997).

Philosophers and Mystics

Other sources of Muslim reflections on vocation are the writings of Muslim philosophers such as al-Farabi (951), Ibn Sina (1037), al-Ghazzali (1111), al-Tusi (1274), al-Dawwani (1502), and Mulla Sadra Shirazi (1640). Many of these writings share Hellenistic ethical concerns with virtue and self-refinement.

The tradition of philosophical ethics rarely takes up the discussion of work or profession *per se*. The focus is rather on the attainment of happiness through cultivating virtue and maintaining moderation and balance. One example is the *Nasirean Ethics* of al-Tusi. Tusi argues that the human species needs both the aid of other species and the cooperation of its own kind to ensure the survival of the individual as well as of the human race.[26] The division of labor allows the livelihood of all to be fulfilled.

Now since the works of man pivots on mutual aid, while cooperation is realized by men undertaking each other's important tasks fairly and equally, it follows that the diversity of crafts, which proceeds from the diversity of purposes, demands (a measure of) organization; for if the whole species were to betake themselves in a body to one craft, there would be a return of the situation against which we have just been on guard. For this reason, Divine Wisdom required that there should be a disparity of aspirations and opinions, so that each desires a different occupation, some noble and others base, in the practice of which they are cheerful and contented.[27]

Al-Tusi further observes that diversity in discernment and capacity allows each individual to undertake his own duty, some in managerial positions, others in subservient ones; thus daily life is ordered.[28]

Like Aristotle, the great Muslim theologian al-Ghazzali identifies happiness with the attainment of the chief felicity or good for humans. Both worldly and otherworldly happiness are taken into con-

26. al-Tusi, *The Nasirean Ethics*, trans. G. M. Wickens (London: Allen and Unwin, 1964), 189.
27. Ibid.
28. Ibid., 190.

sideration in his discussion, although it is the latter which is ultimate and real. According to al-Ghazzali, in order to achieve otherworldly happiness, various levels of virtue must be cultivated—including the external virtues of wealth, kin, and social position. There are four further "virtues leading to success from God":[29] guidance *(hidaya)*, good counsel *(rushd)*, direction *(tasdid)*, and support *(ta'yid)*.[30]

He further declares that "Divine guidance is the foundation of all good. Qur'an 20:50 states that God gave to everything its created nature and then guided it." By good counsel, says al-Ghazzali, we mean "that Divine providence which assists man in turning toward his chosen goals, by strengthening his resolve to do what conduces to his righteousness and deters him from what conduces to his destruction." This counsel is inward, as the Koran asserts in 21:51: "We have indeed imparted to Ibrahim his good counsel *(rushd)* previously and were fully conversant therewith."

Right direction *(tasdid)*, by contrast, consists in man's directing his will and movements toward the desired goal, so as to attain it in the shortest time possible. It differs from good counsel in that the latter is limited to exhortation and advice, whereas right direction involves active assistance and reinforcement.

As for divine support *(ta'yid)*, described in the Qur'an as the "assistance of the Holy Spirit," it is an act of empowering man through granting him insight and the physical capacity to carry out the designs of God's will.[31]

Each of these ideas—guidance, good counsel, and spiritual aid or support—has a Qur'anic basis and informs Muslim understandings of discerning and living out one's vocation. In terms of actively seeking guidance, Muslims recognize a practice called *istikhara*— "seeking help in making a choice or decision"—in which, after a rit-

---

29. *Fada'il tawfiqiyya.* al-Ghazzali defines *Tawfiq* as what is indispensable to a person in all circumstances, that is, having one's will and actions be compatible with the divine decree and measuring out. See al-Ghazzali, *Mizan al-'amal* (Beirut: Dar wa Maktaba Hilal, 1995), 129.

30. Fakhri, *Ethical Theories in Islam*, 201, quoting al-Ghazzali, *Mizan al-'amal*, 129.

31. Ibid., 202, quoting al-Ghazzali, *Mizan*, 130.

ual prayer, a Muslim may ask God for a sign or a form of guidance that is often believed to come in a dream.[32]

There is also an extensive Muslim literature discussing the proper conduct *(adab)* of various occupations—such as Islamic jurists, doctors, and even Islamic spiritual aspirants (Sufis). The concept of moral authority as developed through education, self-cultivation, and religious observance is key in Muslim concepts of *adab*. Sources of moral edification are the religious law *(shari'a)*, philosophical ethics, and works on spiritual development.

Barbara Metcalf remarks on "the radical comprehensiveness" of the Muslim concept of *adab* as follows:

"It is comprehensive in the sense that its rules address all domains of life; it is also comprehensive in its relentless desire to bring all society and all sorts and conditions of humans into consonance with a common core of values underlying all social roles."[33]

The noted historian of Islamic civilization, Marshall Hodgson, observes about this genre, "Muslim writers, accepting the consequences of purposefulness in the creation, have spoken on many levels to the person who finds himself facing solemn responsibilities—as father in a family or judge in a city or seer for a great community."[34]

In Islamic mysticism as well there are various articulations of the idea of vocation. One is that of spiritual conversion. Consider the story of Ibrahim ibn Adham (d. ca. 790), said to have been a prince, who was called one day while hunting in the forest. A deer he was pursuing miraculously turned to him and asked, "Is this why you were created?" At this "call," the prince turned his life around and became a spiritual seeker.[35] Other famous examples of "call" narra-

---

32. Toufic Fahd, "Istikhara," in *Encyclopedia of Islam*, vol. 4, 2d ed., ed. J. H. Kramers et al. (Leiden: E. J. Brill, 1954–), 259–60.

33. Barbara D. Metcalf, *Moral Conduct and Authority: The Place of Adab in South Asian Islam* (Berkeley: University of California Press, 1984), 4.

34. Marshall Hodgson, *Venture of Islam*, vol. 2 (Chicago: University of Chicago Press, 1974), 338.

35. Farid al-Din Attar, *Muslim Saints and Mystics*, trans. A. J. Arberry (Chicago: University of Chicago Press, 1966).

tives include the story of the preeminent theologian al-Ash'ari (935), who was visited in a dream by the Prophet and instructed to adopt a more balanced method for interpretation of the revealed texts.

The words of al-Ghazzali, who struggled with the desire to find religious truth, still resound poignantly today:

> I examined my motive in my work of teaching, and realized that it was not a pure desire for the things of God, but that the impulse moving me was the desire for an influential position and public recognition. I saw for certain that I was on the brink of a crumbling bank of sand and in imminent danger of hell-fire unless I set about to mend my ways.
>
> I reflected on this continuously for a time, while the choice still remained open to me. One day, I would form the resolution to quit Baghdad and get rid of these adverse circumstances; the next day, I would abandon my resolution. I put one foot forward and drew the other back. If in the morning I had a genuine longing to seek eternal life, by the evening the whole host of desires had reduced it to impotence. Worldly desires were striving to keep me by their chains just where I was, while the voice of faith was calling, "To the road! To the road! What is left of life is but little and the road before you is long."[36]

The idea of developing the propensities or potential inherent in each human individual is related in the thought of some mystics— for example, Ibn 'Arabi's emanationist cosmology, in which the pre-eternal creative act of God reflected himself into the world through his divine attributes (1240). The *hadith*, loved by the Sufis for its explanation of the purpose of creation, has Allah saying, "I was a hidden treasure and I wanted to be known. Hence I created the creatures that I might be known."[37] Ibn 'Arabi encouraged the human being to reflect or emulate the creative attributes of Allah in a process known as *takhalluq*.[38]

---

36. Al-Ghazzali, *The Faith and Practice of al-Ghazali*, trans. Montgomery Watt (Oxford: Oneworld, 1998), 59.

37. A "Sufi" *hadith*, known by mystical disclosure but not present in the canonical collections of prophetic traditions. See William Chittick, *The Sufi Path of Knowledge* (Albany: State University of New York Press, 1989), 391, n. 14.

38. Al-Ghazzali, *On Disciplining the Soul*, xxxiv–v. See also al-Ghazzali, *al-Maqsad al-Asna*, trans. David B. Burrell as *The Ninety-Nine Beautiful Names of God* (Cambridge: Islamic Texts Society, 1992).

The Sufi practice of the remembrance of God, *dhikr*, might—in the case of individual spiritual aspirants—be tailored to specific divine qualities that needed to be cultivated in that person. While *dhikr* is generally considered the polish of the heart and a basis for contemplation, the phrases repeated by some Sufis might include divine attributes designed to evoke particular qualities in the person reciting them.

Yet another aspect of Sufi notions of vocation is the tension between taking up some means for earning a worldly living and pursuing a completely ascetic ideal. Islam emerged at a time when Christian ascetic tendencies were known in Arabia, and there are rather specific condemnations in Islam of some aspects of *rahbaniyya*, or monasticism.[39] Thus a tension exists, within the Islamic idea of spiritual vocation, between the ideals of asceticism *(zuhd)*, which is encouraged by the prophetic practice, and the rejection of celibacy and any extreme mortification of the body or total withdrawal from social interaction. Commenting on the need for mystics to remain within society and make a contribution there, a contemporary Muslim scholar, Seyyid Hossein Nasr, writes, "The unitary principle of Islam, however, could not permit this contemplative way to become crystallized as a separate social institution outside the matrix molded by the injunctions of the divine Law or *shari'ah*. It had to remain as an inner dimension of that Law and, institutionally, as an organization integrated into the Islamic social pattern and inseparable from it."[40]

One of the early Sufi manuals, the *Kitab al-Luma'* of al-Sarraj, contains a chapter entitled "Taking up the means for earning a livelihood *(makasib)* and being engaged in earning a living." Citations presented in this chapter include:

---

39. Qur'an 57:27: "but monasticism they invented." And the *hadith:* "There is no monasticism commanded for us," found in Ibn Hanbal's collection.

40. Charles Le Gai Eaton, *Islam and the Destiny of Man* (London: George Allen and Unwin, 1985), 174, quoting from Seyyid Hossein Nasr, *Islam and the Plight of Modern Man* (London: Longmans, 1975), 73.

Sahl ibn 'Abd Allah said, "The person who speaks against earning a living rejects the way of the Prophet *(sunna)* and the one who rejects complete reliance upon God *(tawakkul)* rejects faith."

Ibn Salim in Basra, speaking of the ways of earning a livelihood, said, [*Tawakkul*] complete reliance upon Allah, is the [spiritual] state of the Prophet, whereas earning one's living is the example of the Prophet, peace be upon him. The Prophet left earning a living as an established practice [*sunna*] for his followers, since he was aware of their shortcomings; so that if people were to abandon the level of complete reliance on Allah, still they would not lose the level of earning a livelihood, which was his practice, for otherwise they would perish![41]

According to Ibrahim ibn Adham, Ibn Salim also said, "You must reject idleness and earn a permissible livelihood and spend it on your family."[42] All of these pieces of advice must be viewed in the context of encouraging a balance between the contemplative aspects of the spiritual life and the need to remain a productive member of society.

In Islam there was no church and no institutionalized clergy. Legal scholars, religious experts, Qur'an memorizers, preachers, and Sufis did emerge, but these roles were not sacramental or seen as placing the individual in a higher position because of his office.[43] A contemporary writer had this to say about the hallowing of everyday life, including work, in traditional Muslim societies:

In a quaintly phrased but no less telling comparison, Francois Bonjean, writing of the holy cities of Islam and comparing them to monastic communities, remarks that ordinary artisans and administrators and merchants recall "the mien and manners of our ecclesiastics"; they seem, in other words, more like priests than laymen. "If monasticism is defined as withdrawal for God," says Schuon, "and if its universal and inter-religious character is recognized on the grounds that the thirst for the supernatural is in the nature of normal man, how can this definition be applied in the case of spiritual men who are Muslims and do not withdraw from society?" . . . To

41. al-Sarraj, *Kitab al-Luma,* 259.
42. Ibid.
43. Marshall Hodgson termed this feature of traditional Islamic civilization "contractualism," in contrast to the dignity and status conferred by being the holder of a specific office in European civilization. *Venture of Islam* 2:340.

that the answer must be that one of the *raisons d'etre* of Islam is precisely the possibility of a "monastery-society," if the expression be allowable: that is to say that Islam aims to carry the contemplative life into the very framework as a whole; it succeeds in realizing within that framework conditions of structure and of behavior that permit of contemplative isolation in the very midst of the activities of the world. . . . The famous "no monasticism in Islam" really means, not that contemplatives must not withdraw from the world, but on the contrary, that the world must not withdraw from contemplatives.[44]

In summary, Muslim interpreters have generally held that the spiritual meaning of vocation is ideally actualized in all aspects of life and should not be restricted to priests or contemplative orders.

Metaphors of paths, roads, and journeying pervade the Islamic tradition. The opening chapter of the Qur'an, *al-Fatiha*, which is constantly recited by Muslims, asks God to "guide us to the straight path." The term for the established practice of the Prophet Muhammad, "sunna," means a "well-trodden path." The four legal schools *(madhahib)* are "ways of following or going" and the *shari'a*, the Islamic law code, is "a broad track leading to water." Even the Islamic *Sufi* orders are known as *tariqas*, "roads" or "methods."

Discovering one's vocation in life is a journey in which the way unfolds in the process of traveling. A famous work of Islamic spiritual literature, *The Conference of the Birds,* a Persian Sufi poem by Fariduddin Attar, describes the quest of a flock of variegated birds, each seeking the fabled king or master known as the Simurgh.[45] Each species of bird is represented as encumbered by its particular strengths and weaknesses. Ultimately the most intrepid thirty birds *(si murgh)* arrive at the destination, only to find that the archetypal king bird *(Simurgh)* has lain within them all the time. While ultimately critical of all worldly attachments, the text also takes a pragmatic view of the human contexts of work, relationships, and power.

---

44. Eaton, *Islam and the Destiny of Man*, quoting Frithjof Schuon, *Light on the Ancient Worlds* (Bloomington, Ind.: World Wisdom, 1984), 173.

45. Farid al-Din Attar, *Conference of the Birds*, trans. Afkham Darbandi and Dick Davis (New York: Penguin, 1984).

Contemporary Muslims

Classical Muslim ethicists, although they discussed virtue theory extensively, seem not to have directly addressed issues of an individual's profession or the dignity of labor. Rather, they discussed topics such as the ideal social order, relationships with others, and the cultivation of the soul through knowledge and virtue. A recent collection on ethics within the world religions gives no scholarly sources on the subject of work in Islam.[46] One can see an increasing concern with vocation in more recent Muslim authors, however. A modern Egyptian work on "traits of good character in Islam" holds that the definition of a person's social status includes the individual's wealth, education, and social and political roles.[47] One's status can usually be discerned on the basis of measures such as wealth, knowledge, and power. However, this author affirms that, according to Islam, the one essential marker of status is piety *(taqwa)*.[48] This is explicitly stated in the Qur'an 49:13: "Indeed the most noble of you according to Allah is the most pious." Status seeking is condemned in Islamic moral teachings and by historical example. In fact, there is a strong critique within Muslim ethical and religious teachings of those who desire rule, wealth, or position as ends in themselves.

The South Asian poet Muhammad Iqbal (1938), a twentieth-century Muslim intellectual, made a significant contribution to Islamic concepts of character development through making a contribution to humanity. Iqbal was interested in the entire intellectual heritage of Islam and addressed the problems of Muslims emerging from the colonial experience. In this he encouraged both self-development and creative achievement within the context of Islamic values.

Iqbal's poem *"Rumuz-i beekhudi"* (Symbols of selflessness) may be interpreted as advocating both transnationalism and adaptability,

---

46. John Carmen and Mark Juergensmeyer, eds., *A Bibliographic Guide to the Comparative Study of Ethics* (Cambridge: Cambridge University Press, 1991), 512, 806.

47. Ahmad Abd al-Rahman Ibrahim, *Al-fadā'il al-khuluqiyya fi-l islam* (al-Mansura: Dar al-Wafa, 1989), 97. He also refers to al-Ghazzali's concept of "dignity" *('izz),* discussed in *Mizan al-'amal,* 125ff.

48. See note 11 above.

a message of particular relevance to the experience of Muslim immigrants to Western societies:

> Our Prophet migrated from his homeland,
> Revealing the truth of the Muslim's nationalism.
> His wisdom was establishing a world community
> On the foundations of the *Kalima*[49]

> So that through the bounties of that master of religion
> The whole earth became a mosque for us.
> Take on the form of the fish to flourish in the ocean.
> That is, free yourselves from bondage to one locality
> Whoever frees themself from the prison of directions
> Becomes like the sky encompassing all space.[50]

Modernity and secularism have profoundly influenced contemporary understandings of religious aspects of vocation. In contemporary Muslim thought, concern over the loss of meaning and the sacred in our daily lives sometimes manifests itself in questions about the religious basis and legitimacy of current systems of political order. The vision, however idealistic, of Islam as a total system sacralized all activities, since it dignified work of all sorts in which transactions were to be conducted according to the legal rulings of the *shari'a*. Each individual had a "vocation" of participating in and maintaining the moral order sanctioned by the divine command. The patterning of all life according to the sacred law was felt to inculcate a comprehensive sense of purpose and a link to sacred rhythms.

This may explain in part the evocative quality of the call by today's Muslim reformers and activists to reinstitute an Islamic state, modeled on the community around the Prophet in Medina. Expanding the discussion to professional life and its relationship to religious values might provide an alternative for Muslims living in pluralistic, democratic Western societies.

---

49. The Islamic profession of faith.

50. K. G. Saiyidain, *Iqbal's Educational Philosophy* (Lahore: Ashraf, n.d.), 141, from Iqbal, "*Rumuz-i beekhudi*," in Iqbal, *Kulliyat-i farsi* (Lahore: Shaykh Ghulam 'Ali, 1979), 114.

Exploration of all the ramifications of the concept of "vocation" within Islamic tradition is clearly beyond the scope of a single paper. While I have concentrated on textual and conceptual sources, it would also be useful to view the development of vocation in the light of the social and civilizational patterns of respective religious traditions.

Hodgson characterized the ethos of Islamic civilization as involving each individual's "personal responsibility for the moral ordering of the natural world."[51] Its unique pattern of legitimation was "unitary contractualism," wherein status was conferred by achievement rather than heredity. This allowed individuals living in classical Islamic societies a relatively greater amount of social mobility and choice of occupation. In more recent times, the legacy of colonialism, economic disparities, and political instabilities have often seriously limited the vocational aspirations of Muslims in developing countries.

The Persian poet Sa'di (1292) wrote, "Every soul is created with a certain purpose and the light of that purpose has been kindled in that soul."[52] It is this sense of purpose that needs to be discovered and fostered as an essential element of Islamic concepts of vocation. The challenge that lies ahead, in the eyes of many contemporary Muslim thinkers, is to recover and preserve the authentic heritage while providing the material and educational facilities for individual and social well-being.

51. Hodgson, *Venture of Islam* 2:337.
52. Hazrat Inayat Khan, *The Purpose of Life* (San Francisco: Rainbow Bridge, 1973), 18.

~~⌒⌒~~ Paul F. Harman, S.J.

Vocation and the *Spiritual Exercises* of St. Ignatius of Loyola

Pick up a good standard history of Western education and you will come upon the name of Ignatius of Loyola, the founder of the Society of Jesus (Jesuits). Although the Jesuits have been associated with teaching and learning for more than 450 years, Ignatius never provided them with an explicit theory of education. What he did leave as a lasting gift to the Jesuits and to the Church was a small book that is considered to be one of the classics of Western spirituality: the *Spiritual Exercises.*

Since the sixteenth century, the spiritual insights of the *Exercises* have had an enormous impact on the everyday life of countless men and women in all parts of the world.[1] Though a decidedly Christian and Roman Catholic document, the contents of the *Spiritual Exercises* have proved to be of interest and help to individuals from other

---

1. "According to one plausible estimate worked out in 1948, by then the *Exercises* had been published, either alone or with commentaries, some 4,500 times—an average of once a month for four centuries—and the number of copies was around 4,500,000. Throughout the world today, the *Exercises* are being made by greater numbers than ever before." *The Spiritual Exercises of Saint Ignatius*, trans. George E. Ganss, S.J. (St. Louis: Institute of Jesuit Sources, 1995), 8.

religious traditions as well. This brief essay has as its specific purpose to examine how the instructions of Ignatius of Loyola in the *Exercises* assist individuals in coming to know and understand their *vocation* in life.

Vocation and Ignatius of Loyola

Ignatius of Loyola (1491–1556) was born into one of the ruling families in the Basque country of northern Spain. As a young man he served for a brief while at the Court of Castile and then, for four years, as a soldier. Toward the end of his life, speaking of himself in the third person, he wrote of these early years, "Up to the age of twenty-six, he was a man given to the vanities of the world; and what he enjoyed most was warlike sport, with a great and foolish desire to win fame."[2] At the age of thirty, Ignatius was wounded in a minor military skirmish against French troops at Pamplona. While recovering at the family castle of Loyola, he began to undergo a profound conversion.

Conversion, in religious terms, is the time-honored word describing the inner experience of a person saying "no" to the deceits of the world and saying "yes" to God's truth. The term, of course, has deep roots in both the Hebrew and Christian Scriptures. To look at it in another way, conversion is the process of *coming to understand and accept one's true vocation from God.* It begins in a kind of listening or attentiveness to God and then moves in the direction of a free response on the part of the individual to the creative love of the Creator, calling him or her to a life of intimate relationship with God.

Genuine religious conversion is not an emotion; it is, rather, a personal decision. It is deciding that God, in Jesus Christ, is telling me the truth. Christians believe that in the person of Jesus, the Christ, God repeated the call offered to human beings at the beginning of creation. St. Paul refers to Jesus as the *kalon* (1 Thess. 5:24), the one who calls, offering believers the opportunity to repent, to be

2. From the translation of the *Autobiography* by Parmananda R. Divarkar, in *Ignatius of Loyola*, ed. George E. Ganss, S.J., CWS (New York: Paulist Press, 1991), 68.

reconciled, to return to their original vocation. In putting their faith in Jesus, men and women are reminded of their fundamental vocation: fidelity to a covenant of love with the God who called them into being. Conversion, in the Christian perspective, is a decision to follow Jesus.

If ever there was an instance of how a book changed the way someone looked on his or her vocation in life, Ignatius stands as a prime example. While convalescing at Loyola, he was greatly influenced by reading the only two books that were available to him: a *Life of Christ*, by the fourteenth-century Carthusian Ludolph of Saxony, and *The Golden Legend*, an even older and more popular collection of stories about the saints. Ignatius read and reread these books. At times he began to picture himself imitating the life of Jesus and the saints; at other times he dreamed of returning to the life of a courtier or soldier and winning the attention of a "certain lady." In the *Autobiography* he described his experience this way:

When he was thinking of those things of the world, he took much delight in them, but afterwards, when he was tired and put them aside, he found himself dry and dissatisfied. But when he thought of going to Jerusalem barefoot, and of eating nothing but plain vegetables and of practicing all the other rigors that he saw in the saints, not only was he consoled when he had these thoughts, but even after putting them aside he remained satisfied and joyful. . . . Little by little he came to recognize the spirits that were stirring, one from the devil, the other from God.[3]

As with most people, this conversion and the discovery of his true vocation in life did not happen all at once for Ignatius, but over a period of years. At first he felt drawn to imitate in all seriousness—indeed, with excessive seriousness—the lives of the saints. Of the many paths that lead to an initial understanding of vocation, one of the most easily accessible to anyone is the path of imitation. Perhaps it is only a normal stage of development that before one can become a doer, one must first be an imitator. As with Ignatius, I may see some attractive quality or ability in another person and de-

---

3. Ibid., 71.

cide to "try it on for size," to imitate it. Before I can be my authentic self, I must first imitate or "try on" other selves. At any rate, Ignatius first learned about vocation by imitation.

Vocation and the *Spiritual Exercises*

While still in the process of this personal conversion, Ignatius compiled written notes of his experiences. Just as reading books had helped initiate a conversion of heart, so next he turned to writing. Perhaps, when he was a pilgrim visiting the Benedictine monastery at Montserrat, he had learned of the spiritual practice of using *rapiaria,* little notebooks in which an individual recorded the words of Jesus or the saints or his or her own personal thoughts and observation. Ignatius began to set down in writing his reflections on the conversion he was experiencing. It was these notebooks that became the foundation for his masterpiece, the *Spiritual Exercises.* It is important to remember that Ignatius was a layman when he compiled these notes on the spiritual life. He was not a cleric and he most certainly was not a Jesuit. He was simply, in his own words, a "pilgrim" in search of God who, when he began to find God, longed to share his insights and experiences with others.

The composition of the *Spiritual Exercises* of Ignatius of Loyola is not an isolated phenomenon in the history of spirituality in the West. While the book issued from one man's personal experience, it is also the result of his knowledge and contact with a long tradition. The understanding of call, or vocation, that the directives of the *Exercises* aim to foster and develop in an individual can be traced back through generations of spiritual authors to the Hebrew Scriptures and the New Testament. Recent scholarly research has helped to identify both those elements of the *Spiritual Exercises* that are specific or original to Ignatius and those that are clearly linked to earlier traditions of Christian spirituality in the West.[4]

4. See Javier Melloni, S.J., *The Exercises of St. Ignatius of Loyola in the Western Tradition* (Leominster, Eng.: Gracewing, 2000). Melloni offers a "Genealogical Tree of the Exercises," 12–13.

The *Spiritual Exercises* is not a book to be read; it is really a book of "exercises" to be "done" under the guidance of someone wise and experienced. Ignatius wrote the book in order to assist the guide or "director," rather than for the use of the person "doing" or "making" the *Exercises*. One can, of course, simply read the text, but it only makes good sense if one is actually doing the "exercises."

Ignatius explains at the start what he understands by the term "spiritual exercises":

By the term Spiritual Exercises we mean every method of examination of conscience, meditation, contemplation, vocal or mental prayer, and other spiritual activities, such as will be mentioned later. For, just as taking a walk, traveling on foot, and running are physical exercises, so is the name of spiritual exercises given to any means of preparing and disposing our soul to rid itself of all disordered affections and then, after their removal of seeking and finding God's will in the ordering of our life for the salvation of our soul. (1)[5]

The stated goal or purpose of the *Exercises* is to assist individuals to move from a life experienced as confusion and disarray to a life of order and intentionality, from a life of spiritual darkness to spiritual light. But it is also written with a view to helping someone search and find the will of God about the direction of one's life.

As Ignatius says, the *Exercises* are open to "every method" and "any means" that will assist in removing disordered attachments and enable an individual to seek and find God's will in freedom. The spirit of adaptability is found throughout the *Exercises*. The presumption is that each individual is unique and will seek and find God's will under different circumstances. Ignatius wanted the director to make whatever adaptations are necessary in order to accommodate "the requirements of the persons who wish to make them . . . according to their age, their education, and their aptitudes" (18).

---

5. Parenthetical numbers refer to paragraphs in the *Spiritual Exercises*. Ignatius wrote the *Exercises* in Spanish. The English translation used here is that of George E. Ganss, cited above.

Where the *Exercises* Begin

Thomas Merton, the Trappist monk, wrote in one of his journals: "If you want to identify me, ask me not where I live, or what I like to eat, or how I comb my hair, but ask me what I think I am living for, in detail, and ask me what I think is keeping me from living fully for the thing I want to live for. Between these two answers you can determine the identity of any person. The better answer he has, the more of a person he is."[6] Ignatius would have agreed completely. Early on in the text of the *Exercises* he presents the Principle and Foundation, a consideration of one's basic identity as a human being. What do I understand to be the point of my existence? This question, of course, is where every Christian catechism begins:

> *Q.* Who made me?
> *A.* God made me.
> *Q.* Why did God make me?
> *A.* God made me to know Him, to love Him, and to serve Him in this world, and to be happy with him in the next.

But Ignatius is not looking for rote answers to standard questions. The first goal of the individual who "makes" the *Exercises* is to be able to ask and answer these questions in all freedom. After that, the goal is to become as interiorly free as possible in order to listen more attentively to whatever it is that God is saying and to respond with the greatest possible love and generosity.

There are some key assumptions posited at the beginning of the *Exercises* about the reality and action of God as well as the way the human mind and heart operate:

1. Ignatius fully believes that God, the Creator and Lord of all things, will deal directly with the person making the *Exercises* (15). This was his own experience. Ignatius assumes that God regularly communicates with people in any number of ways, e.g., through

---

6. Thomas Merton, *My Argument with the Gestapo* (1969), quoted in Edward Rice, *The Man in the Sycamore Tree* (New York: Doubleday, 1970), 25.

the created universe,[7] through the Incarnate Son of God (Jesus), through the prophetic word of Scripture, through the dynamics of family and human friendships, through the events of history, and, even more directly, through one's personal experience of God's love.

A distinctive and original characteristic of the *Exercises* at the time of its appearance was the attention and respect Ignatius gives to the individual's own personal experience of God. Ignatius cautions the guide or director of the *Exercises* to have tremendous respect for the direct interaction between God and the individual, and to avoid "getting in the way" (15). He recognizes that, though the guide or director of the *Exercises* may propose certain themes or suggestions for prayer (i.e., certain exercises), ultimately each person should experience God through the fruits of his or her own prayer.

2. Ignatius also assumes that it is of the nature of the human heart and mind to desire to know and to love. This is the way human beings are made. This human desire to know expresses itself in all sorts of ways, from seeking to explore new worlds and new planets, to seeking to understand the human genome. From a faith perspective, this desire to know in human beings includes an inborn desire for God. Whether people are consciously religious or not, this desire is their deepest longing; it is what gives meaning and purpose to human existence. The reason why God communicates with people is because of this built-in capacity for God.[8] In this sense, my vocation is a call from deep within my very nature as a human being. I yearn to seek God and to know myself in God.

What strikes anyone making the *Spiritual Exercises,* or studying them, is that, from beginning to end, Ignatius assumes that an individual's experience of God will be a personal encounter that is *con-*

7. In an interview in the *New York Times Magazine,* Feb. 11, 2001, Avery Dulles, S.J., asked when he first felt "something larger," replied "I was at Harvard Law School, reading at the library, and I got rather tired, so I went out for a walk. And during it, looking at nature, I guess, I began to sense that there was this purpose to it, a governing purpose. It was a matter of becoming aware of this reality behind everything that existed. That evening when I got back to my room I think I prayed for the first time."

8. Cf. part I, chap. 1, *Catechism of the Catholic Church* (New York: Image Books, Doubleday, 1995).

versational. The encounter happens in the context of *dialogue.* The individual is expected not only to "listen" to God but also to speak to God, to converse with God. Ignatius refers to such conversation as a colloquy. "A colloquy is made, properly speaking, in the way one friend speaks to another . . . now begging a favor, now accusing oneself of some misdeed, now telling one's concerns and asking counsel about them" (54). He expected such intimate dialogue to take place daily throughout the entire experience of the *Exercises,* but especially in connection with certain key meditations. What happens in the "colloquy" between God and the individual is of paramount importance in the *Exercises* from start to finish.

It can be said that the theological point of departure for the *Exercises* is the claim that every human life is created to respond to God's invitation to enter into God's own life, i.e., the life of the Trinity. While the *Exercises* were regarded as innovative when first introduced, the implicit theology is firmly rooted in the tradition. The apostle Paul, writing to the Corinthians, says, "It is God who has called you to share in the life of his Son, Jesus Christ our Lord; and God keeps faith" (1 Cor. 1:9), or, in another text, "The God, who said, Let there be light, is the one who has shone in our hearts" (2 Cor. 4:6). For Ignatius, our participation in the life of the Trinity is the deep narrative, the *true story* of the life of each of person. It is the story that begins when the Word of God "catches up" with me and takes me in the direction of my true self.

What helps an individual to know and understand his or her particular call and vocation? In the view of Ignatius, the chief source of guidance or direction for discovering the particular vocation of any man or woman is found in the discovery of the plan or purpose God has—not only for the individual but also for the *whole* of creation. As a way of beginning to answer the question: "Who am I?" or "What am I to do or to be?" Ignatius suggests first that I become "all lost in wonder" at the immensity, the sheer vastness, of the universe God has created. The point is not to experience my insignificance, but precisely my significance, my identity and purpose within the plan of creation. My existence is not something apart from the rest of creation, but wondrously *within* it. My vocation, therefore, is my free response to God's invitation to be a part of, to participate in, the evolution of the divine design—i.e., the history of salvation.

Even though the immediate purpose of the *Exercises* is the conversion of the individual, it is always the whole of humanity that Ignatius has in mind in the many meditations and contemplations he proposes for consideration. God's plan or design is to bring the whole world, not just a part of it, to salvation. For Ignatius, all of creation swings out in a great arc from God, the source, and back to God, the goal. I will come to understand my particular call or vocation by returning again and again to this larger vision of God's purpose and desire for the whole of creation. The British theologian, and now the Archbishop of Canterbury, Rowan Williams, says, "one clue to our identity is this, the idea of *mirroring* God. We have to find what is our particular way of *playing back* to God his self-sharing, self-losing care and compassion, the love because of which he speaks and calls in the first place."[9] Creation is not only the context in which I discover my vocation; it is also the vehicle for fulfilling my vocation. For Ignatius, all of creation is given to human beings as a means of achieving their fundamental goal or purpose in life, namely, to praise, reverence, and serve God. Ignatius invites the individual to ponder this vision of creation and human existence at the beginning of the *Exercises* in the meditation known as the Principle and Foundation (23).

When I approach the whole of creation with the sort of reverential love Ignatius had in mind, I will enjoy created things as God intended that they be appreciated and enjoyed. This reverential love for creation will manifest itself, to the extent possible, in a "poised freedom" with respect to created things (23). Ignatius speaks of making oneself "indifferent . . . in regard to everything which is left to our free will and is not forbidden" (23). To the extent that indi-

9. Rowan Williams, *A Ray of Darkness: Sermons and Reflections* (Cambridge: Cowley Publications, 1995), 150.

viduals are free from disordered attachments (a kind of "addictive-ness") to persons or things, the expectation is that they will be able to choose, again and again, "what is more conducive to the end for which we are created" (23). Growing in this love of God and in freedom from disordered attachments, I am invited to participate in the creative action of God, who desires to bring all things to their fulfillment in God, even as I myself am being brought to my fulfillment. My vocation, then, is discovered at the nexus of reverential love for God, creation, and an appreciation of my goal or *telos* in life.

⌐⌐⌐

This is the understanding of God and of the vocation of human beings in the created universe, with which the *Exercises* begins. It is also, as will be pointed out, where it ends. There is a circularity to the *Exercises* because of Ignatius's vision of how everything does, indeed, come from and return to God. The *leitmotif* of the *Exercises* is both as simple and as complicated as that.

In between the Principle and Foundation and the final "contemplation" with which Ignatius brings the *Exercises* to a close, the individual is led through a series of "exercises," divided into four parts. Ignatius refers to the four parts as "weeks" (though by the term "week" he is not thinking of exactly seven days; the length of each "week" may be much longer than seven days or much shorter, depending on the needs of the individual) (4). How is the understanding of call or vocation developed in each of the four weeks?

The First Week: Having meditated on God's design for the whole of creation, the person "making" the *Exercises* enters upon the first week. Here Ignatius proposes a consideration of the history of sin and rebellion against God's plan. Sin, as presented in the *Exercises,* is not so much about instances of moral transgression as it is about whatever frustrates or derails the purpose for which human beings are created. Ignatius wants the individual to recognize that there are forces pulling me toward the evil I abhor and away from the good I desire. These forces are a part of a long history of sin that would like to destroy God's creation.

The point of the "exercises" of the first week is this: that in the presence of Jesus, the Redeemer who sacrificed his life for me, and with at least the beginning of an awareness of the purpose for which I was created, I now move toward some deep-felt understanding of how, time and again, my choices and actions (or, perhaps, my lack of choices and actions) have in fact been at odds with what God is asking me to be. In the first week, I am directed to take an unsentimental look at my disordered attachments to self-interest, to willfulness, and to control. Ignatius, writing from his own life experience, makes this observation later in the *Exercises:* "For everyone ought to reflect that in all spiritual matters, the more one divests oneself of self-love, self-will, and self-interests, the more progress one will make" (189).[10]

The first week focuses on how my selfish, self-protecting illusions, my reaching for whatever offers security, block the way to answering the call *to be myself.* In the end, sin and disorder are about resisting one's true vocation; they are about preferring blindness to the light of the love of God—the God who, from a desire to share infinite happiness with us, created me for the happiness that is mine, in bringing ourselves and all of creation to fulfillment in God. As Ganss notes, "The *Exercises* bring into play any or all the abilities any [individual] has, such as the intellect, will, imagination, and emotions. All these are stimulated, with a stress on each one at its proper time."[11] Ignatius expected that the one making the *Exercises* would experience movements of noticeable affect (e.g., feelings, impulses of attraction and recoil that come spontaneously to one's consciousness) as a result of entering seriously into conversation with God. His advice to the guide or director is to listen intently to what the individual has to report about such inner movements and then to help the individual assess what he or she is experiencing. Paying attention to these "movements" of the mind and heart can reveal more than a little to an individual as to where he or she stands

---

10. Ignatius in the *Exercises* has as his focus the *interior* life, the life of the Spirit. However, in speaking of "spiritual matters" he does not intend a false dichotomy of the "spiritual" and the "temporal" or mundane.

11. *The Spiritual Exercises of Saint Ignatius,* 6.

in life vis-à-vis call and vocation. Ignatius considered some of these movements to be inspired by God and others to be inspired by spirits that are not of God. To this end, for the benefit of both the director and the person making the *Exercises,* Ignatius provides the "Rules for the Discernment of Spirits" (313).

In the first week, Ignatius encourages the individual and his/her director to discern the movements as follows:

1. The individual who is living a life in obvious opposition to God's call will most likely encounter sharp "stings" of conscience in the context of the first week. In this case, feelings of guilt and remorse may well be understood as a "grace" or visitation on the part of the Creator. Such inner movements can be trusted. On the other hand, if such a person were to feel complacent about his or her past choices and actions, and be inclined to dismiss all thoughts and feelings to the contrary, such movements should not be trusted as coming from God's Spirit.

2. By contrast, an individual who, despite lapses and occasional setbacks, usually strives to live out his or her vocation in keeping with God's design, will most probably experience peace and inner confirmation of desire and will—even when looking at the unhappiness caused by his or her own sinfulness. Again, such inner movements can be trusted. But if this same individual were to begin to experience feelings of disquiet, guilt, and worry, or to become sad and disconsolate—these movements should not be trusted, because this is not how God will deal with a person whose basic orientation is turned in the direction of God.

For Ignatius, the operative rule or norm throughout the *Exercises* is this: are the feelings or movements that the person experiences leading the individual toward God or away from God, toward his or her true vocation in God's design or away from it?

The first week "ends" when I recognize that my relation with God depends on making the decision to be what I am, and to do this because what I am is already known and loved and accepted by God. Karl Barth used to say, "God has chosen us *all* in Christ: at the deepest level we are all called Jesus in the eyes of the Father."[12] This interior knowledge, gained during the first week, is recalled at later stages of the *Exercises* and revisited again and again during a person's lifetime. In terms of developing an understanding of vocation, there is both activity and passivity here: I actively embrace my role in God's plan for creation, but at the same time I let go of the need to be in control. God alone is the Savior of the world and of myself.

The Second Week: The goal of the second week of the *Exercises* is twofold: (1) a deepening of one's personal relationship and commitment to Christ, and at the same time (2) the making of an "election," i.e., seeking, finding, and saying "yes" to God's call to me in the specific circumstances of my life. There are always choices in life, choices about what to do and what to be. For Christians, the most important choice one has to make is how to follow Christ in this world.[13]

Within the second week of the *Exercises,* there are several set meditations that are regarded as containing key elements of Ignatius's spiritual teaching when it comes to making important choices. The first of these pivotal meditations is the "Call of Christ the King." In this meditation, one prays for the grace "not to be deaf to His call, but prompt and diligent to accomplish His most holy will" (91–99).

Once Ignatius's life had been "turned around," once he had been set free of the weight of disordered attachments in his life, what he began to see more clearly, what excited him and filled him with energy and zeal, was Jesus. Using the vocabulary and images of the world in which he grew to maturity, Ignatius pictured Jesus inviting him to be a "companion," by living the way Jesus lived and laboring

---

12. Quoted in Williams, *A Ray of Darkness,* 151.

13. The *Spiritual Exercises* are not choice-centered in the sense that every person making the *Exercises* is expected to arrive at some momentous personal decision about his or her vocation. But insofar as the *Exercises* can be regarded as a "school" of Christian life, a lens through which to view one's entire life in relationship to God, they can be said to be choice-oriented.

the way Jesus labored. Ignatius could not restrain his enthusiasm to accept this call to be of service to the King and Lord of all creation. He felt powerfully drawn to do whatever might be required to be a servant-companion of Jesus.

When Ignatius talked about Jesus as his King and Lord, he was talking about the point where, for him, all the yearnings of his life, from the time of his youth and from the disturbing dreams of his conversion experience, now came together in this utterly compelling figure of Jesus. Just as there is a personal history of our sins over the period of a lifetime, so too, and even more important, each person has a personal history of deep desires and earnest yearnings going all the way back to childhood and coming right down to the present. Dreams of what I could do and be, dreams of love and companionship, dreams of service and sacrifice. What is it that I have always been looking to find? To experience the point where my deepest personal longings meet and coincide with the call I hear from Christ, so that, for my part, I would prefer to be more rather than less like Christ in everything that concerns me—this is the goal Ignatius intends in the second week. "The personal love of Christ, which is the grace of the Second Week, is a love which changes and re-orientates the whole person."[14] What I learn more and more throughout the second week (and it is brought home even more forcefully in the third and fourth weeks) is that my vocation is not something I conjure up for myself in an egotistical way. I do not "invent" myself. As was said earlier, I am called by God to be my true self and I meet that true self in entering into my deepest longings and desires, given all the particular hopes and challenges of the circumstances in which I live.

The Two Standards (136–47) meditation comes after some period of time spent in contemplating Christ's Incarnation, his birth, infancy, and the "hiddenness" or obscurity of his childhood and early manhood. The themes of poverty and humiliation are especially

14. Michael Ivens, S.J., *Understanding the Spiritual Exercises* (Leominster, Eng.: Gracewing, 1998), 75.

highlighted, not as pious abstractions but as concrete manifestations of a love that begins in the heart of the Trinity and ends on the cross at Calvary.

In the Two Standards, Ignatius contrasts "the mind of Christ" with the deceits of "the enemy of our human nature." Ignatius, standing in a long tradition of Christian spirituality, bears witness to the fact that there is a struggle in following the Voice that calls to me. There are false spirits that seek to distract me; there is, for lack of a better word, an "enemy" or "adversary" that seeks to frustrate my knowing and accomplishing God's will. Whatever its nature or origin, the power of the "adversary" is the same: a reduction of human freedom and spiritual disarray. The challenge is to be able to distinguish the "standard of Christ" from the "standard of the adversary." How easy it would be if there were bright and visible markers in life, separating the two: the beauty of Zion, the City of God, and the barren, desolate fields of Babylon. Then I would always be able to recognize one from the other. But the dividing line between the two opposing camps runs invisibly throughout the whole world and through every human heart. This dividing line is the choice waiting to be made wherever God's invitation to a life of poverty, powerlessness, and humility is in conflict with the desire for riches, honor, and pride. The point of the Two Standards meditation is to come to the realization that this choice cannot be deferred.

Next, Ignatius introduces a consideration known as the Three Classes of Persons (149–56). In contemporary terms, the three "classes" are: the procrastinator, the compromiser, and the person who is truly free and generous to choose "what is more to the glory of God and the salvation of my soul." The individual is asked to consider which of these categories best describes his or her present disposition.

Later in the second week, as the one making the *Exercises* continues to ponder and contemplate the life of Christ, an exercise known as the Three Ways of Being Humble (or the Three Modes of Love of God) is presented (165–68). Ignatius is quite clear about the kind of person most likely to persevere under the standard of Christ and be the faithful "companion" of Jesus. It is the individual in whom useless anxiety and self-absorption have been replaced by humble love. Such an individual knows the truth of Jesus' words: "Where your treasure is, there your heart is also" (Matt. 6:21).

The exercises of the second week are intended to foster three areas of realization: (1) an understanding with the *mind* that a free response to God's creative word in Christ is the primary vocation of each human being; (2) an attitude of the *will* to choose what is more in keeping with that vocation in preference to other considerations; and (3) a desire of the *heart* to accept the consequences of this loving choice made in faith. Taken as a whole, the second week is an invitation to intimacy with Jesus, the word of God become human for our sake. But it is also about choosing. All the exercises of the second week, in addition to focusing on the person of Jesus, are directed toward the "election" (169–88).

As was mentioned above, the "election" concerns the choice of a particular vocation or, possibly, some reordering of the priorities in the vocation one already has. During the second week Ignatius proposes certain helps to the individual for decision making. As should be clear from the very start of the *Exercises,* clarity about the goal or purpose of one's existence is the "indispensable hinge on which a sound election [choice] turns."[15] Ignatius is convinced that there are three "times" or situations that are especially conducive to making a good choice: (1) when there is present a kind of self-authenticating experience such that there can be little room for doubt about what God is asking of us. This is more than what one might term a "gut feeling," but on the other hand, the experience offers evidence that the choice is "of God" in a way more "immediate" than mediated; (2) when, although the desire to do God's will is strong and sincere, the individual experiences in her or his heart movements of both consolation and desolation. A careful discernment of these movements will often show quite clearly the choice to be made; (3) when

15. Ganss, *Ignatius of Loyola,* 412.

the individual experiences tranquillity and peace. Then, Ignatius says, I should hold myself "like a balance at equilibrium" and proceed to list not only the reasons for and against the choice, but also the motivation for each reason. When I think the proper choice has become apparent, I still need to seek some confirmation from God (i.e., some consoling movement of the heart).[16] The second week of the *Exercises*, whatever its duration, is a period of intense discernment with regard both to choosing one's vocation and also to discerning the factors that go into the choice (328–36). For Ignatius, discernment has both intellectual and affective components. He knew the need not only to "go beneath" one's emotions but also to unmask what may, on the surface, appear to be serious intellectual arguments proposed by the mind. It is worth noting that confusion, lack of peace, and a troubled spirit are all indications that the time for decision making has not yet come. There is need for greater peace with oneself and with God.

The Third Week: While there is no question that love is central to a life patterned upon Jesus, when we take a closer look we see that the embodiment of that love is Jesus on the cross. The mystery of the cross has already been presented to the person making the *Exercises*—e.g., during the first week, when the individual is directed to look upon the crucified Jesus and converse with him as the sign of both sin and mercy. Again, in the second week, it becomes clear that whoever chooses to follow Jesus is invited into a personal drama of transforming love. To love is to give yourself away. Thus, at the start of the third week, the individual knows the self-emptying that is involved in love, but there can still be resistance to this knowledge be-

16. In practice, it appears that of the three "times" for decision making, the first is rather rare, though there are individuals who make a decision "in the gut," as it were, and experience great peace along with a sense of God's presence and illumination. Most individuals make a decision in the second or third times. The role of the will and affections ("listening to the heart") is more predominant in the second time, while for people who are drawn by what seems rational and reasonable, the third time is likely to be the best. In making some significant decisions of his own, Ignatius seems to have combined the second and third times. Cf. *The Spiritual Exercises of Saint Ignatius*, 177–78.

cause most human beings would like to imagine that life is consistent, straightforward, comfortably navigated.

In the third week, Ignatius proposes that the individual making the *Exercises* contemplate Christ in his sufferings and death so as to gain a deeper interior knowledge of how love suffers all things for the sake of the Beloved. Through my accompaniment of Jesus to Calvary, I also discover the true depth of my faith and commitment or lack thereof. In walking with Christ, I arrive at a place where it becomes clear that my own response to Christ in his suffering has consequences and that there are no easy answers. What I choose to do depends on my humility and courage to respond to the demands that truth and love make on me. Until this point, I may have thought I was open to change, to taking an honest look at my vocation; but in the third week, it becomes clear that God's call to me is not just about making amends, modifying my behavior, making a minor change here or a substitution there. If I choose to go forward with Christ, then I will have to resist trying to construct myself according to my own illusions and yield to God's spirit at work in me. What matters in the end is not only what I have been saying to God, but what God has been saying to me. There is a deeper sense in the third week that I really do not choose a vocation; a vocation chooses me.

The *Exercises* move toward their culmination in the third and fourth weeks. Ignatius anticipates that the nature of the individual's prayer will shift during this time from seeking to know, love, and follow Jesus in the commitment of discipleship to a more immediately participatory involvement—as profound as God wishes to give. In the third week, this manifests itself not so much in seeking suffering as a way that draws me close to Christ, but rather desiring to suffer *with* Christ, who in his love for me draws near to my human afflictions through his own experience of suffering. In contemplating Jesus' sufferings and death on the cross, I learn that my vocation to be *with* Christ is to live in *compassion* with the compassionate Savior.

Ignatius also expects that one's experiences in the third week will confirm again the "election" the individual made in the course of the second week. This confirmation is not for the sake of verifying the choice made earlier, but for the purpose of strengthening the chooser. This strengthening is critical because in contemplating Jesus' self-emptying love, I will be more willing to accept the implications of a love worthy of the name, one which draws me out of myself. Any part of me that holds back, that seeks to keep a little something for myself, undermines the love and the commitment, and makes living out my vocation all the more difficult.

The Fourth Week: If the focus of the third week is suffering with Christ, the focus of the fourth week is to experience joy with the Risen Christ. The claim of Christian faith in the Resurrection is that God's plan for creation will prevail; God's will, as Christians pray in the Lord's Prayer, *will be done on earth as it is in heaven.* The individual making the *Exercises,* having made a free decision about his or her vocation in life, is now invited to savor joy in the conviction that God alone rules and nothing else has any power over us. My past and my present, God's covenant and human history—all of that is the redeemed "stuff" of Christ's victory. We meet Jesus where he has met us before. The experience of joy with Christ Risen is not about the reversal or undoing of all that has gone before, including Jesus' suffering and death. It is the joy of experiencing the healing and the *restoration* of all that had been destroyed or left in shambles by human sinfulness.

The grace or effect of the contemplations of the fourth week, in Ignatius's view, is an inner consolation that moves and strengthens the individual for loving service. One's vocation in life moves outward, impelled by the Spirit. In the fourth week, I experience a call to active participation in the work of redemption, to carry the "Good News" of God's Kingdom to others. For Ignatius, the authenticity of the experience is always measured in terms of depth and strength rather than emotional exuberance. If the joy stays with oneself or is merely ephemeral, Ignatius is not inclined to trust it. A lasting joy and confidence in God's final victory should function as a kind of yeast in the day-to-day living out of our vocation.

Where the *Exercises* End

At the end of the *Spiritual Exercises* there is what Ignatius called the Contemplation to Attain Love (226–37). In a sense, one is back where one started, caught up in the awareness of how everything turns on the two meanings of the love of God: God's love for me and my love for God. As was said earlier, vocation is the intimate relationship between the Creator who lovingly calls one into being and the individual who freely and lovingly answers "yes" to the call. It is Love that calls us into existence. Love, then, is the deepest meaning of the human vocation.

The Contemplation at the end of the *Exercises* touches on the giving and receiving of this love in the "now," in each present moment. *Now,* in this moment of time, God gives; I receive the gift of love and I offer, in return, the gift of my love. If God gives me the grace of the Contemplation, it is ultimately what will push me out the door in the morning and bring me home tired at the close of the day. The Contemplation is about desire, choice, and action—all rolled into one.

In the Contemplation, Ignatius proposes four "points" for prayer and consideration, though they all form a single vision: (1) I will call to mind all the gifts I have received from God. The whole of life is a gift. Not a day should go by without our pausing to take note of all that we have received and to respond with loving gratitude to the God who gives everything. (2) I will consider how God not only gives everything, but God dwells in everything. The deep conviction that "God is in this place" or this person or this thing, that "all we do is go from one bit of holy ground to another," grows in us as we look at everything through the prism of God's love. God is everywhere and everything; and therefore, can become the medium within which the exchange of loves itself takes place. (3) I will consider how God labors and works in everything. At every moment and in everything, God is at work in creation. Every love is "a piece of work." It takes some doing and, often, some heartbreak. Ignatius knew from personal experience that the proof of love, both God's love for us and our love for God, consists not in words but in deeds. (4) I will consider how God is both the source and fulfillment of everything. God's love is a summons to give ourselves to the only vocation worthy of our efforts: loving service in bringing all creation to its fulfillment in God.

⌒꙳

Commenting on the final stages of the *Exercises,* Ganss writes:

By now the [individual] has reviewed God's entire plan of creation and re-demption evolving in the history of salvation, from creation, through the fall of the angels and Adam, as well as the Incarnation and Redemption which lead one all the way to the destiny of the beatific vision. The [indi-vidual], too, has been striving to fit himself or herself cooperatively into this divine plan. . . . This whole sequence of exercises has produced a pow-erful psychological impact and given a new orientation of life.[17]

What have people over the centuries learned about call and voca-tion in their experience of making the *Spiritual Exercises?* First, in this intense personal encounter between individuals and God they have registered their deepest desires and hungers to know and be known, to love and be loved. Moreover, they have discovered a deeper level of interior freedom that has made it possible for them to appreciate more fully all existence as the gift of love that it is. Per-haps they would also say that, at the deepest levels of vocation, it is not so much that one asks; rather, that one is asked. In the experi-ence of interior freedom, they have found it possible to respond "yes" in love to God and to the ongoing work of becoming them-selves through the specific choices that life presents.

Rowan Williams makes a telling point:

Vocation may be to be *what* we are, but that doesn't leave us *where* we are. We shall need to work to find the structure and form of life that is most our own because it leaves us most alert, most responsive, most open to the never-failing grace of God. We have to find the meter for our poem, the key in which to sing our song to God, the cell where we can pray to him, the person in whom we can love him, so as to give a "local habita-

17. *The Spiritual Exercises of Saint Ignatius,* 7.

tion and a name," face and flesh, to our own particular following of Christ.[18]

When a person completes the *Spiritual Exercises,* the journey is only beginning, not ending. To respond to God's call, to make a decision about vocation, to commit oneself to a work or a direction in life, is not to make a prediction. Ignatius chose to give himself completely to God in loving service, but he could never have imagined the particular circumstances in which he would actually live out his vocation. Over a lifetime, he continued to see himself as a pilgrim on the road to God. It is the same with all of us.

> With the drawing of this Love and the voice of this Calling
> We shall not cease from exploration
> And the end of all our exploring
> Will be to arrive where we started
> And know the place for the first time.[19]

18. Williams, *A Ray of Darkness,* 159.

19. From T. S. Eliot's poem "Little Gidding," in T. S. Eliot, *Collected Poems 1909–1962* (New York: Harcourt, Brace & World, 1963), 208.

Mark A. McIntosh

Crying to Follow a Call

Vocation and Discernment in
Bunyan's *Pilgrim's Progress*

If we think of vocation in terms of our own particular
choice of a career in life, then John Bunyan's seventeenth-century
Puritan allegory, *The Pilgrim's Progress from This World to That
Which Is to Come*, must seem an odd tool for exploring vocation. It
is, after all, about a journey from damnation to salvation, and involves a fairly dire critique of the very world in which most of us are
trying to follow our individual callings. But suppose what we usually think of as our "vocation" were really only an emerging thread—
which sometimes we can follow and sometimes only guess at—in
the developing pattern of our lives? Religious thought tends to
think of vocation this way, not simply in a narrow and technical
sense (vocation as job), but as calling in the deepest sense—calling
out of illusions and pretenses, calling into the fullness of who we
each have it in us to be.

Vocation as the Calling to Exist

In more overtly theological terms, we might see vocation as a dialogue.[1] On one side there is God's calling everything that exists into the fullness of being. And on the other side there is the "response" that each thing makes to that calling, in the first place simply by coming *to be,* but also by coming to be very particularly the *kind* of being that each thing is. When the things in question have some degree of mindfulness about them, then this dialogue between divine calling and our response is more exhilarating and more challenging, involving as it does our abilities to feel and reason, to choose and reject, to commit and evade. God's calling to us "happens from birth to death, and what we usually call vocation is only a name for the moment of crisis within the unbroken process."[2] It might make sense to regard our whole life as a pilgrimage in response to divine calling, and our particular vocation as a journey into those patterns of life that allow us to be truthfully and wholly the persons God is calling into being. But what that might mean at any given moment is not always clear: "crises occur at those points where we see how unreality, our selfish, self-protecting illusions, our struggles for cheap security, block the way to our answering the call to be. To live like this, to nurture and develop this image of myself, may be safe, but it isn't true."[3]

⤳

To pursue one's vocation in this sense, then, means becoming more real, moving beyond a kind of stymied, half-life caricature of oneself. It means moving beyond a response to calling that is merely a biological drive to go on existing and toward a listening, responding, choosing, delighting personhood. This kind of personhood in-

---

1. For good introductory reflections on this idea, see, e.g., Noel Dermot O'Donoghue, *Heaven in Ordinarie: Prayer as Transcendence* (Edinburgh: T. & T. Clark, 1979), chap. 3; and Rowan Williams, *A Ray of Darkness: Sermons and Reflections* (Cambridge: Cowley Publications, 1995), 147–59.
2. Williams, *A Ray of Darkness,* 150.
3. Ibid.

volves the risk of setting out from the self given to us by our biology, or constructed for us by our culture, and embracing the call to relationship with others who stretch us beyond the limits even of what we thought of as our selves, and on into a deeper truthfulness of being. This is the calling, the vocation, that religious thought understands as the calling into being, by virtue of a calling into relationship with God.

If we take vocation in this broader sense, then Bunyan gives rise to helpful reflection. For he dramatizes the journey into the truth of one's being precisely as a pilgrimage into a more truthful response to God's calling—a pilgrimage, that is, into a less fearful, less driven, less illusory, and more personal form of existence. Bunyan is adept at unmasking the artificial stopping points, the inauthentic concretions of selfhood that mesmerize and numb us. And he illustrates what we might call path-finding vocational skills. These habits of discernment and interpretation permit one to read the world not as a concatenation of mute objects and opaque events but as the landscape of a journey—with discernible landmarks, inspiring vistas, and a population of important companions for the way.

Allegory in a Reifying World

It is not coincidental that allegory was so popular a genre among Puritan writers. *Pilgrim's Progress* and many other works in the same vein were designed to pry open the range of meanings inherent in everything, and to do so in a world increasingly ill at ease with ambiguity. Founding figures in the new science of early modernity like Francis Bacon were happy to employ allegory as well. But Bacon's allegorizations of ancient myths were designed to cloak the real political and scientific implications of his teaching; they are essentially a rhetorical training in subtlety and calculation. Bunyan's allegory, by contrast, is more nearly a narratival metaphysics; *Pilgrim's Progress* is a way of recovering entire dimensions of meaning that, in Bunyan's view, were being washed out of the picture.

Early modernity is marked by an epistemological crisis, by an urgent "search for new forms of language to replace traditional logic and rhetoric."[4] For Bacon, for Hobbes, and for the influential founders of the Royal Society, language had been too much infected with the teleological momentum of Aristotelian logic and the seemingly artificial plausibility of the rhetorical tradition. For language to be useful again it would need, in their view, a nominalizing purification, a pruning away of all metaphorical and analogical penumbra. And the point of this was not simply to chasten language, but to purge our conception of the reality that language names. Hobbes is very clear about wanting to jettison all the linguistic habits of thought that might conduct the mind toward anything infinite, anything not subject to knowledge of the senses.[5] Establishment religious thought, despite its occasional opposition to Hobbes, was of a very similar view. Archbishop Tillotson (himself the son-in-law of one of the founding members of the Royal Society) argued strenuously for the elimination from religious discourse of all "sublime notions and unintelligible mysteries, with pleasant passages of wit, and artificial strains of rhetoric; and nice and unprofitable disputes, with bold interpretations of dark prophesies."[6]

And yet Bunyan was convinced that it was precisely the work of puzzling over such dark mysteries that could fit the mind to encounter a truth not graspable by a plain, discursive, nominalizing rationality. In the "Apology" that prefaces *Pilgrim's Progress,* Bunyan addresses himself as if directly to Tillotson:

> Solidity, indeed becomes the Pen
> Of him that writeth things Divine to men:
> But must I needs want solidness, because
> By Metaphors I speak; was not God's Laws,

4. Barbara J. Shapiro, *Probability and Certainty in Seventeenth-Century England: A Study of the Relationships between Natural Science, Religion, History, Law, and Literature* (Princeton: Princeton University Press, 1983), 227.

5. See especially Thomas Hobbes, *Leviathan,* ed. Edwin Curley (Indianapolis: Hackett, 1994), part I, chap. 2 ("Of Imagination"), chap. 3 ("Of the Consequence or Train of Imagination"), and chap. 4 ("Of Speech").

6. John Tillotson, "The Necessity of Repentance and Faith," in *Works* 8:233, quoted in Shapiro, *Probability and Certainty,* 255.

His Gospel-laws in older time held forth
By Types, Shadows and Metaphors?[7]

The practice of figural reading trains the mind to search for hidden depths of meaning in ordinary life. To discover a hidden purpose in your life, to "read" the choices you make in terms of that goal— these are vocational habits that allegory is able to teach in a way that more discursive argumentation cannot. Partly this is so because of how the interpretive task of allegory forms the mind, but it is also true in a more ontological sense: what Bunyan draws to our attention may in fact not *be* apprehensible apart from an analogical frame of mind. Or as Bunyan puts it in his preface to the second part of his work:

And to stir the mind
To a search after what it fain would find,
Things that seem to be hid in words obscure,
Do but the Godly mind the more alure;
To study what those Sayings should contain,
That speak to us in such a Cloudy strain.
I also know, a dark Similitude
Will on the Fancie more it self intrude,
And will stick faster in the Heart and Head,
Then things from Similies not borrowed. (139)

For Bunyan, this "fancie" is a creative, imagining faculty capable of receiving a "dark Similitude" and being drawn thereby into a new level of understanding and insight. "Words obscure, / Do but the Godly mind the more alure," and so conduce toward a multidimensional sense of the world. For Hobbes, by contrast, such fancy or imagination "is nothing but decaying sense."[8] Hobbes's materialism and nominalism have no conception of the imagination playing a constructive role; it is in his view, but the ever-fainter impression

7. John Bunyan, *The Pilgrim's Progress*, ed. N. H. Keeble, Oxford World's Classics ed. (Oxford: Oxford University Press, 1984), 4; all references to *Pilgrim's Progress* are from this edition and will hereafter be noted parenthetically.
8. Hobbes, *Leviathan*, part I, chap. 2, 8.

left on our senses of whatever is now absent from us. This is important to Hobbes because he fears that any interpretive openness about the world leaves a dangerous opening for challenges to the epistemological dominance of the state. The modern world badly needed to shut down rival visions of reality if it was to achieve peace and order.[9] But what if rival visions are precisely what we need in order to hear an authentic calling, one not, perhaps, engineered for us by the culture? All of this is instructive because it may help us to understand why discernment seems such a challenge for us today, why vocational awareness seems inaccessible: when the mind reifies the world and sees everything as reducible to one datum after another, then the world becomes opaque and mute. It becomes extremely difficult to sense any "more" to the world if it has no more interpretive depth to it, no more quality of sign-fullness.

This is excruciatingly demonstrated by a later writer of Puritan descent. Daniel Defoe's *Moll Flanders* (1722) arrived a generation after *Pilgrim's Progress* (1672), and its warning against the mainstream cultural absorption of a Hobbesian frame of mind is searing. *Moll* is the original "Pilgrim's Regress," depicting the rapid descent of the anti-heroine into a moral autism of confused identity, loss of purpose, and persistent duplicity. For when nothing has any enduring significance, everything becomes capable of meaning anything, all is simply what you make it: everything is reducible to different denominations in one common coinage and available to the largest purse. Whereas Bunyan's pilgrim still struggles toward discernment, Moll's submersion beneath the unrecognizable significance of her endlessly compromising circumstances reduces her efforts at personal and vocational judgment to a suspiciously amusing charade of excuses for debauchery. Moll's ability to notice and respond to authen-

---

9. Fuming over the threat posed to civic control by traditional Christian teaching about grace, Hobbes writes: "they say that faith, and wisdom, and other virtues are sometimes poured into a man, sometimes blown into him from Heaven . . . and a great many other things that serve to lessen the dependence of subjects on the sovereign power of their country. For who will endeavour to obey the laws, if he expect obedience to be poured or blown into him?" (Hobbes, *Leviathan*, part IV, chap. 46, p. 460).

tic personal vocation is reduced to the flatness of a materialist biological drive, in which her conduct is merely the result of whatever
appetite or aversion is most immediately brought to bear upon her
at any given moment. The sustaining vocational directionality of
Bunyan's Providence (figured in such characters as the Evangelist,
Faithful, and the Shepherds) has been replaced in Defoe by a series
of characters who can imagine no end for Moll other than the basest
devices of their own urges, and who teach her to hope for nothing
better. Our ambivalence about doctrines of predestination today
perhaps obscures their positive function in vocational discernment;
as one commentator puts it, weaken predestination "and you are
heading towards Defoe."[10] Perhaps we could say that Bunyan's allegorical thinking brings out the providential, directional function of
predestinarian Puritan thought; for it illuminates life in terms of a
guiding calling and goal—or at least serves as a marker, holding
open the world to a meaning from beyond it. Certainly the absence
in *Moll* of any hope of that transparency of life to its deeper meaning
reminds us of how painful the loss of a discerning capacity can be.

Bunyan's use of allegory, therefore, is an important step in re-
training the mind to navigate life, not as one thing after another but
as invested with meaning and directionality, irradiated with a light
of eternal significance. In fact, we could say that by conceiving life
allegorically in terms of pilgrimage, Bunyan is not merely telling us
about the possibility of our lives' deeper meaning, but engaging us
in a literary practice of sign reading, path-finding, and depth-dis-
covering—all of which are important skills at work in vocational reflection.[11]

Learning to Recognize Illusion

Having considered the implications of Bunyan's chosen genre, let
me now attend to the critical faculty he seeks to teach us. Later I

10. Roger Pooley, "Spiritual Experience and Spiritual Autobiography: Some Contexts for *Grace Abounding*," *Baptist Quarterly* 32 (Oct. 1988): 393–402, at 396.

11. For more on Bunyan's development of an allegorical rationality, see the fine

will focus more directly on the more positive skills of vocational discernment themselves.

Bunyan spent more than a third of his adult life in prison for continuing to preach without a license, so he knew very well that his interpretive vision of life was threatening to both the cultural and the individual status quo. The world does not especially like to notice the "more" of God's invitation. Bunyan wants to make sure that his readers reckon with their tendencies to illusion about this. He wants to warn us about the power of counterfeit goals to beguile us from efforts toward vocational authenticity. Real calling, divine gift that it is, in Bunyan's experience is likely to be heard by the world only as a repugnant threat to its autonomy. The interpretive space, the graceful multidimensionality of life lived toward a radical call, is perceived as a dangerous mark of epistemological instability by a reifying world—just as the same calling renders us politically unstable, unwilling to confine our loyalties to the state. Because Bunyan is so aware of this he makes the recognition of "substitute" callings an important part of his teaching on discernment.

We might begin with the most obvious attacks on vocation and move toward an awareness of the subtlest. Undoubtedly, the most overt threat to Christian and his own self-understanding comes from the "foul fiend" Apollyon. This monstrous figure (whom Bunyan adapts from biblical references) assails Christian with a telling combination of frightful appearance and a cunning reasonableness; he is shown to be the pilgrim's hateful adversary but also his secret, unacknowledged master. When Christian announces that he has come from the City of Destruction, Apollyon exults malignantly: "By this I perceive thou art one of my Subjects, for all that Countrey is mine; and I am the Prince and God of it. How is it that thou hast ran away from thy King? Were it not that I hope thou maiest do me more service, I would strike thee now at one blow to the

---

essay by Barbara A. Johnson, "Falling into Allegory: The 'Apology' to *The Pilgrim's Progress* and Bunyan's Scriptural Methodology," in *Bunyan in Our Time*, ed. Robert G. Collmer (Kent, Ohio: Kent State University Press, 1989), 113–37.

ground" (47). There is a horrible shock here as Christian is made to realize who *claims* at least to have been the dominant power in his life so far.

Even more disconcerting, however, are Apollyon's well-oiled counsels, charmingly accommodating and even consolatory in tone. He fears Christian will find his new calling a hard one, promises good things upon Christian's undoubted return to his old king, and assures him that "it is ordinary for those that have professed themselves his [Christ's] Servants, after a while to give him the slip; and return again to me; do thou so too, and all shall be well" (47). Here is the strangely comforting poison of despair, holding before us a hopeless picture of our apparently inevitable failure and so giving us permission to skulk back cozily into the old and familiar servitude, forsaking any effort to test the real depths of our calling.

Apollyon tightens the noose further with an excruciatingly accurate rehearsal of all the ways in which Christian has already been unfaithful to Christ (and is therefore unlikely to persevere in his calling). The fiend saves his most insidious swipe for last: "and when thou talkest of thy Journey, and of what thou has heard, and seen, thou art inwardly desirous of vainglory in all that thou sayest or doest" (48). Even Christian's highest calling, says Apollyon, is morbidly tainted with self-preoccupation. But Christian answers freely and fearlessly, "All this is true, and much more, which thou has left out; but the Prince whom I serve and honour, is merciful, and ready to forgive" (48). Surely if Christian *had* tried to argue with Apollyon, finding mitigation for this or that little infidelity, he would have been lost. He would have been swept into a collaboration with all his weaknesses, and gradually brought to a destructive choice between a ceaseless and exhausting denial of truth or else a paralyzing state of self-condemnation. Vocational judgment is not possible, Bunyan seems to suggest, if we pretend that flawed motivations are entirely absent from our journey; but neither can we let our shortcomings be the measure of our hope. The hope of our calling lies quite beyond ourselves: "the Prince whom I serve and honour, is merciful."

In the episode of Apollyon, Bunyan alerts his readers to the danger of a distortion of their calling; he does this by depicting the menacing power of the world, both in its beguiling calls to a false and lesser goal and by its insinuations that the pilgrim has really been seeking only these lesser goals all along anyway. Apollyon is depicted finally as a bully who begins by using believers' own self-doubts against them and then escalates to naked threats of violence in order to keep would-be pilgrims back in their accustomed places.

The underlying systematic structure of control, which Apollyon merely personifies, becomes even more apparent in the famous adventures of Christian and Faithful at Vanity Fair. In this great sequence, Bunyan shows with what difficulty the world has even to *imagine,* let alone pursue, a vocation beyond the commerce of the world. For what Bunyan unmasks here are the commodifying structures of the world, which seek to convert every desire to a purchasable form and thus constrain all our aspirations and goals to the limits of a worldly purse: "at this Fair are all such Merchandize sold, as Houses, Lands . . . Kingdoms, Lusts, Pleasures, and Delights of all sorts, as Whores, Bauds, Wives, Husbands, Children, Masters, Servants, Lives, Blood, Bodies, Souls, Silver, Gold, Pearls, Precious Stones, and what not" (73).

The fact that the pilgrims refuse to enter into the "commerce" of the fair creates a terrible hubbub. Their refusal to name a price or quantify their callings in commodifiable terms is a threat to the world system; for their refusal opens the eyes of some "that were more observing, and less prejudiced then the rest" (75) to the possibility that there may *be* real goals not fully attainable on the world's terms. And thus it shows the very idea of vocation to be a sign of transcendence, a marker of an ungraspable calling to "more" in a system that would like to assimilate everything and everyone within the scope of its own measures.

At Vanity Fair no one attempts to convince the pilgrims, as Apollyon did, that their goals are really only pious expressions for worldly ambitions; rather, here Bunyan simply depicts the stark incomprehension of any ideals that might threaten to extend beyond material terms. The pilgrims are regarded frankly as dangerous lunatics; they are beaten, put on public display in cages, and tried on trumped-up charges with a parade of false witness. Bunyan's magnificent trial scene—presided over by Lord Hategood and receiving testimony from such sober citizens as Envy, Superstition, and Pickthank—portrays the world's vicious discomfort with authentic vocation as rooted in bitter pusillanimity. The world's soul is literally too small *(pusilla anima)* to embrace the glory of a hope beyond its own tight-fisted management and control. If it cannot buy and sell the thing, it despises it. Christian and Faithful threaten to open the world's eyes to the real depths of its desires, depths it prefers not to notice because they lie beyond its own powers.

One of the paradoxes that Bunyan repeatedly explores is that a deep and wonderful calling, which seems so foolhardy, dubious, and deadly to the world, is really the only thing capable of prying open the world's otherwise continually constricting hopes. Conversely, the goals that the world holds out as worthy callings, says Bunyan, inevitably collapse into vain and ever-narrowing pursuits of self-interest. While most of us might wish to affirm the naturalness of religious belief and its perfect congruence with true human happiness, Bunyan always points to the danger that our authentic callings will be suborned by lesser ones.

The climate was not auspicious for Bunyan's warnings. Bishop John Wilkins, one of the founders of the Royal Society, had written a highly influential work, *Of the Principles and Duties of Natural Religion*, which appeared just three years before *Pilgrim's Progress* and emphasized how harmoniously religious faith and human success might go together. His goal, he wrote, was:

to persuade Men to the Practice of Religion, and the Virtues of a good life, by shewing how natural and direct an influence they have, not only upon our future Blessedness in another World, but even upon the Happiness and Prosperity of this present Life. And surely nothing is more likely to prevail with wise and considerate Men to become Religious, than to be thoroughly convinced, that Religion and Happiness, our Duty and our Interest, are really but one and the same thing considered under several notions.[12]

Bunyan seems to be satirizing Wilkins's argument pretty directly when he presents numerous self-declared pilgrims who, despising Christian's risky and difficult route, keep falling by the wayside into more pleasant paths. One good example is By-ends, who claims as his relatives a Mr. Smooth-man, Mr. Facing-bothways, and Mr. Any-thing. Having discoursed upon his enviable relations, By-ends adds blithely, "'Tis true, we somewhat differ in religion from those of the stricter sort, yet but in two small points: First, we never strive against Wind and Tide. Secondly, we are always most zealous when Religion goes in his Silver Slippers; we love much to walk with him in the Street, if the Sun shines, and the people applaud it" (81).

Vanity Fair, suggests Bunyan, is the state of the world when it has finally accommodated all its real hopes in this way. First, there is a barely perceptible debasement of authentic calling into a more immediately prosperous counterfeit version, and then at last comes total incomprehension and antagonism toward any call that refuses to fit in. By-ends and his friends Mr. Hold-the-World, Mr. Mony-love, and Mr. Save-all accuse Christian of being rigid and censorious, a threat to liberty. And yet, as their own conversation continues, Bunyan depicts them as falling progressively into the most laughably self-serving platitudes imaginable. "'Tis best to make hay when the Sun shines," opines Mr. Hold-the-world cheerily to his friends:

you see how the Bee lieth still all winter and bestirs her then only when she can have profit with pleasure. God sends sometimes Rain, and sometimes Sunshine; if they be such fools to go through the first, yet let us be content to take fair weather along with us. For my part I like that Religion best, that will stand with the security of Gods good blessings unto us; for who

12. John Wilkins, quoted in Isabel Rivers, "Grace, Holiness, and the Pursuit of Happiness: Bunyan and Restoration Latitudinarianism," in *John Bunyan: Conventicle and Parnassus, Tercentenary Essays*, ed. N. H. Keeble (Oxford: Clarendon Press, 1988), 53.

can imagin that is ruled by his reason, since God has bestowed upon us the good things of this life, but that he would have us keep them for his sake? (83–84)

For Bunyan, a world in which the depths of authentic vocation are left unexplored is a world in which the profoundest hopes becomes unhearable and one's calling degenerates into crassness. And this loss of deep vocational acuity leads to a real epistemological numbness, an inability to conceive of or interpret reality beyond the bounds of the obvious and the quantifiable. Bunyan seems to be telling us that if what is truly great can only be present in this world in the form of our human yearning for it, then should that longing be falsely satiated, we will suffer a terrible absence of what is real beyond all measuring. Platitude assumes the place of wisdom.

The Self Become Its Own Prisoner

Bunyan deepens the paradox still further, for he shows this vocational autism, which tries to be happy by hearing nothing beyond the clamor of self-aggrandizing desire, as always at risk of falling yet more grievously into nihilism and despair. It is as if the self, deprived of a real calling *beyond* itself, becomes the prisoner of its own anxieties and doubts. If the human will exists in a mere echo chamber of its own desires, in which the authentic voice of the other has been silenced in favor of an "other" that is merely my own self-interest projected outward, then my will becomes, paradoxically, self-annihilating. Nowhere is this clearer than in the episode of Doubting Castle and its lord, Giant Despair.

Christian falls subject to this terrible figure through nothing but his own self-seeking will. Bunyan sets the scene with astuteness. Christian and his new companion, Hopeful, (Faithful having given his life for his calling at Vanity Fair) have been enjoying a period of refreshment and consolation beside the River of Life. But as they take up their journey again they discover to their sorrow that their way parts from the river: "Now the way from the River was rough, and their feet tender by reason of their Travels; So the soul of the

Pilgrims was much discouraged, because of the way. Wherefore still as they went on, they wished for a better way" (91). Yet this desire to make joy their possession leads them to a false path and a way that is no way at all. They see a delightful meadow on the other side of a fence and immediately Christian cries out, "Tis according to my wish . . . here is the easiest going" (91). And of course it is delightful walking, but with nightfall a tremendous storm and flood overtake them and in their lostness they fall asleep. With the morning, they are awakened by the "grim and surly voice" of the owner of the grounds upon which they have trespassed, Giant Despair. In his "nasty and stinking" dungeon, they are kept for days without any light or food or drink. "In this place, Christian had double sorrow, because twas through his unadvised haste that they were brought into this distress" (93).

Bunyan is very subtle at this point, for he allows the fairytale-like conventions to play themselves out realistically, testing the reader's ability to read between the lines. The giant terrorizes them, and they are starving with their wounds untreated, and so on. Yet gradually it appears that the giant's power over them is somehow linked to their own fear; he browbeats them with the hopelessness of their plight and urges them to take their own lives: "for why, said he, should you chuse life, seeing it is attended with so much bitterness" (94). Now Christian begins to succumb, and the voice of Despair becomes indistinguishable from his own thoughts.

Bunyan had hinted at this most sinister ventriloquism once before. When Christian was passing through the Valley of the Shadow of Death, one of the demons had crept up so covertly and closely to him that the horrible blasphemies and dismally obsessive murmurings that the demon was whispering into Christian's ear seemed to him as if they "proceeded from his own mind" (52). Bunyan's vision is quite telling. The supposed bastion of rational judgment and enlightened self-interest, the human self turns out to be much less stable than we might like to think; the isolated ego, busily pursuing its own path, is far more susceptible to unperceived motivations than it usually admits. But whereas in the episode of the whispering demon

Christian is still being accosted (albeit covertly, from without), now, in Doubting Castle, the threat has truly found its interior nest and begins to incubate in the pilgrim's own heart. All vocational judgment begins to be undermined and infested with despair, and these thoughts really are now proceeding from the pilgrim's own mind. The self, having been led into decay and debasement through the pursuit of counterfeit goods (the beguilingly soft meadow) is left in a vacuum. The voice that had continually called out to the self and made it alive and awake to a reality beyond itself has been walled out; the self now feels itself cut off and tyrannized by its own fears.

It is at this point that Bunyan makes movingly clear how truly vocation can only ever be a communal journey. We may each have to travel as individuals, but we are lost if we travel alone. Just as Christian has reached the point of irrevocable despair, Hopeful comforts him, reminding him of all the great wonders he has seen and passed through already. And most important, he simply calls Christian "My Brother," and says, "Thou seest that I am in the Dungeon with thee, a far weaker man by nature than thou art: Also this Giant has wounded me as well as thee; and hath also cut off the Bread and Water from my mouth; and with thee I mourn without the light" (95). In spite of the world's attempts to divert the pilgrims by falsely constricting their callings within the limits of the self's own natural desires, that self is not quite left entirely alone; there is always a fellow sufferer whose presence holds open a door out of the self that the world has tried to construct for us, whose voice is the voice of a calling beyond the limits of what we thought was our selfhood.

Encouraged by Hopeful's words, Christian joins him in praying through Saturday night "till almost break of day" (96). Then suddenly, in amazement, Christian cries out that he realizes he has all along had in his possession a key "called Promise, that will, (I am perswaded) open any Lock in Doubting-Castle" (96). Perhaps Bunyan sets this moment of liberation deliberately in the time sequence of Saturday vigil to resurrection morning, suggesting how Christian's recovered fellowship with Hopeful draws him again more deeply into a community of new life that has learned to live precisely by living no longer for itself alone, but for another who has suffered with and for it.

Clearly, for Bunyan, the deepest cause for concern about vocation relates to this very intrinsic tendency, which is to fall prey to solipsism and to a culture that holds itself together precisely by holding us apart, by abetting isolation and obsessive self-interest. If calling is to remain clear and healthy and vocational discernment to remain robust and free, they will need a fellowship that permits everyone to discover the true depths of their "own" callings in mutuality with one another.

Communities of Vocational Discernment

It would take us beyond the bounds of this essay to examine all the instances in which Christian is taught or inspired by others to have a deeper understanding of his calling. But leaving aside such memorable figures as the mysterious Interpreter and the kindly Shepherds of the Delectable Mountains, let me consider just the great episode of Christian's visit to the Palace Beautiful.

This extended episode comes immediately prior to two of Christian's most desperate trials (Apollyon and the Valley of the Shadow of Death) and provides the formation and encouragement in his calling without which he would have very likely perished. Taken as a whole, the episode comprises three distinct sequences: an initiatory trial, a dialogue on experience, and a confirming immersion in the historical and communal context of the pilgrim's calling.

The episode begins in extreme ambivalence: night has fallen on Christian, he has just been warned of ravening beasts ahead, and yet "while he was thus bewayling his unhappy miscarriage, he lift up his eyes, and behold there was a very stately Palace before him, the name whereof was Beautiful, and it stood just by the High-way side" (37). We can sense very well the tension and conflicting emotions that beset the early stages of any vocational journey. An image or foretaste of the hoped-for goal is in sight, but at the same time

there are considerable hindrances, chief among them the fear and
uncertainty about whether one can truly sustain the journey, or
whether it would be better to turn back. This all comes to a climax
as Christian approaches the gates, and Bunyan intensifies the significance of the moment for the reader by informing us that the lions
Christian hears roaring are actually chained, although—because of
the darkness—Christian is not able to see this.

By letting us in on the actual state of affairs, Bunyan is training
the reader. He is conjoining the ability to see the real truth of things
(the chains hidden by the darkness) with a reasonable ground for
hope and confidence (the lions cannot actually harm us); and by
linking these in the reader's mind, Bunyan teaches us a basic vocational stance, namely, that the more deeply we perceive the circumstances of our lives, the more we will realize the true basis for hope.
In other words, this time of testing is not just an occasion for scar-
ing off the faint-hearted; it is really a means of forming confidence
and endurance—even in the face of what we cannot yet see how to
cope with or understand.

And this confidence, says Bunyan, is most likely to be mediated
to us by others. Christian was on the point of turning back, "for he
thought that nothing but death was before him" (37), when the
Porter at the gates sees him and calls out to say that the lions cannot
harm him. Watchful, the Porter, briefly questions Christian, informing him that "This House was built by the Lord of the Hill . . .
for the relief and security of Pilgrims" (38). Watchful's presence and
help are the beginning of Christian's new sense that he is not alone
in his journey, that there are possibilities of friendship and mutual
support and unexpected refreshment all along the way.

Watchful calls out one of the household, "one of the Virgins of
this place, who will, if she likes your talk, bring you in to the rest of
the Family, according to the Rules of the House" (38). This young
woman is named Discretion, and she does indeed introduce Christian in turn to her sisters, Piety, Prudence, and, at last, Charity. It is
quite possible that Bunyan was consciously deploying these figures
in their accustomed traditional roles. Certainly there is a kind of

logic in having the pilgrim exposed first to two of the Gifts of the Holy Spirit—Discretion and Piety—and then move on to two virtues, culminating in Charity. Christian needs literal inspiring, gifting with grace, before he can begin to realize—within his calling—the strengths of the virtues. In any event, Bunyan does portray the sisters as conversing with Christian in a friendly and loving manner that draws out from him some crucial features of his journey so far, features upon which he needs to reflect more deeply. One of Bunyan's foremost modern interpreters explains the vital importance of this examination of Christian's experience:

A basic element in the expressions of the Puritan's interest in past experience was the profound belief that experience formed the kind of rational whole in which God's activity could be descried as an explication and confirmation of biblical statement. In his private experience, as much as in the Word, the Puritan discerned God's voice speaking instruction and doctrine. Indeed, insofar as he made edifying use of his past, he tended to read it as *logos,* as an elaborate allegory of intelligible statement.[13]

There is a very clear progression in the kinds of questions the sisters put to Christian, designed to move him to a new awareness of the divine meaning implicit in his journey, and so help him intuit the deep structure of his calling.

Discretion begins by asking Christian to reflect on the most basic features of his life hitherto, helping to hold before his mind's eye the fundamental shape of his calling. Her questions lead him at last to a realization of how much he longs now to rest there. And in silent, poignant response, "she smiled, but the water stood in her eyes" (39). Perhaps this woman of good counsel is moved by the authenticity and yearning she senses in the pilgrim, glad that he will, at least for the time being, have a chance to explore and confirm the true depth of his calling. Piety's questions are much more detailed, and seem designed to clarify and savor the very real changes and in-

13. U. Milo Kaufman, *The Pilgrim's Progress and Traditions in Puritan Meditation* (New Haven: Yale University Press, 1966), 201; see also more recently, Kaufman, "Spiritual Discerning: Bunyan and the Mysteries of the Divine Will," in Keeble, *John Bunyan,* 171–87.

sights that have come to Christian's life already. All of this corresponds to the advice Bunyan gives his readers in the preface to his own autobiography:

It is profitable for Christians to be often calling to mind the very beginnings of Grace with their Souls. . . . Yea, look diligently, and leave no corner therein unsearched, for there is treasure hid, even the treasure of your first and second experience of the grace of God toward you. Remember, I say, the Word that first laid hold upon you; remember your terrours of conscience, and fear of death and hell: remember also your tears and prayers to God; yea, how you sighed under every hedge for mercy. Have you never a Hill Mizar to remember? Have you forgot the Close, the Milkhouse, the Stable, the Barn, and the like, where God did visit your Soul?[14]

Just as Bunyan's allegorical vision in *Pilgrim's Progress* teaches the reader to see the underlying meaning in everything, so this meditation on experience teaches pilgrims how to read their lives as the landscape of a journey, to recognize at last the pattern and shape of God's calling out to them.

With this foundation of trust and hope, it becomes possible with Prudence to ask rather more probing and analytical questions. "Do you not think sometimes of the Countrey from whence you came?" she begins (41). Not only do her questions invite Christian to be honest about the ways in which negative movements seem to hinder him, but they also help him to recognize what contrary motions seem to help him: "Can you remember by what means you find your annoyances at times, as if they were vanquished?" (41). What helps Christian most to get past the resistances are the thoughts of what Jesus had given him and the future to which he is being drawn. Thus it is reflection on features we might characterize as external gift and definite future that help to alleviate the interior doubts and feelings of helplessness or unworthiness. Significantly, Prudence's last question leads Christian to achieve some interior appropriation of that confidence and joy: "And what is it that makes

---

14. John Bunyan, *Grace Abounding*, ed. John Stachniewski, with Anita Pacheco (Oxford: Oxford University Press, 1998), 4–5.

you so desirous to go to Mount Zion?" (41). This moment of reconnecting with the deep desire of his heart again leads Christian to
break out in tender affection toward the one who is the source and
ground of his calling. It is just at this moment, when Christian has
reached some clarity about his deepest feelings and the role they
play ("For to tell you the truth, I love him, because I was by him
eased of my burden" [42]), that Charity takes over the dialogue.

Perhaps not surprisingly, Charity's questions are in fact the most
probing and in some ways the most painful of all, for they direct
Christian away from himself and toward those whom he has left behind. Her questions force Christian to consider whether the disso-
nance between his calling and his commitments to his family is really inescapable or is in fact the result of a failure in charity on his
part. Asking why the pilgrim has come without his wife and children, Charity demands to know whether Christian had truly made
every effort to bring them, and whether the former pattern of his life
did not render his new sense of calling simply unintelligible to his
loved ones: "But did you not with your vain life, damp all that you
by words used by way of perswasion to bring them with you?" (42).

We can see here the aptness in depicting Charity as the one who
sets our calling in the context of our relationships. Her questions re-
frame the pilgrim's sense of vocation, enlarging it and investing it
with a mature sense of the costs and sorrows of an authentic pursuit
of calling. For in the end, Charity does not disclose so much a lack
of love in the deepest heart of Christian but rather a more general
and universal need for love. We know that in part two of *Pilgrim's
Progress,* Bunyan will indeed recount the happy journey of Christian's family to join him; but at this point Charity finds that Christian's vocation must be to set out ahead of them, and by the painful
separation force both himself and his family to cast themselves all
the more entirely upon the charity of God. The urgency of vocation
is truly pressing, and it can only avoid hardening into fierceness and
zealotry if it understands itself in the milieu of a universal love.
There are no easy algorithms for calculating the justness of this or
that step in the working out of an authentic vocation, and some-

times it will be necessary not to *cease* loving one's own but perhaps to place our little love in the context of a much greater love, and trust that that greater love can alone supply what is most truly needed. Surely we see such difficult stages of awareness in the vocations of most married folk and vowed religious with respect to their families of origin. None of us can manipulate precisely the perfect balance of "mine" and "theirs" in the pursuit of our callings; we can only, Bunyan suggests, be terribly mindful of the need to test the love that moves us and remember that our callings never leave those around us unaffected.

We come to the final portion of Christian's stay at the Palace Beautiful by way of a lovely transition. From the poignant conversation about Christian's family left behind, Bunyan takes us immediately into a new kind of fellowship: the family of the house gathers Christian with them to their table "furnished with fat things, and with Wine that was well refined; and all their talk at the Table was about the Lord of the Hill" (43). In this way the ecclesial and indeed eucharistic fellowship makes possible the pilgrim's transfer from one life to another, from one basis of relationship to another, from one kind of hope to another. And though Christian is indeed eager the next day to begin these momentous passages, the family politely urges him to stay, to strengthen and confirm the new life that has begun to take root in him.

For three glorious days the sisters immerse Christian in the many wonders and "Rarities" of the place. They show him marvelous records of all the many good things wrought by the Lord of the Hill and of all the fellow pilgrims whose lives have been changed. They bring him into the armory and let him see and handle the strengths of faith and the "engines" used by faith's champions of old (Moses' rod, Gideon's trumpet, and David's sling among them). They take him to see incredible views into the Delectable Mountains and Immanuel's Land in the distance beyond. And, of course, they continue to talk with him about the experiences of his calling and how to interpret it all. In these many ways we could say that the sisters of the Palace Beautiful afford Christian a formational community in which his authentic vocation can be nurtured and clarified and shaped. They give him a history in which his calling's deepest significance can become clear and its solipsistic tendencies overtaken by the light of a communal struggle and a corporate hope.

What Is "Vocation" in *Pilgrim's Progress?*

Perhaps it is this mingled thread of struggle and hope that weaves the vocational theme together in Bunyan—the struggle to see and speak honestly about calling and the hope that keeps calling fresh and lively. Bunyan's own experiences of religious persecution, coupled with his sense of the self-deluding sinfulness of humankind, make him a highly critical interpreter of vocation. Few could have a more discerning eye when it comes to picking out the distorting influence of culture and self-interest upon vocation. So, while the source and ground of one's calling is very strong, a vocation is in Bunyan's view always a living, changing, growing, and provisional dimension of one's being. Its unfolding is never mechanical or fixed; and if it is subject to negative misshaping, so by the same token, the living out of our calling is also open to new clarity, intensification, and maturation.

We have also seen, however, that we name the one who calls us into fuller being, into the truth of ourselves; for Bunyan, it is this divine ground of our calling alone that can fund the certainty and perseverance needed for vocational fruition. While it is the self that grows into truth by leaving earlier versions of itself behind, the growth, the pilgrimage, are sustained by the caller. And this otherness, which must ever be the proper milieu of vocation, is figured in Bunyan by the many occasions when the pilgrim would certainly perish without companionship. Vocation emerges in Bunyan as a fully social phenomenon, in which the deep trajectory of the self becomes perspicuous in terms of the mutuality of calling.

⟨⟩ D. H. Williams

Protestantism and the Vocation of Higher Education

For American Protestants, there is nothing new about the concept of vocation. It has been the driving force, often implicitly, behind the Protestant imperative during the nineteenth and twentieth centuries to orchestrate a moral, spiritual, and educational climate within our culture. The very idea of possessing a providential calling is what once fueled commitment for reforming the social order, moral responsibility, and the founding of institutions of higher learning. What characterized that "calling" and how its obligatory nature slipped away from Protestant hands into near oblivion is a story that needs to be told. It is chiefly a story not of the forces of secularization versus religion, but of the predominance of antitraditionalist religious ideals over others. We have reached the point in today's academic atmosphere when the concept of vocation, should it possess a specific religious content, has become problematic unless it is confined to purely personal discussions. As many Roman Catholic universities are already following the same course that Protestant schools pursued a century or so earlier, it is timely that the subject matter of vocation be raised again within higher education. I want to argue, as a Protestant who formerly taught within a

Roman Catholic context, that the place of confessionalism—
shunned in principle by the majority of schools as an embarrassing
vestige of social and religious intolerance—ought to be given a new
hearing in order to avoid the inevitable loss (except in some nomi-
nalist sense) of a distinctive Christian character within church-originated institutions. It may be objected that this is to shut the barn
door once the horse has gotten out. How far the horse has run away
is, however, a matter of ongoing discussion. Approaching the notion of vocation within an ostensibly religious context of academia
underlines the imperative of holding such discussions.

Consider the leading article by Dwight Bradley in a 1932 issue of
the *Christian Century*, which extols the blessings and responsibilities
of Protestantism in America. Supremely confident of Protestantism's
well-defined course and normative cultural status, the essay reads
more like a manifesto than a set of descriptive arguments.[1] The
Protestant achievement, ostensibly begun by the sixteenth-century
Reformation, is said to be located in its "irresistible desire to regain
the lost simplicity and immediacy of religious experience," which resulted in a return to the Bible and freedom from the Roman ecclesiastical establishment. Its goal is to produce a simple and purified
faith, now fully loosed from the external shackles of "paganism" (i.e.,
Rome), opposing any mediating structures that might derogate from
the cultivation of the individual's responsibility in moral and spiritual affairs. While Bradley acknowledges that individualism leads easily to sectarianism and denominationalism, which are perceived as
undesirable, the benefits of "a new emphasis upon education and a
tremendous growth of general intelligence," which naturally lend
themselves to democratic principles, outweigh the risks. In fact,
American democracy and Protestantism share a marvelous align-
ment of purpose, because democracy too is essentially individualistic
yet progressive, best thriving without the pressures of any external

---

1. Dwight Bradley, "What's Coming in Protestantism?" *Christian Century* 49 (June
6, 1932): 10–13. Bradley was minister of the First Church of Christ in Newton, Mass.,
and a regular contributor to the *Christian Century*.

authority imposed upon it.[2] Protestantism is *de facto* a religious and moral extension of democratic principles.

In order to secure the future, Bradley adjures Protestants to take an aggressive stand on the key points of their identity—namely, the centrality of direct religious experience (which ought "to go even beyond the limits reached by past tradition"), thereby allowing the Holy Spirit to direct one's path rather than human authority; revival of worship through the intensification of private prayer; simple practices of devotion; and the reclaiming of a prophetic and ethical faith that eschews mysticism or sacramentalism. No less important for liberal or free religion is the acknowledgment that "the really Protestant church" is bound up intimately with the development of science in every field. Herein is said to lie the future for theology and the church, as Protestantism becomes the leading interpreter of scientific data in terms of spiritual experience. A sacred status is bestowed upon scientific inquiry as a means of fulfilling the divine calling. Spiritual intensity, moral passion, and progressive attitudes are superior to any claim of sectarian loyalties, which might abrogate the new canons of personal freedom of faith and the possibility for unity on a democratic basis.

Even if the optimistic tone typical of liberal a-millennial attitudes and the platitudes of democratic idealism were removed, the writer is proclaiming nothing less than the conjunction of providential operation and the agenda of American Protestantism. Like John Dewey's political philosophy, the formation of values is inherent in the process of democracy, as is faith in the capacities of human nature and the call for its liberation from all external and organizational coercion.[3] The stress on individualism as a political necessity in order to

2. Ibid. "Catholicism on the one hand, and fascism or communism on the other, threaten the individual with unreasonable restraints; while Protestantism offers to the individual an opportunity to think, to speak, and to conduct his affairs with the maximum of liberty."

3. "Democracy Is Radical" (1937), in *The Essential Dewey: Pragmatism, Education, Democracy,* vol. 1, ed. L. Hickman and T. Alexander (Bloomington: Indiana University Press, 1998), 337–39. Dewey valued the freedom of the individual, but not as its own end and only as it contributed to the maintenance of liberty within society.

pursue God-given destinies, however, owes just as much—if not more—to the Protestant spirit in its exaltation of unmediated religious experience and anti-institutionalism.[4]

Particularly noteworthy is the negative assessment of the ecclesiastical establishment and its "wholly archaic" tradition as irrelevant to the present and future vitality of Christian faith.[5] Despite the fact that a crucial part of the Protestant task is perceived as the recovery of the historical Jesus and the application of biblical teaching, these goals are viewed in a way detached from doctrinal history, such that their "recovery" means a remapping of their significance via the believer's religious experience. From this standpoint, realization of human rational and moral potential, once freed from external constraints (such as religious standards specific to church affiliations), becomes possible. Scientific, political, and ethical progress is thus attained, as is agreement among all enlightened individuals about the value of this progress. Inherent in this ideology we find what one historian has identified as the three persistent elements of modernist thought in Protestantism: a conscious adaptation of religious ideas to modern culture, the belief in the immanence of God in human nature and cultural development, and an optimistic assumption that society is being formed as a Kingdom of God on earth.[6]

At least in the earlier stages of the American Protestant program of reform, it was this combination of ideas, replacing the alleged constrictions of confessional theology, that governed educational perspectives. One finds in Bradley's article a number of working presuppositions that formed a kind of epistemological canon among a

4. It is particularly fascinating to find strong condemnations of "mysticism" in the face of such emphasis on the direct religious experience as the expression of an authentic faith.

5. Throughout this essay I will be using "tradition" in two distinguishable ways: in the broad or categorical sense of the term, to mean how a past system of rationality provides operating guidelines for present experience; and in a more specific sense, meaning a definitive qualification of the Christian faith that entails normative beliefs and practices.

6. W. R. Hutchinson, *The Modernist Impulse in American Protestantism* (Cambridge: Harvard University Press, 1976), 32.

great number of institutions of higher learning that originated within Protestant foundations. Another article, in the *Christian Century* of the previous year, offers a brief application of these presuppositions, specifically to the concepts of education: "[T]he ruling concepts of modern education are freedom of the individual from disciplines and patterns of conduct based solely upon tradition, the right of the individual to realize his own possibilities and to discover the best means of realization by his own experience."[7]

⌒⌒

One hears in this, among other things, the voice of academic freedom that was in vogue by this time. This was not merely a freedom from the dictatorial powers of university trustees or the pressure of political agencies, for which the American Association of University Professors (AAUP) had so forcefully advocated in the beginning of the century, but a freedom from religious tradition(s) as the more serious threat.[8]

We will return to the notion of academic freedom. For the moment, we may observe in passing the ironic position of liberal Protestantism, that as it diligently sought to be a Christianity freed from all sectarian prejudices or forms of confessionalism, it became quite sectarian in practice as a process of bracketing doctrinaire forms of Protestantism and Roman Catholicism as inimical to rational inquiry and personal freedom. In its own reaction to fundamentalist evangelicalism—which, by the 1930s, had the reputation of being hostile toward modern science and cultural and intellectual freedom—liberal religion was proving itself to be no less fundamentalist in attitude and approach. The reality of divine revelation and the intersection of the supranatural and natural orders were routinely marginalized or discounted altogether as reliable sources of knowledge.

7. "What Are Education's Ruling Concepts?" *Christian Century* 48 (Feb. 11, 1931): 197–98.

8. R. Hofstadter and W. Smith, eds., "General Declaration of Principles of the AAUP" (1915), in *American Higher Education: A Documentary History* vol. 2 (Chicago: University of Chicago Press, 1961), 860–78.

The more central question here, however, is in what ways did the modernist Protestant "calling" help to create an educational philosophy that was formed in its own antisectarian image? Alasdair MacIntyre has trenchantly argued that "liberalism" successfully excluded parties that did not conform to its particular platform of rationality. The liberal ethos held that if human rationality could be freed from external constraints—such as religious and moral tests—the result would be not only progress in inquiry but also agreement among all rational persons about the nature of rationally justifiable arguments.[9] There has thus often been, in the academic context, the illusory appearance of unconstrained rational agreement. One result of this post-Enlightenment philosophy is that only certain kinds of conversations and statements about what constitutes knowledge are permitted to take place in the classrooms of the modern university.

What I want to argue is that the notion of a calling, so pervasive in American Protestantism's program for social and pedagogical reform in the early twentieth century, was slowly yet inexorably undermined as Protestantism's quest for a latitudinarian religion was displaced by an alien agenda—namely, secular modernity.[10] Once this agenda was in place, the religious character of a call (and, eventually, the need to inform institutions of higher education with this concept) became superfluous.

⸺⸺

The only vestige of the older enterprise today is the notion that education ought somehow also to address moral formation. Despite the elimination of religious or ecclesiastical confessions, the nagging sense persists on college and university campuses that the intellectual enterprise cannot afford to neglect completely the impartation of an ethical consciousness. Education should, *inter alia*, prepare young men and women to take responsible places in society for the civic good.

Built into liberal educational models is the principle that respon-

9. Alasdair C. MacIntyre, *Three Rival Versions of Moral Enquiry: Encyclopaedia, Genealogy, and Tradition* (Notre Dame: University of Notre Dame Press, 1990), 225.

10. By "secular" I do not necessarily intend a negative connotation such as

sible inquiry should include some formation of self-understanding. This principle derives, of course, from classical epistemological theory about the cultivation of the intellect depending upon a moral formation of the knowing self. But in the absence of agreement on what constitutes the good, the beautiful, and the just, this enterprise, too, has become impossible. As concrete notions of morality became ephemeral, even accidental, to the goals of higher education, it was still assumed that students would somehow construct for themselves a practical and compatible ethical code through intellectual discipline and social integration in the university community. Such an assumption was and is obviously unfounded, as institutions today are constantly searching for ways to provide a core of instruction in the arts and sciences that meaningfully imparts "values." At the same time, the search to identify and elevate some set of "core" values invites charges of bigotry and bias from the politically correct and relativist camps.

⤳

Indeed, the process underway since the 1960s has been to discount normative claims as nothing more than statements of personal preference. Allan Bloom points out that every education system has a moral goal, whether it claims to or not, and aims to produce a particular kind of human being. On the postmodern American university campus, the prevailing moral code is based on the relativity of moral judgments and indeed of "truth" itself. Relativism "is the virtue, the only virtue, which all primary education for more than fifty years has dedicated itself to inculcating."[11] If there is one danger that students have been taught to fear from absolutism, it is not error but intolerance of difference and "otherness."

Fundamental to the liberal project is the opening of political and intellectual space in which all substantive agendas have an equal chance to compete. Of course, that "space" is necessarily circum-

---

"decline," although secularization is clearly a departure from former ways of conceiving of the universe and of morality.

11. Allan Bloom, *The Closing of the American Mind* (New York: Simon & Schuster, 1987), 26.

scribed, as all political orders are, according to specific principles of exclusion. Attempts to reshape public life according to a specific vision of the good are out of bounds in most colleges and universities today.[12] Systems that suggest moral intolerance cannot be tolerated. Values proposed as normative or absolute are perceived as arbitrary and tyrannical. According to Bloom, we have taught our students to be more vexed by the potential tyranny of normative values than by the abandonment of such values.

For the past decade, in reaction against the tide of relativism and in the attempt to return institutions of higher education to their earlier vocation of inculcating certain values in students, the John M. Templeton Foundation has published a biennial "honor role" of universities and colleges. The foundation's goal in this enterprise is to foster in a programmatic way the development of virtue and moral character on college campuses.[13] Exactly what constitutes "character" is never spelled out, but clearly the project is informed by Enlightenment assumptions, à la Dewey, about civic duty and other forms of idealism. Projects such as Templeton's only arise, of course, once the values they hope to encourage are already dangerously attenuated. But it is unclear whether the noble ideology behind Templeton's humanist mission can succeed, the whole idea of virtue and character having been so roundly attacked by the postmodern relativists that the concepts have become benignly meaningless in many quarters.

The new task of discerning the role of vocation within colleges and universities of Protestant origins—and that means most U.S. schools of higher learning—represents a "toned-down" return to well-trodden paths. The religious origins and early vocational mission of these institutions have been all but forgotten. It is, obviously, much too late for a return to these original vocational ideals, nor

12. Peter Leithart, "Review of Stanley Fish, *The Trouble with Principle*," *First Things* 102 (April 2000): 56.

13. That is, "those habits of mind, heart and spirit that help young people to know, desire and do what is good . . . a primary goal of educators." *Honor Roll for Character-Building Colleges 1997–1998* (Radnor, Pa.: John Templeton Foundation, 1997), xi–xii.

is such a return necessarily desirable. I do not want to argue that we should return to a lost golden age, if there ever was one. In any case, it is the very nature of Protestantism's traditional sense of calling that serves as the major source of antagonism between advocates of cultural pluralism and defenders of religious foundationalism in the culture wars over truth claims. It's not difficult to see in hindsight how the liberal Protestant agenda for education provided support for both positions.

It would be simplistic to argue that "secularism" accounts for the efforts to ban or relativize absolutist concepts of morality or religious norms in academia. There is no simple cause-and-effect explanation here; and we must not forget that Protestant universities jettisoned their own confessional and denominational identities in their quest for academic respectability. In *The Soul of the American University*, George Marsden has convincingly documented that the theology of nineteenth- and early-twentieth-century Protestantism itself gave rise to pragmatic and positivist approaches to pedagogy as much as scientific methodology did.

While Protestantism was not the only factor shaping the intellectual heritage of those who founded and governed the major universities, other educational ideals—those based on scientific and progressive enlightenment, democratic populism, romantic principles of individual development—were mediated through the American Protestant context. Likewise, the liberal Protestantism that came to dominate American education was shaped by these ideals and perceived them as indigenous to sound biblical interpretation and to the essence of the Christian calling. The irony is that this Protestant establishment—motivated by virtues of freedom, democracy, reform, and inclusiveness—set out to create a system of higher education that excluded all but liberal Protestant or "nonsectarian" perspectives, relegating alternatives (Protestant evangelical and Roman Catholic institutions) to the periphery. But the greater irony came when the very nonsectarian logic set in motion by liberalism eventually turned against the liberal Protestant establishment itself. The result, according to Marsden, was a supposedly "inclusive" ethic that virtually banned religious perspectives from academic life.[14]

The Protestant perspective that lay behind so much of higher education in the United States cannot be understood apart from its roots in the Free church or "believers' church." What Marsden calls "low-church" Protestantism was key in shaping American universities' characteristic traits. In fact, he observes, the United States is the only modern nation in which the dominant culture was substantially shaped by low-church Protestantism. "So with respect to American universities, their pragmatism, their traditionlessness, their competitiveness . . . their emphasis on freedom as free enterprise for professors and individual choice for students, their anti-Catholicism, their scientific spirit . . . their tendency to equate Christianity with democracy and service to the nation, all reflect substantial ties to their low-church Protestant past."

By way of example, Marsden points to the educational vision of William Rainey Harper, a Baptist and the first president of the University of Chicago.[15] Harper had a passion for cultural reform through Bible study. His was a biblicism that belonged to the previous century, fueled by the notion that sanctification of the mind and the heart meant returning to the purity and simplicity of the primitive faith. Typical of Free church theology and essential to primitivistic ideals was an emphasis on freedom from ecclesial and traditional intellectual authority, a general disdain for tradition, and a focus on individual moral responsibility.[16] Harper's effort to restore the centrality of the Bible in higher education stemmed from his conviction that American democratic and individualistic values were derived from Scripture, which he saw as a firm foundation for science and the investigation of truth. Harper's enemy was not pagan America but Christian "superstition"—i.e., the beliefs of fundamentalist Christians, whose prescientific reading of Scripture and

14. George Marsden, *The Soul of the American University: From Protestant Establishment to Established Nonbelief* (Oxford: Oxford University Press, 1994), 4–6.

15. The University of Chicago, which Marsden calls "a quintessential Protestant institution," was organized by the Chicago Baptists of the American Educational Society and initially funded by John D. Rockefeller Sr., himself a Baptist layman.

16. Marsden, *The Soul of the American University*, 243–44.

pessimistic views of modern culture brought discredit to Christianity, in his view. One of Harper's most frequently reiterated themes was that traditional biblical teaching was unworthy of the faith of enlightened modern persons, and that it certainly had no place in an institution of higher learning. The Protestant calling to sacralize the nation was being jeopardized by the narrow vision of obscurantist Christian churches. Harper aimed for a more liberal reading of the Bible, one more in keeping with the scientific and other secular trends of the broader culture.

Marsden tracks similar movements of "progressive Christianity" in a number of universities—Chicago (Baptist), Vanderbilt (Methodist), Syracuse (Methodist), Johns Hopkins (Quaker), Boston University (Methodist)—all in one way or another seeking to elevate their academic stature and become eligible for funding from the Carnegie Foundation by eschewing their denominational positions. Religion, while still relevant for training in liberal arts, needed to be freed from its confessional moorings to become suitable to the identity that was emerging in the twentieth-century university. But, as so often happens with progressive reforms, the dismissal of doctrine had unintended consequences, and exacted a high price. Modern Protestantism did not ultimately achieve a more objective and culturally amenable faith; instead, it was confronted with a new hostility toward *any* Christian norms. The liberal Protestant virtue of freedom had become so central to the faith that the distinctive aspects of that faith simply could not survive within the academic institutions of a free society.[17] Even the replacement of religious doctrine by ethical ideology became an impediment to the progressive attitudes that now reigned in the once-Protestant universities. By the early twentieth century, the goal of nonsectarian religion had been translated into "nonreligious education."

⟨≥⟩

The Protestant attempt over the past century and a half to establish an impartial and unbiased religion has backfired. There is no

17. Ibid., 398.

such thing as a truly latitudinarian religious perspective, for this always comes to mean modernity's own quest for scientific objectivism. The watering down of religion has created not the broader base of agreement that was its goal, but a pious insipidness that can satisfy neither the intellectual community nor the community of faith.

Many colleges and universities have nevertheless relinquished their confessional identity in exchange for the broader recognition of academic guilds or commissions of higher education (such as Carnegie). James Burtchaell has recounted at length the ways in which institutions' "flight from sectarianism" since World War II has gradually driven them from theological specificity and commitment into a vague sort of "personal" piety, and thence into religious indifference, and finally to the secular rationalism we see today, which is hostile to religion in the academy.[18]

At the heart of the liberal Protestant experiment with education lay ideological assumptions about the nature of freedom. Freedom guaranteed an authentic faith because it allowed for the exercise of self-awareness and self-criticism, a view structured according to liberal notions of divine immanence—the presence and working of God *within* the world rather than upon it. This kind of freedom assumed that human beings were capable of discovering and conforming to the divine plan, that they would choose to follow the path to human dignity rather than degradation. The liberal establishment feared that dogmatic Christianity, as represented in its historic creeds and doctrines, worked against freedom by its authoritarian nature. The dogmatic character of traditional Christianity prohibited, or stunted, the religious freedom inherent in the liberal Protestant view.

Uncritical exaltation of freedom in liberal Protestant circles has

18. James Burtchaell, *The Dying of the Light: The Disengagement of Colleges and Universities from Their Christian Churches* (Grand Rapids: Eerdmans, 1998). Seventeen case studies are presented from seven denominations: Congregationalist (Dartmouth, Beloit); Presbyterian (Lafayette, Davidson); Methodist (Millsaps, Ohio Wesleyan); American Baptist (Wake Forest, Virginia Union, Linfield); Lutheran (Gettysburg, St. Olaf, Concordia); Roman Catholic (Boston College, New Rochelle, St. Mary's of California); and Evangelical (Azusa Pacific, Dordt).

not been without its critics. Reinhold Niebuhr, admittedly of a liberal perspective himself in some ways, had warned against what he called "extravagant estimates of freedom," for these create the illusion that human beings need no longer be subject to natural necessity but can become the masters of their destiny.[19] Religious tradition, by contrast, confronts the modern mind with the unacceptable proposition of its own impotence and corruption.

As long as academic freedom and tradition are seen as competing opposites, the misguided paradigm of the rational versus the confessional will continue. The foundation of the AAUP has its origins in just such a paradigm. Largely the creation of liberal Protestant academics, the AAUP takes an antisectarian view of religion and, not surprisingly, sees religious commitment and academic inquiry as basically antithetical to each other. The AAUP does pay lip service to the legitimacy of a vague sort of religiosity; the organization's "General Declaration of Principles of 1915" acknowledges that there are fields of human endeavor in which our knowledge is only at a beginning, including our knowledge of ultimate realities and values. On this subject the document mentions the epistemological value of "spiritual life" and the discovery of the "general meaning and ends of human existence." But if this passage signifies some acceptance of religion, it is "religion" in its broadest possible sense. The declaration is silent on the subject of what tangible forms such "religion" might actually take.

While religious knowledge may be said to constitute a legitimate form of understanding, it must not infringe on the greater good of academic freedom, which must be "complete and unlimited," according to the AAUP. And indeed the declaration of principles states unequivocally that "In the early period of university development in America the chief menace to academic freedom was ecclesiastical."[20] Apparent here again is the influence of Dewey, who sought

19. Reinhold Niebuhr, *Faith and History: A Comparison of Christian and Modern Views of History* (New York: Chas. Scribner's Sons, 1949: 79.

20. Hofstadter and Smith, eds., "General Declaration of Principles of the AAUP" (1915), 868.

to construct an alternative to religious faith in the elevation of the scientific method, which he claimed was the "sole authentic mode of revelation." The result has been an anthropocentric idea of religion, which is deemed palatable as long as its strictures stay within reasonable bounds of morality and do not curtail intellectual freedom.

The restatement of the AAUP's 1915 declaration in the 1940 "Statement of Principles on Academic Freedom and Tenure" is even more negative on the subject of religion, although for this reason it is clearer. But this statement simply states as fact that religion limits academic freedom, without explaining why this is so.[21] Any sort of governing tradition is deemed problematic. A college or university is "a marketplace of ideas, and it cannot fulfill its purposes of transmitting, evaluating, and extending knowledge if it requires conformity with any orthodoxy of content and method." Ironically, faculty members should be completely free to engage in *political* activities and, moreover, ought to be given a leave of absence to mount a political campaign or serve a term of office.[22] Evidently, politics does not limit academic freedom as religion does. Whatever kind of inquiry academic freedom is meant to protect, it clearly protects the academy from confronting its own blind spots and biases.

Some of these blind spots, nevertheless, have become apparent. The scientific and technological inquiry for which academic freedom was sought now figures as the greatest threat for undermining its much-vaunted independence and scholarly integrity. As federal money has decreased, high-tech corporations are pouring money as never before into university departments where the promise of commercial application (e.g., in computing, biogenics, and so on) is greatest. The alleged autonomy of disinterested academic research is vulnerable to being co-opted by commercial interests that are in turn determining the educational mission and academic ideals of universities.

And as education is being construed by certain major universities

21. Section b, under Academic Freedom.

22. Section 12 of "Recommended Institutional Regulations on Academic Freedom and Tenure" (revised in 1968).

as a commodity in the marketplace of business, the academic freedom to explore ideas that have no obvious or immediate commercial value is being vitiated.[23] The slow process of gaining knowledge, the methods by which one gains knowledge, and the question what one should do with knowledge are circumvented by utilitarian agendas. The university has become less a setting in which inquiry and self-discovery occur than a delivery system for desired "goods and services." Already in the 1930s Abraham Flexner and Robert Hutchins were criticizing the university for becoming a "service" station for the general public, thus confusing the aim of a liberal arts education with the goals of a trade school.[24] Their deepest concerns have been more than realized today.

These developments are hardly surprising. Despite the fact that the AAUP was founded to discourage this compromising of higher education's aims, the dependence of academic freedom on some kind of "orthodoxy of content and method" is unavoidable. Academic research has never been a truly "disinterested" enterprise, and academic freedom has never been truly free of bias. The real fight is not between academic freedom and religious authority or "tradition," but between competing versions of authority and competing traditions. And the authority higher education chooses to honor directly affects how it construes the concept of vocation.

There can be no doubt that much of the antagonism between academic freedom and the heavy hand of "tradition" results from modern educators' confusion and uncertainty about the concept and function of tradition. When Jaroslav Pelikan delivered the National Endowment for the Humanities' 1983 Jefferson lectures on the subject of tradition, he began in the assumption that none of his listeners knew what tradition really was.[25] There is no point in talk-

---

23. See E. Press and J. Washburn, "The Kept University," *Atlantic Monthly* 285 (March 2000): 39–54, which provides telling information about the commercialization of technological research in universities such as Berkeley, Stanford, Chicago, Michigan State, and others.

24. "Abraham Flexner Criticizes the American University, 1930," *American Higher Education* 2: 907.

25. Jaroslav Pelikan, *The Vindication of Tradition* (New Haven: Yale University

ing about the loss of tradition in modern scholarship, he said, if its identity and meaning are unknown. The very idea of tradition suffers from caricatures that have become an indissoluble, though not necessary, part of Protestant rationality and religious epistemology since the late sixteenth century.

I have chronicled the historical development of these caricatures elsewhere,[26] but it is important to note here that, for Protestant thinking, the axiom on which the post-Reformation turned was a sharp distinction between gospel and tradition. The former is equated with the timeless and divine truths recorded in the New Testament, whereas the latter is an artificial accumulation of human machination and religious practices. The gospel is the primitive and simple message of fundamental religious experience, whereas tradition is derived from doctrinal systems, political institutions, and ceremonial rituals that arose during the late first and second centuries, that is, from early Catholicism.

It is in this dichotomous version of early Christian history that Protestant liberalism and conservatism come closest together. For completely different reasons, both share a view of relative discontinuity when it comes to a historically applied understanding of doctrine. While the Protestant liberal model of epistemology denies the existence of a narrative that links contemporary faith experiences with the concrete expressions of that faith in the past,[27] evangelical Protestantism nullifies a tangible connection by its tendency to em-

---

Press, 1984). "For even if—or especially if—the tradition of our past is a burden that the next generation must finally drop, it will not be able to drop it, or understand why it must drop it, unless it has some sense of what its contents is and of how and why it has persisted for so long" (19).

26. D. H. Williams, *Retrieving the Tradition and Renewing Evangelicalism: A Primer for Suspicious Protestants* (Grand Rapids: Eerdmans, 1999), chaps. 4 and 5.

27. Historian Francis Young, for example, has argued for the problematic nature of ascertaining "orthodoxy" because all doctrinal development is environmentally conditioned and determined by such factors as politics, philosophical presuppositions, and the chances of history. The disjunction between present-day forms of faith and that of the earliest Christians is an undeniable, if regrettable, fact. See Young, "A Cloud of Witnesses," in *The Myth of God Incarnate*, ed. John Hick (Philadelphia: Westminster Press, 1977), 23.

brace the "true" faith through an immediate (and often ahistorical) appropriation of the New Testament era.[28]

In both cases, antitraditionalist and antidogmatic perspectives are built into the Protestant religious ethos, whether liberal or conservative, implicitly or explicitly, and these determine what should be included and what excluded in a responsible educational pedagogy. Both are stamped by the influences of Romantic modernism (with its roots in reaction against the Enlightenment), as witnessed in their emphasis on individualism, egalitarianism, and low tolerance for the practices and beliefs of antiquity. Epistemological principles, such as the right to private judgment, or the elevation of personal experience as an arbiter of worth and meaning, have become definitive—for the liberal, because experience is the chief means of acquiring knowledge, and for the conservative, because the priority of every believer's individual judgment, or conscience, ultimately guarantees freedom of the spirit and mind. John Henry Newman's criticism of the Protestant understanding of religion as consisting in sentiment or feeling and practical morality[29] is still valid for characterizing both perspectives, at least as it pertains to the absence of historic Christian *credenda*, as well as *agenda*, for informing the knowledge of faith.

⟨∂⟩

If the Protestant American experience has taught leaders of higher education anything, it should be that the vocation of any institution seeking to instill in its students the value of religious faith *must* be confessional if it wishes to preserve its identity within the prevail-

28. A primitivistic or restitutionist view of history underlies the belief that a connection between the apostolic and present church exists, but largely in a spiritual sense. Since most of church history is "fallen" or corrupt, it is necessary that the "true church" of the present age find its own predecessors in select instances or figures of the past, while rejecting the main body of the historical narrative. The rise of the episcopacy, dependence on tradition rather than the Bible or the Holy Spirit, the use of creeds, and so on, all bespoke a faith that had become misaligned and detached from the pristine and simple spirituality of the Bible.

29. John Henry Newman, Discourse II.4, in *The Idea of the University Defined and Illustrated* (London: Longmans, Green, and Co. 1902), 27–28.

ing context of pluralism and relativism. A specific Christian constitution—whether Protestant or Roman Catholic—cannot succeed
unless it unapologetically sets forth certain points of theology as the
philosophical cornerstone of the school's identity. Otherwise it will
repeat the failure of religious liberal or latitudinarian approaches,
which ended up supplying little more than the wants of human nature, to paraphrase Newman.[30]

At the very least, universities founded on Christian principles
ought to retain what I will call an essentialist Catholicism: basic
transdenominational propositions that pertain to the historical core
of Christian identity. A working definition of essentialist Catholicism can be found in the recent restatement of *Ex Corde Ecclesiae,*
which argues for "a shared baptismal belief in the truths that are
rooted in Scripture and tradition, as interpreted by the church, concerning the mystery of the Trinity: God the Father and Creator,
who works even until now; God the Son and incarnate Redeemer,
who is the way and the truth and the life; and God the Holy Spirit,
the Paraclete, whom the Father and the Son send."[31] Virtually every
church-originated institution, regardless of its denominational affili-
ation,[32] can espouse these truths about God and his unique revelation—truths that also insist on the importance of theology when it
comes to determining the emphasis of university curricula. One
might equally point to the Apostles' Creed, which functions in a
way similar to the rule of faith used by the Church in the second
and third centuries. Origen of Alexandria informs us that the rule
(or "canon") consisted of fixed and flexible elements that enabled
any Christian in any place to learn the most basic components of
doctrine.[33] Some differences in formulation, given varying circum-

---

30. John Henry Newman, *The Idea of the University* (London: Bombay, Longmans, Green, and Co., 1902), 28.

31. U.S. Bishops' Meeting, "*Ex Corde Ecclesiae:* An Application to the United
States" in *Origins* 29 (1999): 404.

32. As illustrated in the ecumenical concord achieved in *Baptism, Eucharist, and
Ministry* (1982), which represented the input from virtually all the major church traditions as it sought to express a common understanding of the apostolic faith.

33. Origen, *De principiis,* prologue, 4–10.

stances, were not unexpected, but there was no question that the rule was sufficient for conveying the constituents of the Christian identity and its definition of authority. Here was a clear and specific guide for moral and spiritual reckoning, which made clear that creation is ultimately accountable only to its Creator, and that the natural and the supranatural are not closed off to each other. In whatever ways the diversity of the human response is conveyed (and it should be conveyed) in an educational curriculum, maintaining an essentialist Catholicism preserves the place of Christian doctrine within the realm of knowledge. Theology and religion thus become legitimate objects of study in a liberal arts education, no less practical or important to the understanding of the human person and society than the other disciplines. This kind of essentialist Catholicism prevents the study of theology from being reduced to a phenomenology of religion that has little toleration for confessional Christianity or, conversely, that is prone to an individualistic piety that evades critically confronting the intellectual content of the Christian faith.

In practice, the role of Christian tradition in its specific confessional sense within the university need not be antithetical to rational inquiry and intellectual freedom. Just as no discipline can achieve complete objectivity, so total freedom from all forms of tradition or authority is impossible. It is one of myths of modernism and postmodernism that religious tradition has been replaced by rationalism. But the question, again, is the nature of the tradition to which we submit our inquiries.[34]

This is the question that Augustine found himself asking in his own pursuit of wisdom. His *Confessions* present a select sketch of an epistemological inquiry, *inter alia,* into the nature of God and himself (*Conf.* I. i.1; X. i.1). One finds here a series of intellectual transitions, as Augustine came finally to embrace a tradition that he claims provided the basis for freedom of the intellect. In books

34. Mark Schwehen, *Exiles from Eden: Religion and the Academic Vocation in America* (Oxford: Oxford University Press, 1993), 58ff.

I–IX, the narrative part of the work, Augustine takes us with him in his search for knowledge and belief:[35] first is his empty acquiescence to his mother's Catholic faith, which he rejected for the primacy of experience, only later, and gradually, to turn away from mere physical and emotional experience to encounter "the immortality of wisdom" and convert to Manichaeanism. In an act of epistemological despair, Augustine eventually rejected all of this, eight or nine years later, for the skepticism of the Academics, who believed "that everything is a matter of doubt, and that an understanding of truth lies beyond human capacity" (V. x.19). A corner had to be turned before he could go any further in his search. Thus Augustine came to discover the value of belief as the result of a rational position, since he found that he already believed innumerable things that he supposed to be true: "Unless we acted on what we were told, we would do nothing at all in this life" (VI. v.7). From here he is open to understand the tradition of the Catholic faith, the reception of which is itself a critical and informed act. It was not the abrogation of criticism and discovery that enabled him to value the place of faith in the mind; on the contrary, it was through a rationality of faith that he claimed to have found the freedom of the will. In other words, the tradition actually enabled Augustine to believe again in the possibility of knowledge and of finding truth.

"Tradition" need not be opposed to rational inquiry, but it can understand freedom as the creative exercise of the will within an acknowledged circle of governing first principles; indeed, such principles enable the very process of rational inquiry. Tradition, as MacIntyre would insist, is always subject to correction and change, since tradition is itself a dynamic of self-reflection as it becomes aware of new needs for greater internal coherence or for responding to inadequacies raised by changed circumstances. What is important is that there remains a core belief, which survives and holds together the

35. Of course the progression as I outline it was not nearly so smooth, as the stages of Augustine's transition from one position to another often overlapped for long periods of time.

identity of the tradition (in the specific or broad sense) such that corrections are able to be made.[36]

If we are going to uphold consistently a broad-minded notion of academic freedom, then it must include the freedom to be religious, and to be specifically confessional or traditional. A religious posture does not and should not of itself rule out participation in enlightened and critical inquiry. To take this a step further, following MacIntyre's argument for rationality of tradition, it can be reasonably argued that tradition (religious or otherwise) provides a cohesive framework such that rational arguments for and against a viewpoint are possible. Even if one does not share a certain confessional position, meaningful dialogue on the issue is at least possible. Antagonists who work from completely different conceptions of reality, or who believe that there is no unifying conception of rationality, cannot even debate the point. Since the formation of traditions is itself a dialectical process, there must always be room for disagreement and debate, evolution and change.[37]

The vision of American liberal Protestantism for higher education has not come to pass in the way that it was intended, nor was its vision as self-evident as its proponents believed. It had strong biases against confessional or doctrinal theology, biases paraded as commitments to academic freedom and progressive thinking. But these biases became clear in time and, as a result, ideals of intellectual freedom and rationality were erected on an anticonfessional platform that remains intact today. To claim that the alleged synthesis of science and Protestant theology that once inspired the reform of American higher learning is largely moribund[38] does not adequately represent the almost total alienation between the two. Not only has the older liberal vision *not* given us a unified and harmonized approach to learning within the arts and sciences, but progressive

36. See J. Herdt, "Alasdair MacIntyre's 'Rationality of Traditions' and Tradition-Transcendental Standards of Justification," *Journal of Religion* 78 (1998): 528.

37. McIntyre, *Three Rival Versions*, 10ff.

38. Edward Schaffer, "The Protestant Ideology of the American University: Past and Future Prospects," *Educational Theology* 40 (1990): 20.

Protestantism, by means of its sacralization of culture and scientific method, has been displaced by a secular ideology of progress through technology and the "values" of pragmatic strategies. With this displacement, there is no longer any need for a "call" (religious or otherwise). We must conclude that the ultimate end of intellectual formation lies in a source outside itself, and that pragmatic ideology and the use of technology are not conceptually neutral practices, but exist within a definite framework of conceptions that are often contrary to higher goods.[39]

What the liberal Protestant educational experience has shown us is that Protestantism's absorption of the national culture, with the aim of shaping and unifying it, led to the loss of distinctive confessional parameters as Protestantism was demoted to play a supporting role in that culture. Religion is still regarded as somehow "useful," but commitments to religious doctrine too easily interfere with cultural and intellectual freedom. Once the "call" of God, which was given to God's people for fulfilling a covenantal relationship, was stripped of its particular content and became a bland, unobjectionable set of moral propositions, the concept of a calling ceased to have any distinctive meaning. The notion of "calling" devolved into a vague moral idealism and flabby pietism that, now devoid of doctrinal identity, could not ultimately sustain itself. Against the chaos of the undefined benefits of "diversity," the core *credenda* of the Christian tradition keeps before us the imperative that the call to seek the good, the true, and the beautiful is the ultimate goal of human achievement, as it is of the arts and sciences. As the dialogue about the role of church-originated institutions of higher learning takes new steps forward, the place of confessionalism must be given a new hearing. The imbalance of academic opinion must be righted.

---

39. In part, this is what Norman Postman warns us against as the rise of a cultural technopoly eschews moral and religious commitments for efficiency, interest, and economic advance. "It [the technopoly story] casts aside all traditional narratives and symbols that suggest stability and orderliness, and tells instead of a life of skills, technical expertise and the ecstasy of consumption . . . saying that the story of Western civilization is irrelevant" (Norman Postman, *Technopoly: The Surrender of Culture to Technology* [New York: Knopf, 1992], 179).

∽ John P. Neafsey

Psychological Dimensions of the Discernment of Vocation

At the heart of the vocation of St. Ignatius of Loyola was a conviction that he was called to "help souls."[1] Although he responded to this calling in a variety of ways during his lifetime (1491–1556), the unique method that Ignatius developed for helping souls, known as the *Spiritual Exercises*, has become his greatest legacy to soul searchers of subsequent ages.[2] This psychologically sophisticated sys-

1. *The Autobiography of St. Ignatius Loyola*, trans. Joseph F. O'Callaghan, ed. John C. Olin (New York: Harper & Row, 1974). The call to "help souls" is referred to throughout Ignatius's autobiography.

2. David J. Fleming, S.J., *The Spiritual Exercises of St. Ignatius: A Literal Translation and a Contemporary Reading* (St. Louis: Institute of Jesuit Sources, 1978). The *Spiritual Exercises* contain Ignatius's "Rules for the Discernment of Spirits." The *Exercises* are designed to help people to listen deeply for the inner voice of the Spirit and to learn to differentiate feelings associated with the divine voice or Spirit from feelings associated with other kinds of unhelpful voices or "spirits," all with the aim of making life choices that are in accord with the authentic inner voice of vocation, with the call or leading of the Spirit. The *Exercises* were originally designed as a thirty-day retreat process to be led by an individual spiritual director like Ignatius or one of his early Jesuit companions, a process seen as particularly helpful for people discerning a vocation or call. The process is divided into four weeks—the first week centering around a personal confrontation with one's own sinfulness and a reorientation toward God, and the remaining weeks focused on discerning a call in the context of prayer and medita-

tem of spirituality and spiritual guidance is still in use and is intended to help people to discover or discern their true vocation or calling,
to find and follow the path that best embodies who they are meant
to be and what they are meant to do in their short life on this earth.

Though I live in a very different age and work in a profession
more associated with modern science than with spirituality, I believe that my own calling as a clinical psychologist bears some re-
semblance to the vocational pattern of Ignatius. My calling to "help
souls" has been expressed primarily through my work as a psychotherapist. The emotionally demanding process of psychotherapy, like the journey of spiritual growth, often requires considerable
discernment in order to understand and interpret the mysterious
and complex crosscurrents of our inner emotional experience. Interestingly, the root meaning of the word *psychology* is "study of the
soul," and the root meaning of *therapist* is "servant" or "attendant."
The vocation of the psychotherapist, therefore, can be understood
as a calling to be a servant or attendant of the soul, a kind of secular
helper of souls in the modern world.[3]

I have had some personal experience with Ignatian methods of
prayer and discernment through receiving spiritual direction and
making retreats under the guidance of spiritual directors trained in
the Ignatian tradition. These experiences, along with my professional clinical training, have been profoundly formative and influential
in nurturing my own evolving sense of vocation. I have also had a
longstanding interest—both personally and professionally—in the
dialogue between psychology and religion and in the relationship of
spirituality to emotional health and growth.

The spiritual dimension, however, is usually more implicit than

---

tion on the life, death, and resurrection of Christ. For solid, readable introductions to
Ignatian spirituality and discernment, see David Lonsdale, S.J., *Eyes to See, Ears to
Hear: An Introduction to Ignatian Spirituality* (Chicago: Loyola University Press,
1990), and *Listening to the Music of the Spirit: The Art of Discernment* (Notre Dame:
Ave Maria Press, 1992). See also the essay by Paul F. Harman, S.J., in this volume.

3. See David N. Elkins, *Beyond Religion* (Wheaton, Ill.: Quest Books, 1998), 168.

explicit in the psychological work I do. By this I mean that even when spiritual matters are not explicitly discussed, my belief is that it is nonetheless possible for a deep sense of the sacred to be implicitly present in the therapeutic process. This could be said, for that matter, about any situation in which people come together to engage in an honest and careful search for compassionate understanding, for insight, for healing, or for an authentic sense of personal meaning and direction in life. In this broad sense, spirituality has less to do with the particular language that is used, or with the religious tradition that is followed, than with the depth and integrity of the listening, the self-examination, the discerning, and the efforts to make intelligent life choices in accord with the truths that have been uncovered or revealed.

As I see it, a central feature of this implicit spirituality in the psychotherapeutic process is the collaborative, disciplined effort involved in helping people to listen carefully to their inner experience, with the aim of learning to recognize and follow the calling of their own "inner voice." Whether this voice is conceived in psychological or spiritual terms, it can be understood as a source of inner wisdom and guidance that can be consulted and relied upon in discerning important matters of the heart and finding our way in life.

Various psychological and spiritual traditions have offered different names and explanations for the source of the inner voice and the felt sense of vitality and authenticity associated with it. For example, in contemporary psychoanalysis, this center of emotional truth and health at the core of the human person has been referred to as the "true self."[4] C. G. Jung and his followers have called it the

---

4. The term "true self" is associated with the British analyst D. W. Winnicott, an innovative and influential figure in the psychoanalytic object relations psychology tradition. See his essay "Ego Distortion in Terms of True and False Self," in *The Maturational Processes and the Facilitating Environment* (New York: International Universities Press, 1965). Although Winnicott did not discuss spiritual matters, other authors have elaborated on the profound spiritual implications of his thinking. See John McDargh, "The Drama That Is Prayer: A Psychoanalytic Interpretation," in *A Hunger for God: Ten Approaches to Prayer*, ed. W. A. Barry and K. A. Maloney (Kansas City: Sheed &

"Self."[5] Other contemporary authors call it the "soul," an ancient term with more obvious spiritual resonance and associations.[6] In the Ignatian tradition, this positive and helpful source of inner guidance and direction is understood as a manifestation of the wise and loving inner presence of God. In her recent book on Ignatian spirituality, Margaret Silf uses the metaphor of the "inner compass" to capture the essence of the guiding, orienting function of the inner voice in the process of discernment.[7]

My interest in this essay is to explore the psychological dimensions of the experience of vocation in some detail. Vocation will be broadly understood, in keeping with the original meaning of the word, as a universal or archetypal human experience that has been spoken of through the ages by way of the metaphor of hearing and following a call or voice. As Jung wrote, "The original meaning of 'to have a vocation' is 'to be addressed by a voice.'"[8] In the sense that I will be using the term, *every* human person has a vocation and *all* of us—whether we are aware of it or not and whether we respond to it or not—have the potential to hear and follow the inner voice.

Ward, 1991); and James W. Jones, *Contemporary Psychoanalysis and Religion: Transference and Transcendence* (New Haven: Yale University Press, 1991).

5. Throughout his writings, Jung refers to the Self as the mysterious, sacred center or core of the human personality, an inner source of guidance, orientation, and meaning that symbolizes the unique potential that the individual person is called to realize or become through the process of individuation. See C. G. Jung, *Memories, Dreams, and Reflections* (New York: Vintage Books, 1965).

6. For writings representative of what might be called "soul" psychology, see James Hillman, *The Soul's Code: In Search of Character and Calling* (New York: Random House, 1996); and Thomas Moore, *Care of the Soul: A Guide for Cultivating Depth and Sacredness in Everyday Life* (New York: HarperCollins, 1992).

7. Margaret Silf, *Inner Compass: An Invitation to Ignatian Spirituality* (Chicago: Loyola University Press, 1999).

8. C. G. Jung, *The Development of Personality* (New York: Bollingen Foundation, 1954), 176. From the perspective of pastoral psychology, Sellner says, "The word *vocation* itself comes from the Latin *vocare,* which means 'to call.'" See the chapter "The Call of Life" in Edward C. Sellner, *Mentoring: The Ministry of Spiritual Kinship* (Notre Dame: Ave Maria Press, 1990), 83. A recent perspective on vocation is offered by Parker J. Palmer, who says, "the word *vocation* itself . . . is rooted in the Latin for 'voice.'" See *Let Your Life Speak: Listening for the Voice of Vocation* (San Francisco: Jossey-Bass, 2000), 4.

The call gives rise to inclinations to be a particular kind of person or to do particular things, and is accompanied by an invitation to follow or obey by living one's life in accord with what the inner voice seems to be desiring or asking.

In exploring this complex phenomenon, I will attempt to move as fluidly and flexibly as possible between a number of psychological and religious vantage points. My interest is not so much conceptually to explain the psychology of vocation as to explore and appreciate the experiential dimensions of what an authentic sense of vocation *feels* like to the person attempting to discern the call. This emphasis on experience and practice over theory is also consistent with the Ignatian approach. As Lonsdale says about Ignatius, "he was far more interested in the practice of discernment than in theory. His concerns were primarily pastoral: to develop the skills which would enable him, as he put it, 'to help souls.' He was interested in theory, not for its own sake, but only insofar as it grounded and supported his practice and made him a more effective spiritual guide."[9]

Throughout, I will draw relevant parallels between psychological insights from contemporary psychology and spiritual insights from the Ignatian tradition of discernment. My aim is not to replace the language of Ignatian spirituality with psychological terms or to reduce mysterious, transcendent spiritual realities to psychology. Rather, I will try to demonstrate that some solid psychological understanding of vocation tends to confirm, complement, and add further depth and perspective to the insights of Ignatian spirituality.

Understanding the psychological dimensions of vocation can be useful for a number of reasons. First, in the Ignatian spirit of "finding God in all things," is to recognize the potential for God to be encountered in and through the emotional or psychological dimensions of our human experience.[10] A grasp of relevant psychological

9. Lonsdale, *Listening to the Music of the Spirit*, 159.

10. For thoughtful discussions of the Ignatian ideal of "finding God in all things," see the chapter "The Religious Dimension of Experience," in William A. Barry, *Spiritual Direction and the Encounter With God* (Mahwah, N.J.: Paulist Press, 1992); and Lonsdale, "Ignatian Prayer," in *Eyes to See, Ears to Hear.*

concepts can be useful to both spiritual directors and spiritual seekers in discerning the complexities of inner experience. Likewise, some grasp of spiritual dynamics can also be useful for mental health professionals who wish to be sensitive to the spiritual dimension in their clinical work. Second, although there has been a great deal of skepticism in modern psychology toward religion, a considerable number of psychological theorists have arrived at insights into vocation that seem to represent striking parallels to insights from Ignatian spirituality. Finally, for people who are either uncomfortable with or alienated by the use of religious language, the development of a phenomenological, nonreligious language for vocation could potentially be very helpful by providing more accessible words and concepts for thinking and talking about these important matters.

Four main questions will be considered: (1) How is the inner voice or call of vocation experienced psychologically? (2) How can one discern or tell the difference, on an emotional or psychological level, between the authentic voice of vocation and other kinds of voices or "spirits" that may confuse or cloud the picture? (3) What are the psychological signs and symptoms that suggest that a person may be ignoring or living at odds with his or her true calling or vocation? (4) What are the emotional or psychological indicators that a person *is* living in accord with his or her vocation?

How Is the Inner Voice Experienced Psychologically?

As has been noted, a core principle of Ignatian spirituality is the belief that God can be found in all things, that the call or voice of the Spirit can potentially be recognized or heard in *all* aspects of our human experience. Although I am concerned primarily with the inner dimensions of vocation as a voice that speaks to us through the internal world of our psychological experience, it should be kept in mind that God can also speak to us through the external events and experiences of our lives. That is, the voice of God can be heard not only through the feelings, thoughts, images, and dreams of our inner world, but also through significant life events, people, and circumstances we encounter. The key issue for discernment in considering any life experience, however, still centers on the need for careful reflection on the various kinds of feelings that the experience arouses or evokes in us. The simple yet profound insight of Ignatius is that we should reflect carefully on the feelings evoked by our life experiences because God may be speaking to us through them.

In *Eyes to See, Ears to Hear: An Introduction to Ignatian Spirituality*, David Lonsdale highlights the central place of the *affective* dimension of experience in the Ignatian tradition of discernment. He notes that thoughtful awareness and consideration of our deeper feelings is at the heart of the endeavor to discern the presence and action of the Spirit within the complex crosscurrents of our inner experience and the various outer involvements of our lives:

Discernment of spirits in everyday life involves us in a process of sifting our daily experience by noting and reflecting regularly on our affective responses to God and to life and its events. It means noting, for example, situations and events in which we experience joy or sorrow, peace or turmoil, attractions or revulsions, an opening out to others or a narrowing in on ourselves, a sense of God's presence or absence, creativity or destructiveness. The purpose of observing and reflecting on these patterns of responses is that they deepen our sense of ourselves and they can show us where, for each of us . . . the Spirit of God is leading.[11]

Before moving further, some examples of how God can be seen to speak through life experiences and the feelings they evoke may be helpful. In an insightful little book on prayer titled *God Is More Present Than You Think*, Robert Ochs offers numerous helpful illustrations of the Ignatian view that all of our life experiences can, with a little religious imagination, be viewed as potential means for encountering God.[12] For example, on the internal cognitive level of experience, Ochs suggests that the experience of a helpful thought

---

11. Lonsdale, *Eyes to See, Ears to Hear*, 69.
12. Robert Ochs, *God Is More Present Than You Think* (New York: Paulist Press, 1973).

coming into our consciousness when we are struggling with a personal dilemma could be interpreted not just as our own thought, but also as the answer to a prayer. From this vantage point, the thought is something that is *spoken to us* within our mind by God, who *gives* us the thought in order to help us with our problem. To use another example, during an emotionally trying time, the thought "No matter what happens, God still loves me" might come into our mind, accompanied by a feeling of reassurance and consolation. This thought itself, with all its emotional poignancy and meaning, could be viewed as God's personal communication of reassurance to us.

A person might also hear God speaking to him through experiences in the external world. For example, a person might experience a calling to do something to help the poor, perhaps through a personal experience of feeling pained by injustice or feeling moved by the suffering of the poor. In this case, the voice is heard through the poor or, perhaps more precisely, through the *feelings* that are evoked in the person's heart through contact with the poor.

A call might also be heard through a life event. For example, a workaholic person who suffers a serious illness or injury might experience it as a "wake-up call" from God, and consequently engage in some serious soul-searching and rearrangement of her life priorities in order to make more time for leisure or meaningful contact with people. Another example might be the experience of feeling deeply accepted and understood by another human being, which, on a spiritual level, could be taken as an assurance that one is accepted and loved by God. In the context of vocation, the experience of an important mentor figure recognizing and affirming one's unique talents and gifts could be taken as a sign that one has a calling to a particular path of study or work.

In the Ignatian spirituality of discernment, the particular interest is in our deeper emotional responses to life experiences.

In discernment of spirits it is the deeper levels of affectivity that we are concerned with: those which actually influence our behavior; the areas where our affective life and the life of the spirit interpenetrate; the places from which spring our commitments, our most significant choices and the fundamental directions that we give to our lives. Discernment is mainly about these more significant areas of our affective life.[13]

It is evident that an authentic sense of vocation—a genuine hearing of the voice of God or the Spirit—must be rooted in or flow from the deeper currents of feeling and desire within the human person, the kinds of feelings that give rise to and influence the most significant choices, commitments, and directions of our lives. According to Ignatius, the process of learning consciously to acknowledge and reflect in a discerning way on the meanings of our deepest feelings amounts to a "schooling of the heart."[14]

But what are these deeper feelings, these more significant areas of our affective life, and what is this place within ourselves where our emotional life and the life of the Spirit interpenetrate? A number of major psychological traditions and figures have suggested, with a few variations in language and emphasis, that this inner place of emotional and spiritual depth is the fundamental core, center, or essence of our human identity—our deepest and truest self.

Theorists like D. W. Winnicott from the psychoanalytic object relations tradition refer to this inner reality as the "true self."[15] Winnicott saw the primary goal of psychotherapy for people who are alienated from themselves and out of touch with their deepest feelings as the gradual uncovering and expression of the true self in the context of an emotionally secure, growth-promoting therapeutic relationship. In a thoughtful essay that uses Winnicott's concept of the true self to develop a psychology of prayer, John McDargh attempts to integrate psychological and spiritual perspectives by examining parallels between psychoanalytic insights into emotional healing and growth and ancient Christian understandings of prayer. He sees both as processes involving the gradual uncovering and expression of the true self, which, in Christian spirituality, is under-

---

13. Lonsdale, *Eyes to See, Ears to Hear,* 70.
14. Barry, *Spiritual Direction and the Encounter with God,* 82.
15. See Winnicott, "Ego Distortion."

stood as the *imago Dei*, or image of God, within the human person.[16] The true self, or *imago Dei*, is seen as emerging in the context of a nurturing, growth-promoting, transformative relationship. In psychotherapy, the therapeutic relationship provides the emotional environment conducive to genuine self-acceptance and self-expression. In prayer, the deepest and truest inner identity of the person is brought into being through the healing and transformative dialogue with God.

To illustrate these parallels between prayer and the inner connection with the true self, McDargh uses a poignant example from the diary of Etty Hillesum, a thoughtful young Jewish woman from the Netherlands who was sent to the death camps by the Nazis during the Holocaust. Hillesum wrote that, for her, prayer involved "a silly, naive or deadly serious dialogue with what is deepest within me, which for convenience sake I call God."[17] For Etty Hillesum, the connection with God was experienced in and through her connection with her own deepest and truest feelings, her own deepest authenticity as a person.

Jung also saw this deep center of authenticity as reflecting the image of God within the human person. He referred to this mysterious inner reality as the "Self," even going so far as to capitalize the word in order to highlight its association with the emotionally stirring effects of the sacred or "numinous."[18] Other contemporary authors, like James Hillman and Thomas Moore, refer to this same level of depth and sacredness within the human person as the "soul."[19] All seem to agree, regardless of terminology, that this inner reality from which our deepest and truest feelings arise is the place of contact with God.

16. McDargh, "The Drama That Is Prayer."

17. Quoted ibid., 90. Original reference is from *An Interrupted Life: The Diaries of Etty Hillesum 1941–1943* (New York: Pantheon Books, 1983).

18. Jung was strongly influenced by the thinking of the German theologian Rudolph Otto on the emotional impact of the sacred or "numinous" on the human person. See Otto's classic book, *The Idea of the Holy* (London: Oxford University Press, 1923).

19. Hillman, *The Soul's Code*, and Moore, *Care of the Soul.*

In *The Varieties of Religious Experience*, William James refers to this place within us where the psyche and spirit meet as the "wider self": "we have in *the fact that the conscious person is continuous with a wider self through which saving experiences come . . .* a positive content of religious experience, which it seems to me, is literally and objectively true as far as it goes."[20] James further suggests that such "saving experiences" can be consciously *felt* through their emotional impact on us, that is, through the deep feelings that are stirred within us when we have such "saving" contact or connection with the sacred. He conceives of the sacred as a saving power that transcends the self but that is nonetheless experienced in and through the connection with the deeper or "wider" self, a power that is mysteriously both beyond *and* within.

James provides an interesting inventory of the psychological "effects" of the sacred, of the *kinds* of feelings associated with the "saving experiences." These include "a new zest which adds itself like a gift to life"; a sense of "lyrical enchantment" or "earnestness" or "heroism"; "an assurance of safety and a temper of peace"; and, "in relation to others, a preponderance of loving affections." James suggests that people who are living in union or "harmonious relation" with themselves and with God tend to experience such feelings more intensely and frequently.[21]

Interestingly, a number of the affective responses that James includes in his list are reminiscent of a much earlier inventory found in St. Paul's Letter to the Galatians, which lists the various emotional effects of the Holy Spirit on the human person. These included "joy, peace, patience, kindness, goodness, trustfulness, gentleness and self-control."[22] Paul suggested that such feelings and attitudes, which are traditionally referred to as the "fruits of the Spirit," seem to grow naturally within the consciousness of the person who is living in touch with the enlivening and transformative power of the

20. William James, *The Varieties of Religious Experience* (1902; New York: Simon & Schuster, 1997),398.
21. Ibid., 377.
22. Gal. 5:22.

Spirit. When he says in the same letter, "It is no longer I who live, but Christ who lives within me," it appears that Paul may be speaking of a saving and transformative reality within himself that is directly analogous to what James calls the "wider self through which saving experiences come" or to what Jung refers to as the "Self."[23]

In the *Spiritual Exercises*, Ignatius also described a variety of feelings that he believed were experienced as a natural emotional consequence of living in harmony with God. Ignatius referred to this category of feelings as "consolation." Deep feelings of gratitude, trust, joy, and peace, or desires that lead in the direction of spiritual growth or an increase in our capacity for genuine love, would all be seen as emotional indicators of the consoling, inspiring, animating presence of the Spirit. The main feature of such feelings, says Lonsdale, "is that their direction is towards growth, creativity and a genuine fullness of life and love in that they draw us to a fuller, effective, generous love of God and other people, and to a right love of ourselves."[24]

From another vantage point, feelings associated with consolation can be seen as an indication that a person is hearing and living in accord with the inner voice. Hearing the wise and loving voice of God within ourselves has consoling, healing, and morale-building psychological effects on us. In this vein, spiritual author Henri Nouwen has suggested that the essence of prayer is the process of learning to listen deeply within ourselves for the consoling inner voice of love.[25] The idea is that each human person has the potential to hear within himself or herself something like the tender, affirm-

---

23. Gal. 2:20. For an insightful Jungian perspective on the New Testament, see John A. Sanford, *Healing Body and Soul: The Meaning of Illness in the New Testament and in Psychotherapy* (Louisville: Westminster/John Knox, 1992). In analyzing Paul's statement from Galatians, Sanford writes, "The fact that he said that Christ lived in him shows the closeness between the Self and God. In fact, Jung said that the idea of God emerges spontaneously from the Self, which is like an *imago dei,* an image of God, that lives within our very souls."

24. Lonsdale, *Eyes to See, Ears to Hear,* 71.

25. Henri Nouwen, *The Life of the Beloved: Spiritual Living in a Secular World* (New York: Crossroad, 1992).

ing voice that Jesus is said to have heard at the moment of his baptism, a voice that assured him that he was beloved and pleasing to God.[26]

It is important to note that the experience of warm, positive, or pleasant feelings is not, on its own, a reliable indicator of genuine consolation. The ultimate aim of the spiritual journey is not just to "feel good." A person might experience a superficial sense of peace and relief from anxiety by avoiding a challenging situation that could actually be an occasion for emotional or spiritual growth if it was faced more directly. In such a case, a feeling of "peace" or an absence of anxiety could be misinterpreted as consolation.

In Ignatian discernment, it is not the particular feelings in themselves—positive or negative—that are most important, but the meaning and significance of the feelings in the context of the *direction* in which a person is moving that is most important to interpret. A more reliable sign of genuine consolation would be the experience of a sense of peace that, after careful discernment and consideration, is interpreted as a sign that a person is moving in a direction of growth that is in harmony with God, in accord with the inner voice. In Ignatian spirituality, it is the movement toward God or away from God that is seen as having repercussions in our feelings or affective life. "Thus our affective movements and responses," says Lonsdale, "which we can relatively easily be aware of and name, are signs of how we actually stand in relation to God, at a deeper, more hidden level of ourselves."[27]

On another level, spiritual growth or progress is seen in the Ignatian tradition as consisting of a movement away from self-centeredness or egocentrism and toward an ever-deepening capacity for

26. See Mark 1:11 and parallels in Luke 3:22 and Matthew 3:17. Interestingly, in Mark and Luke the voice is addressed *personally* to Jesus, saying: "*You* are my beloved son, in whom I am well pleased," suggesting that Jesus may have experienced it privately as an *inner* voice. In Matthew, the voice is described as a kind of public announcement to the crowd gathered at the Jordan river, saying, "*This* is my beloved son."

27. Lonsdale, *Listening to the Music of the Spirit,* 72–73.

"fuller, effective, generous love of God and other people." It follows that the inner voice of the Spirit is seen as guiding and encouraging the human person through a process of personal growth characterized by a progressive overcoming and surrender of egocentric concerns. The ultimate aim of this process is the development of people who are able to live, work, and love ever more creatively, deeply, and freely. It goes without saying that becoming such a person is not easy and that this process requires considerable humility and courage from the human ego, which may have to overcome many of its own fears and resistances and subordinate some of its own desires in order to respond to a deeper or higher calling.

Edward Whitmont offers some helpful insight from the Jungian tradition on the distinction between the ego or "smaller self" and the larger inner Self, and the association of this larger Self with the inner voice of God:

> Jung called the sum total of our potential being the Self. He contrasted this larger Self with the smaller self, namely our conscious self-image, sense of personal identity and personal hopes and expectations. The Self operates as though generating an evolutionary will and intended pattern of its own, quite often at variance with the conscious ego personality. From the Self flow our "lower" instincts as well as our spiritual aspirations. It generates the individuation drive, the urge to become what we are, as well as the genuine individual conscience, which, in its psychological significance, is likened to *vox Dei*, the "voice of God."[28]

Whitmont's view of the structure of our inner experience suggests that our "conscious ego personality" or "smaller self" is the part of us that is responsible for the task of listening to and following the inner voice, a reality that comes from a source within ourselves that is greater than our ego. Whether this reality is viewed psychologically as the voice of the larger inner Self, or spiritually as the voice of God, the call of the voice is to *individuation*. According to Jung, this process of "becoming what we are" involves both self-discovery and self-expression. Individuation requires, first of all, that we become con-

---

28. Edward C. Whitmont, *Return of the Goddess* (New York: Crossroad, 1984), 206.

scious of who we are, and then calls upon us to find ways to actual-
ize or express the unique truth of who we are within the unique circumstances and realities of our life situation. It is evident from
Whitmont's reflections that the demands of individuation may
sometimes involve "listening" to things we would rather not hear,
that the "will" or wishes of the inner voice may at times be at vari-
ance with our own will or wishes, and that following or obeying the
voice may sometimes lead us to places that our ego would normally
resist going.

In *Healing Body and Soul: The Meaning of Illness in the New Testament and in Modern Psychotherapy,* John Sanford provides some
remarkably detailed and sophisticated psychological and spiritual
insight into the role of the human ego—for better or for worse—in
the individuation process and the spiritual life.[29] Sanford describes
numerous ways that the ego can defensively avoid or resist the demands of psychological and spiritual growth, thereby becoming
alienated from the inner Self and God and diminishing its own capacity to enter into loving relationships with others. He also, however, discusses the potential for the ego to submit willingly to and
cooperate with the inner voice of the Self and God. If the ego is able
to let go of its self-protective fears, defenses, and resistances, it can
become a vehicle that allows for the expression of the deeper truth
and life that is calling for expression or actualization from within.

Sanford's view is that psychological insight into the defensive,
self-protective, and self-promoting concerns of our own ego is a
painful but necessary step in the process of developing an ego that is
more emotionally flexible, more open to and capable of expressing
the fuller reality of the inner Self. His psychological view of the correlation between egocentricity and sin is directly analogous to the
Ignatian emphasis in the first week of the *Spiritual Exercises* on acknowledging and taking responsibility for one's own sinfulness and
willfulness.[30] Developing a detailed knowledge of and feeling for the

---

29. Sanford, *Healing Body and Soul,* 121–22.
30. Ibid. Says Sanford, "Psychologically, the egocentric state corresponds to the

particularities of one's own sin and egocentrism—for all of the ways one says "no" to the call of God—is seen by Ignatius as a humbling but necessary prerequisite or preparation for becoming a person who is spiritually ready to be more discerning and responsive to God's call.[31]

Our resistance to individuation, this process that, according to Sanford, necessitates the "breaking down of our egocentric egos," is quite understandable when we consider the numerous reasons this can feel so humbling and potentially dangerous to the ego.[32] To begin with, the process of becoming conscious of ourselves, of growing in self-knowledge, often requires that we face uncomfortable, painful, or even embarrassing truths about ourselves that we might prefer *not* to acknowledge. Also, the path of self-discovery inevitably seems to lead to a point where we are called upon to take responsibility for what has been discovered.

For example, if we become aware that the deepest desires of our heart seem to incline us in a particular direction, and if the inner voice seems to be calling us in that direction, then we are faced with the choice of whether to obey or refuse the call. If we choose to follow the call, we must then find within ourselves the courage to *become* the person we know ourselves to be, or to take the risk of *doing* the thing we feel that we are meant to do. Learning to love, becoming a loving person, also understandably stirs up considerable fear and resistance in the ego, because opening ourselves to love is an inherently risky venture that makes us emotionally vulnerable to loss and hurt and disappointment. Love may also sometimes call upon us to make the sacrifice of putting the needs of others before the needs and wishes of our own ego.

---

religious notion of original sin, for it is a state of affairs from which we must be saved if we are to live creatively and know God" (6).

31. *Spiritual Exercises.* For example, see the second contemplative exercise of the first week: "I see myself as a sinner—bound, helpless, alienated—before a loving God and all his gifts of creation. . . . I let pass before my mind all my sins and sinful tendencies that permeate my life from my youth up to the very present moment. I let the weight of such evil, all stemming from me, be felt throughout my whole being" (Ex. 56–57).

32. Sanford, *Healing Body and Soul,* 122.

Finally, listening to and following the inner voice may sometimes require that we let go of our own will or wishes in order to submit or surrender to the will of an authority or power greater than our own ego—potentially at considerable personal cost. The psychological process of the ego or "smaller self" learning to acknowledge and serve as a vehicle for the expression of the larger Self directly parallels the spiritual process of the human will attempting to discern and submit to the will of God. The most poignant scriptural example of this is Jesus' anguished prayer in the garden of Gethsemane: "Not my will, but yours be done."[33]

Discernment of Spirits and Voices

The heart of Ignatian spirituality, then, centers on the effort to discern or tell the difference between different kinds of feelings or affective inclinations. The aim is to determine which feelings seem to be leading us in directions consistent with the call or leading of the Spirit and which are not. Ignatius referred to his system of evaluating these different inner affective currents as the "discernment of spirits."[34] As has been discussed, he referred to feelings that arise within a person who is moving in a direction that is in harmony with God as "consolation." By contrast, Ignatius referred to feelings that arise within a person who is moving in a direction that is at odds with or out of tune with God as "desolation." Lonsdale provides a psychologically minded description of the feelings associated with consolation and desolation:

Ignatius identified two contrary kinds of feelings or affective movements among those we experience. They are contrary in that, when they affect us, they move us in opposite directions. In the tradition of discernment, which Ignatius grew familiar with, they are called "consolation" and "desolation." . . . Very briefly, consolation is any affective movement or state that draws us to God or that helps us to be less centered upon ourselves and to open out to others in generosity, service, and love. . . .

33. Matt. 26:39; Mark 14:36; Luke 22:42.
34. *Spiritual Exercises*. See the "Rules for Perceiving and Knowing in Some Manner the Different Movements Which Are Caused in the Soul" (Ex. 313–36).

The feelings and affective movements that come under the heading of "desolation" are the contrary of these. Their characteristic tendency is to draw us away from God and things which have to do with God, and to lead us to be self-centered, closed in and unconcerned about God and other people. So, for example, we might feel a depressing inner darkness and restlessness; life ceases to have meaning; God and other people seem to count for nothing; paralyzing feelings of failure, guilt, and self-hatred can threaten to set us on a downward spiral of neglect of ourselves, other people and God; or we might experience other states and movements of feeling which seem to undermine our capacities for faith, hope and love and to lead us into destructive forms of behavior towards others and ourselves.[35]

Ultimately, the aim of discernment is an ever-increasing sense of self-knowledge, sensitivity, and skill in distinguishing between feelings of consolation and desolation, all for the purpose of being better able to choose to move in the direction in which the Spirit is believed to be calling us through the different kinds of feelings we experience within ourselves.

Ignatius believed that feelings associated with consolation and desolation were stirred up or aroused through the invisible influence of different types of unseen "spirits." Feelings associated with consolation were seen to arise from the influence of "good spirits" or the Holy Spirit. Feelings associated with desolation were seen to arise from the influence of "evil spirits" or Satan. Lonsdale discusses the potential problem that Ignatius's terminology of "spirits" may pose for modern, psychologically minded people.[36] He suggests that one

---

35. Lonsdale, *Eyes to See, Ears to Hear*, 69–70.

36. Ibid. Lonsdale says, "the term 'discernment of spirits' harkens back to a previous age of psychology. The term itself comes from the time when the variety and changes of often contrary feelings within the human person were attributed to the presence and action of 'good spirits' (the Spirit of God and the angels) and 'evil spirits' (Satan and his minions). Naturally, Ignatius, being a man of his pre-Freudian time, accepted this framework unquestioningly and built it automatically into his writing on discernment. But of course we do not have to accept that particular theoretical framework in order to believe in and practice discernment. A difficulty is, however, that we have not yet found a very adequate terminology to replace the traditional one, and people still use the language of 'spirits.' So it is important to distinguish between this language and the outmoded theoretical framework from which it springs, and to know what in fact we mean by the language of spirits" (69–70).

way to handle this issue is to use more forward-looking criteria for discernment that focus more on where feelings seem to be *leading* us or *drawing* us than on identifying whether the feelings have good or evil sources or origins.

Following this framework, it may be less useful to know that a certain feeling comes from the "evil spirit" than to recognize that it is leading us in an egocentric direction. Similarly, identifying the source of a particular inner voice as "demonic" may be less helpful than recognizing that the thought process it is associated with seems to be drawing a person into an emotionally destructive state of hopelessness, demoralization, or despair. In a more positive vein, our assessment of whether a feeling or inclination seems to be leading us in a direction of deeper personal authenticity, or a more mature love for other people, is probably the most reliable indication that the feeling is consistent with the direction in which the Holy Spirit is calling or leading.

Although such forward-looking criteria for discernment seem wise and useful, they still may not completely resolve the problem of the terminology of "spirits" as a theoretical explanation for where our feelings come from. The view that unseen forces or spirits can have a powerful influence—for better or worse—on the emotional and physical health, well-being, and behavior of human beings was widespread in the ancient world and persists in many cultures to the present day. This view seems to be particularly prevalent in cultures where the spirituality and healing practices of shamanism are encountered.[37] Belief in spirits was also common in the world of the New Testament, as is evidenced in the gospel accounts of Jesus' dialogues with Satan and in the stories of Jesus' healing encounters with people who were seen as being possessed by demonic or "unclean" spirits. For example, Jesus' first healing miracle in the Gospel of Mark is an exorcism. A few chapters later, Jesus heals the Gerasene demoniac, a man who, in the modern world, would be

37. For an excellent cross-cultural overview of shamanic beliefs from an anthropological perspective, see David Kinsley, *Health, Healing, and Religion: A Cross-Cultural Perspective* (Upper Saddle River, N.J.: Prentice-Hall, 1996).

seen as a severely mentally ill homeless person who is dangerous to himself and others.[38]

In an interesting essay titled "The Presence of Spirits in Madness," psychologist Wilson Van Dusen offers some rather unconventional reflections on the parallels between religious experiences of good and evil spirits and the hallucinations of the severely troubled psychotic people he worked with at a state psychiatric hospital.[39] Van Dusen suggests that the auditory hallucinations of psychotic patients (i.e., people who "hear voices"), especially those who are tormented and demoralized by hostile, disparaging inner voices, are remarkably similar to the experiences of people who, in previous ages, would have been viewed as possessed by or under attack from malicious evil spirits. Van Dusen refers to such destructive and unhelpful inner voices as "lower order hallucinations."

Interestingly, Van Dusen makes the point that not all the hallucinations of the mentally ill are destructive in nature. He documents a number of cases in which voices were characterized by a more respectful and caring emotional tone toward the patient. Such "good voices" said things that had *positive* effects on the patient's morale and were often seen as giving wise, constructive advice and support. Van Dusen referred to these constructive and helpful inner voices as "higher order hallucinations," seeing them as parallel to religious experiences of God, angels, or "good spirits." Jung reported similar observations in his account of a case he encountered in his early work in a psychiatric hospital: "I once had to treat a schizophrenic old woman. . . . She heard voices which were distributed throughout her body, and a voice in the middle of the thorax was 'God's voice.' 'We must rely on that voice,' I said to her, and was astonished at my own courage. As a rule, this voice made very sensible remarks, and with its aid I managed very well with the patient."[40] Such clinical observations suggest that the terminology of spirits

38. See Mark 1:21–28 and 5:1–20.

39. Wilson Van Dusen, *The Presence of Spirits in Madness* (New York: Swedenborg Foundation, 1983).

40. Jung, *Memories, Dreams, and Reflections*, 126.

found in the *Spiritual Exercises* may not be so outmoded as they might initially seem to the skeptical modern mind. My interest in this essay, however, is not primarily in the extreme, externalized manifestations of voices, such as are encountered in the psychotically mentally ill. It is rather in the more subtle, internal experiences of average people on the more healthy or "normal" end of the spectrum of psychological functioning. One way to explore these more subtle, inner phenomena is to look for concepts in modern psychology that represent parallels to Ignatius's view that different kinds of feelings and thoughts have their sources in different kinds of spirits. Along these lines, various psychological schools of thought have developed theories based around hypothesized distinctions between different structures or "parts" of the mind, and have made qualitative differentiations between various types of thoughts and feelings that seem to have their sources in different aspects of the mind.

For example, Jung's idea of the distinction between the conscious ego and the unconscious inner Self has already been discussed as a direct psychological parallel to the spiritual distinction between the human will and the will of God. This distinction between ego and Self seems to have considerable potential for use as an alternative explanatory framework for the sources or origins of at least some of our feelings in the process of discernment. Sanford is careful to caution against viewing the ego itself as inherently demonic, and it may be that direct parallels between the ego and the "evil spirit" or the Self and the "good spirit" are not always fitting. The conscious effort to distinguish between feelings arising from the superficial ambitions and self-protective concerns of the ego versus the deeper, more authentic desires and inclinations of the inner Self, however, seems to represent a potentially quite useful alternative criterion for discernment.

In his recent book *Let Your Life Speak: Listening for the Voice of Vocation*, Parker Palmer captures the essence of the qualitative distinction that can be made between the "willful" ego and what he calls the "true self" by the person who is listening carefully for the voice of vocation in his or her inner experience:

Vocation does not come from willfulness. It comes from listening. I must listen to my life and try to understand what it is truly about—quite apart from what I would like it to be about—or my life will not represent anything real in the world, no matter how earnest my intentions. . . . That insight is hidden in the word vocation itself, which is rooted in the Latin for "voice." Vocation does not mean a goal that I pursue. It means a calling that I hear. . . . Behind this understanding of vocation is a truth that the ego does not want to hear because it threatens the ego's turf: everyone has a life that is different from the "I" of daily consciousness, a life that is trying to live through the "I" who is its vessel. This is what the poet knows and what every wisdom tradition teaches: there is a great gulf between the way my ego wants to identify me, with its self-protective masks and self-serving fictions, and my true self. It takes time and hard experience to sense the difference between the two—to sense that running beneath the surface of my life, there is a deeper and truer life waiting to be acknowledged.[41]

According to Palmer, if we are to grow in our ability to acknowledge and express the "deeper and truer life" within us, we must be willing to go through the process of learning to recognize and tell the difference between the voice of the ego and the voice of the true self, between the superficial or "phony" feelings associated with the "self protective masks" of the ego and the deeper, truer feelings emerging out of our authentic selfhood.

Such a truth-seeking attitude is also essential for the person who is sincerely attempting to "discern the spirits." Lonsdale says that this requires "searching honestly for the most authentic truth, not just knowledge that makes little difference to how we live, but also the deeper gospel truth that makes little sense in fact until it becomes the truth that governs our lives."[42] The implication is that this type of discernment calls for considerable honesty, courage, and a willingness not only to face but to *live* this "deeper gospel truth," to let it "govern" our lives.

Some further psychological theory may be helpful to clarify some other aspects of the inwardly felt sense of authenticity that is an in-

---

41. Parker Palmer, *Let Your Life Speak: Listening for the Voice of Vocation* (San Francisco: Jossey-Bass, 2000), 4–5.
42. Lonsdale, *Eyes to See, Ears to Hear,* 63.

dicator of the presence of the true self. D. W. Winnicott made a distinction between the true self and what he called the "false self on a conformity basis."[43] The true self, according to Winnicott, is rooted in the experience of the primary, undistorted, spontaneous, moment-to-moment unfolding of our own inner emotional reality. The true self is our personal emotional truth, our real feelings, what we actually think and feel about things. It has to do with the emotional reality of what *is* rather than what we think we *should* be feeling. The true self, in this sense, consists of what William Lynch has called our "psychological facts," whether or not we like them, express them, or even admit them to ourselves or others.[44]

What Winnicott means by the "false self," on the other hand, develops during childhood out of fears that one's actual emotional reality is unacceptable, out of the feeling that one's parents or family or world cannot or will not tolerate or accept who one actually is. The experience is that it is emotionally dangerous to actually *be* oneself or to have and express one's real feelings. Consequently, in order to cope and survive emotionally, the person develops a kind of inauthentic mask that is motivated by the need to please or adjust or conform to the expectations and wishes of others in order to win their acceptance or avoid their rejection. This mask, which Winnicott refers to as the "false self" (or the "false self on a conformity basis"), serves both to conceal and to protect the true self, which remains hidden and, in extreme cases, perhaps even forgotten or repressed within the unconscious of the person.

It is evident that such a defensive, fear-driven way of being inevitably gives rise to marked feelings of inauthenticity, self-alienation, and disconnection from one's inner emotional reality. The search for the true self, or the recovery of a connection with it that has been lost, necessarily involves efforts to remember what one's true feelings once were or to recognize and feel what they are right

---

43. Winnicott, "Ego Distortion."

44. William F. Lynch, *Images of Hope: Imagination as Healer of the Hopeless* (Notre Dame: University of Notre Dame Press, 1965). See especially the chapter "The Science of the Bare Fact."

now. Such efforts are often at the heart of the painstaking and painful process of psychotherapy for people who never had the feeling that it was safe or permissible to actually be *themselves*.[45]

The distinction between the false self and the true self may also represent a useful psychological parallel to the discernment of good and evil spirits. Although the nature and degree of "false self" development or self-alienation in most people does not reach the severe pathological proportions of the cases described by Winnicott, many people can easily relate to the distinction between fear-driven inclinations toward conformity, or "hiding" of our true feelings, and freer, spontaneous inclinations toward authentic self-expression and self-actualization. The issue for discernment centers around differentiating emotional truth from emotional falsehood, recognizing the difference between authentic and counterfeit ways of being in the world. In this framework, it may be less helpful to draw an automatic parallel between the false self and the evil spirit than to recognize the emotional and spiritual dangers that develop when our self-protective and self-concealing inclinations unduly influence our choices, thereby limiting and restricting our emotional, relational, and spiritual development.

Another potentially useful psychological parallel to the discernment of spirits centers around the distinction between the "super-ego" and the "true conscience." These psychological concepts most clearly embody the phenomenon of something like an inner voice. Freud's original theory of the superego centered around the notion of a structure within the mind that developed through a process of the internalization of parental or societal moral standards, judgments, and prohibitions. According to Freud, these internalized standards of right and wrong eventually become the superego, which operates, for all intents and purposes, like the inner voice of conscience. The particular parental or familial or societal standards that are internalized during one's upbringing determine the content

45. For an interesting application of Winnicott's ideas to the process of psychotherapy, see Alice Miller, *The Drama of the Gifted Child: The Search for the True Self* (New York: Basic Books, 1981).

and emotional tone of the superego judgments or "corrections" one might expect to hear from within one's mind.

For example, a person who grows up with parents who have a flexible, relaxed approach to morality might be expected to develop a correspondingly flexible superego. On the other hand, a person who grows up with harsh, rigid, or punitive parents might be expected to develop a superego characterized by a correspondingly negative emotional tone. She might hear a critical or judgmental voice from within, something resembling the original voice and emotional tone of her parents, which perhaps induces intense feelings of guilt and anxiety whenever she happens to think or feel or do the "wrong" thing. In *The Ego and the Id,* Freud expressed a kind of puzzlement and dismay over the potential for a rigid, critical superego to induce a neurotic sense of guilt: "How is it that the super-ego manifests itself as a sense of guilt (or rather, as criticism—for the sense of guilt is the perception in the ego answering to this criticism) and moreover develops such harshness and severity towards the ego?"[46]

In his book *Voice Therapy,* Robert Firestone discusses the potential for pathological forms of the negative superego voice to have a profoundly destructive emotional impact, which, in severe cases, can give rise to annihilating feelings of depression, guilt, worthlessness, despair, self-destructiveness, and inhibition of a person's natural inclinations toward emotional growth and self-realization.[47] The traditional religious term for such a rigid, overactive superego is "scruples," a problem that is manifested in obsessional, guilt-driven ways of thinking and behaving that give the superficial appearance of virtuousness but that are actually pathological and self-destructive. For a time, Ignatius himself suffered from a severe case of scruples that nearly drove him to suicide.[48] His own inner struggles

46. Sigmund Freud, "The Ego and the Id," in *The Standard Edition of the Complete Psychological Works of Sigmund Freud,* vol. 19, ed. J. Strachey (1923; London: Hogarth Press, 1961), 53.

47. Robert W. Firestone, *Voice Therapy: A Psychotherapeutic Approach to Self-Destructive Behavior* (New York: Human Sciences Press, 1988).

48. *Autobiography of St. Ignatius Loyola,* 33–37. Also see discussion of this period of

taught him some important lessons in discernment between differ-ent kinds of guilt-inducing inner voices.[49]

Firestone also makes a useful distinction between "neurotic guilt" and "existential guilt." Both forms of guilt, he says, are generated by a guilt-inducing inner voice, but the two kinds of guilt have differ-ent meanings and origins. Neurotic guilt, he says, arises from the vi-olation of superego standards or "rules," consistent with Freud's original theory. Existential guilt, by contrast, arises not because one has violated internalized parental prohibitions but because one has betrayed *oneself.* One is guilty, in this sense, of being inauthentic—of going against one's own inner nature. Irving Yalom, a representa-tive of the existential psychology tradition, says this: "Most simply put: One is guilty not through transgressions against another or some moral or social code, but *one may be guilty of transgressing against oneself.*"[50]

In contrast to destructive forms of the rule-oriented superego voice that induces neurotic guilt and emotional inhibition, Yalom and others in the existential psychology tradition suggest that the source of existential guilt may be a *constructive* inner voice that "cor-rects" us from within when we have deviated or strayed from our authentic path in life. Yalom says that "existential guilt is a positive constructive force, *a guide calling oneself back to oneself.*"[51]

John Sanford offers similar insights from the Jungian tradition on the origins of different kinds of guilt in different kinds of inner voices. In an interesting chapter on guilt in his book *Between People,* Sanford distinguishes between what he calls "false guilt" and "real guilt."[52] In his view, false guilt is similar to neurotic guilt, and it is induced by a similar superego-like voice that Sanford refers to as the "Inner Critic." The Inner Critic tends to speak in moralistic gener-

---

inner torment and crisis in Ignatius's life in W. W. Meissner, S.J., *Ignatius of Loyola: The Psychology of a Saint* (New Haven: Yale University Press, 1992), 73–78.

49. *Spiritual Exercises,* Ex. 345–51.

50. Irving D. Yalom, *Existential Psychotherapy* (New York: Basic Books, 1980), 277, emphasis added.

51. Ibid., 281, emphasis added.

52. John A. Sanford, *Between People* (New York: Paulist Press, 1982).

alities, in the language of "shoulds" and "oughts." The feelings of false guilt that this critical, accusatory inner voice evokes in us tend to have destructive, demoralizing, and inhibiting effects on our sense of emotional well-being and growth.

Real guilt corresponds more closely with existential guilt, and is seen by Sanford as stemming from a voice that offers constructive criticism and guidance from within. He sees the source of real guilt as a helpful inner voice that is interested in our development as an authentic person—something like the voice that, according to Yalom, "calls oneself back to oneself." Sanford calls this the "true Conscience" or the "voice of our real Self," and offers some useful guidelines on the matter of differentiating between false guilt and real guilt, between the destructive Inner Critic and the wise inner counsel of the true Conscience:

There is indeed a true Conscience within us, a voice that can be said to come from our real Self and that tries to correct us when we deviate from our proper path in life. When this voice comes to us we need to listen. But corrections from this voice do not annihilate us. Painful though such corrections may be, they lead us back to our true Self, not away from it. For these corrections come, not from false guilt feelings, but from a violation of our true and deepest nature. When we deviate from our true nature, we hear what amounts to the voice of God within us.[53]

53. Ibid., 64. Sanford offers some further thoughts on guilt-inducing inner voices that are relevant to discernment: "This brings up the question of the relationship between the accusing voice and what we can call the voice of our real Self, the contrast between the Inner Critic and our true Conscience. After all, are we not supposed to have a conscience? Is there not supposed to be something like God's voice within us that admonishes us when we do evil and tries to keep us on the right path in life? Of course. The problem is that the accusing voice poses as the true moral authority but isn't. That is one thing that gives the accusing voice such power: it acts as if it were God, and pretends to be our true conscience. But it isn't, and there is one way we can tell: the accusing voice of which I'm speaking can only be destructive. It has no power to build us up, or lead us to our true Self. It can only tear us down, and will infallibly say things that are annihilating. Its admonitions are full of 'shoulds' and 'oughts' and are phrased in generalities that condemn us as a person. They are the sort of accusations that leave us with the feeling 'I guess I am just no good . . . I guess I am just a failure.' In short, though this voice seems like God's it acts more like the devil of the New Testament whose name in Greek, *diabolos,* means 'the accuser'" (64–65).

Sanford's distinction between the true Conscience and the Inner Critic is a clear parallel to the distinction between good and evil spirits in Ignatian spirituality, and between the qualitatively different kinds of advice or commentary on our lives that are offered by these different types of inner spirits or voices. For example, in his "Rules for the Discernment of Spirits," Ignatius suggests that the evil spirit tends to stir up discouraging feelings of false doubt and anxiety (false or neurotic guilt) in people who are on the path of genuine spiritual progress and growth.[54] In people who are moving in the wrong direction, by contrast, the good spirit is seen as arousing feelings of genuine remorse (real or existential guilt) which are experienced as the "sting of conscience."[55]

Living "In Tune" or "Out of Tune" with Our Vocation

All of the various psychological and spiritual terminologies that have so far been discussed (ego vs. Self, false self vs. true self, neurotic vs. existential guilt, superego vs. true conscience, evil spirit vs. good spirit) have their unique limitations and potential to serve as useful criteria for discernment. In this final section, I will offer a few concluding thoughts on the psychological dimensions of discernment, centering around the question of how it is possible to tell whether or not we are living in tune with our true vocation or calling. What are the emotional or psychological indicators, the feelings we might expect to experience, that suggest that we are living in harmony with the inner voice? And what are the psychological signs and symptoms that suggest that we may be ignoring or living at odds with our vocation?

For several reasons, the question of knowing with any kind of certainty whether or not we are on the "right" path must be approached with a sense of humility. It is evident that matters of discernment are often quite mysterious and complicated on both the psychological and spiritual levels of our experience. We human be-

54. *Spiritual Exercises*, Ex. 315.
55. Ibid., Ex. 314.

ings have a difficult enough time knowing our own minds, let alone the mind of God. We also need to be mindful of our own potential for self-deception, recognizing that egocentric concerns, defensiveness, or psychological blindness in ourselves might obscure or distort the inner voice and possibly lead us in directions that deviate from our true calling.

Acquiring a wise and discerning mind and heart also requires considerable self-knowledge, which can only be obtained through long and careful reflection on the ups and downs of our life experiences and long and patient listening for the inner voice. William Barry does a good job of capturing the spirit of humility and willingness to learn that is needed in order to cultivate the art and skill of discernment:

> I must be willing to start slowly, to let God train my heart as he did Ignatius', through painstaking trial and error. . . . I must learn to pay attention to the movements of my heart and mind, to reflect on them wisely and carefully with the help of others . . . and to test them over time. In the process I must learn two equally difficult and seemingly incompatible attitudes: to trust myself and my reactions and to recognize how easily I can delude myself.[56]

Traditionally, discernment has been associated with "finding the will of God." An obstacle sometimes encountered by spiritual seekers is the widespread simplistic view that the discernment of God's will involves the discovery of a secret, predestined "plan" that God has for one's life, followed by efforts to comply by trying to fit one's life into this plan. Lonsdale offers some helpful perspective on how this narrow understanding of God's will tends to diminish the exercise of human freedom in giving shape to our lives by the choices that we make. He suggests that a more complex, creative view of the will of God takes into account the responsible exercise of human judgment and choice in the context of a living dialogue or partnership with God:

---

56. Barry, *Spiritual Direction and the Encounter with God*, 82–83.

God's will is that we should exercise our freedom responsibly and well by choosing what honestly seems the best course of action in a given set of circumstances, using all the relevant aids that we have been given for that purpose. There is a sense in which we create, in terms of concrete action in given circumstances, the will of God in this exercise of freedom. There is no blueprint in God's mind with which we have to comply. Discernment of spirits, within a living relationship with God, is one of the gifts that we have been given to help us to exercise our freedom in the choices that we make and so come to "find the will of God" for us.[57]

As Lonsdale suggests, discernment is often a very personal and individual matter of attempting to discover—or perhaps even participate in creating—the unique will of God *for us,* given all of our unique potentials and limitations and in the context of the unique particulars of our personal life history, opportunities, and circumstances. Although various spiritual or psychological criteria for discernment can be helpful in this process, there is no absolute set of guidelines for making choices that can guarantee that we will always make the "right" choice, the choice that is consistent with the will of God, and not make a mistake. Discernment and decision making, therefore, require a willingness to experiment, to engage in a process of trial and error, to take the risk of making the best choice we can with the knowledge we have after careful consideration of all the options. As Jung wrote:

When one follows the path of individuation, when one lives one's own life, one must take mistakes into the bargain; life would not be complete without them. There is no guarantee—not for a single moment—that we will not fall into error or stumble into deadly peril. We may think there is a sure road. But that would be the road of death. Then nothing happens any longer—at any rate, not the right things. Anyone who takes the sure road is as good as dead.[58]

That said, however, a knowledge of certain kinds of psychological signs and symptoms may sometimes help us to recognize when

---

57. Lonsdale, *Eyes to See, Ears to Hear*, 65–66.
58. Jung, *Memories, Dreams, and Reflections*, 297.

we are falling into error or living in a way that is not in harmony with the inner voice of vocation. Barry refers to this as being "out of tune" with the action or intention of God.[59] As we have seen, Ignatius believed that affective experiences of desolation are a sign that a person is moving in the wrong direction or living in a way that is out of harmony with God. From the perspective of humanistic psychology, Abraham Maslow has suggested that people are vulnerable to becoming emotionally "sick" in some way when their deeper needs and desires are not acknowledged and taken into account in their ways of living: "If this essential core of the person is denied or suppressed, he [or she] gets sick, sometimes in obvious ways, sometimes in subtle ways. . . . This inner nature . . . is weak and delicate and subtle and easily overcome by habit, and cultural pressure. . . . Even though denied, it persists underground, forever pressing for actualization."[60]

In *Care of the Soul*, Thomas Moore expresses a similar view that certain kinds of painful or troublesome feelings can be interpreted as "symptoms" of a kind of emotional or spiritual sickness in the essential core or soul of the person. Such symptoms, he says, might include feelings of spiritual emptiness, meaninglessness, depression, guilt, disillusionment, restlessness, boredom, anger, dissatisfaction with work or relationships—virtually any feeling that suggests that something may be wrong or missing in some area of our life. Rather than taking the approach of quickly trying to "fix" or get rid of such uncomfortable symptoms, Moore suggests that such feelings should be honored by carefully *listening* to them and reflecting on their meanings in the context of our life. The idea is that such feelings potentially contain a message that we need to hear, that the "voice of the soul" may be using the annoying or disruptive symptom to get our attention or communicate with us. Appreciating the meanings and messages contained in our symptoms not only helps us to diagnose what is wrong, but may also help us to recognize what is

59. Barry, "The Religious Dimension of Experience," 76.
60. Abraham Maslow, *Toward a Psychology of Being* (New York: Von Nostrand Reinhold Company, 1962), 3–4.

missing in our life, perhaps by making us aware of the kinds of experiences our soul may be longing for.[61]

For example, a person's choices may be overly influenced by needs for emotional safety or financial security, with the result that more risky longings for love and meaning are not given enough weight in their decisions. Consequently, they may experience a nagging sense of emptiness or lovelessness that money, possessions, status, or a safe and secure lifestyle do not take away. Or perhaps neurotic guilt and fear have stifled or inhibited a person's inclinations toward personal authenticity and individuation, with the result that she feels emotionally and spiritually trapped or constricted in the circumstances she has chosen for herself. Or maybe the self-protective mask of the false self has resulted in a life focused so much on conformity and pleasing others that we have forgotten who we really are, perhaps failing to recognize that other ways of living could be more satisfying and pleasing to *us*, to our true self, to our soul.

In Ignatian spirituality, negative feelings corresponding to such symptoms might initially appear to be manifestations of "desolation," and could perhaps be interpreted as evidence that the evil spirit is trying to undermine a person's morale or progress by stirring up emotional trouble for him. An alternative interpretation to consider, however, is that such troublesome feelings could potentially be a form of communication from the *good* spirit—a manifestation of the inner voice of God. This is analogous to Moore's view that the "voice of the soul" may sometimes use what appear to be dark or negative feelings as a way to give us a message from within, perhaps to help us recognize the error of a direction we have taken or a choice we have made. This voice has our best interests at heart, and ultimately aims to guide us or correct us so that we can find a path that is more fitting for us, a way of living that is more conducive to our emotional and spiritual health and growth.

How then, do we know when we are on the right path, when we are living in tune with the inner voice of vocation? Ignatius believed

---

61. Moore, *Care of the Soul.* See especially the first chapter, "Honoring Symptoms as a Voice of the Soul."

that affective experiences of consolation—such as feelings of deep peace or joy related to a particular life choice or direction—may be good signs that it is consistent with the will of God for us. In his interesting book *Callings: Finding and Following an Authentic Life*, Gregg Levoy offers other experiential criteria for discernment: integrity, authenticity, sense of connection to self and others, intuitive rightness, and aliveness.[62] Each of these criteria is strongly evident, either explicitly or implicitly, in the *Spiritual Exercises* as well as in the alternative psychological frameworks for discernment that have already been explored.

The feeling of *aliveness*—the experience of a sense of joy and vitality and enthusiasm in relation to vocation—deserves to be emphasized. Mythologist Joseph Campbell's oft-quoted, refreshing advice that we should "follow our bliss" is rooted in the belief that feelings of deep joy and aliveness are important qualitative criteria for discerning whether or not we are on the path of our true calling.[63] Such feelings in connection with the recognition of a genuine calling are poignantly captured in a lovely passage from James Joyce: "His heart trembled in an ecstasy of fear and his soul was in flight. . . . This was the call of life to his soul, not the dull gross voice of the world of duties and despair."[64]

A similar sentiment, expressed in a quote from the great psychologist of religion William James, seems to be a fitting conclusion to this essay. In a letter to his wife, James wrote of the emotional quality of certain special, unforgettable life experiences that are marked by a feeling of intense authenticity and aliveness. "At such moments," he said, "there is a voice inside which speaks and says: '*This is the real me!*'"[65]

62. Gregg Levoy, *Callings: Finding and Following an Authentic Life* (New York: Harmony Books, 1997), 39.

63. The reference is to an oft-quoted statement by mythologist Joseph Campbell in an interview with Bill Moyers for the PBS television series *The Power of Myth*.

64. James Joyce, *A Portrait of the Artist as a Young Man* (New York: Viking Press, 1964).

65. Henry James, ed., *The Letters of William James* (Boston: Atlantic Monthly Press, 1920), 199.

⤳ Mary Elsbernd

Listening for a Life's Work

Contemporary Callings to Ministry

As a member of a religious congregation for many years, I have been surprised and inspired by the frequent reference to call as a reason for application into the Master of Divinity (M.Div.) program that I direct at the Institute of Pastoral Studies (IPS) at Loyola University Chicago. The M.Div. is a professional degree that prepares persons for major ministerial leadership in the church, church-sponsored institutions, or in the marketplace. Although the M.Div. is widely recognized as the degree for ordained ministry, the M.Div. at the Institute of Pastoral Studies grows out of the baptismal call to ministry. In other words, almost all of the graduates are professional ministers who are not ordained for ministry but who work in the church, its sponsored institutions, and the marketplace as leaders and professionals. The ministries that these graduates take up include:

a. Pastoral associates in parishes
b. Chaplains for hospitals, hospice, retirement homes, funeral homes, and universities
c. Directors of religious education

d. Heads of archdiocesan offices (Parish Councils, Family Life, Hispanic Ministries, Peace and Justice, Lay Ministry Training, Diaconate Formation)

e. Directors of young adult volunteer programs

f. Retreat providers and spiritual directors

g. Teachers and administrators in high schools and colleges

h. Pastors/pastoral coordinators

i. Freelance authors and speakers

Participation in the Lilly faculty seminar on vocation provided me the opportunity to explore some of the dimensions of call as it is used by applicants to this M.Div. program.[1]

A personal essay is part of the application process for acceptance into the M.Div. program at the IPS. Although applicants are not required to address the question of call, the vast majority of them speak to their sense of calling. The vocabulary and concept of call usually surface in their narratives when they describe the roots of their faith, previous ministerial experiences, reasons for seeking an M.Div. degree, or issues of concern to them in church and world.

I hope with this study to contribute to a working understanding of vocation or call by looking at essays written by persons who readily speak of a calling to ministry. Since the essays also address the personal circumstances surrounding the call to ministry, it may be possible to glean some sense of the environments that nurture an understanding of one's life work as a vocation.

While it is quite possible that the application essays for admission to other professional schools include references to a calling to other professions, I have looked only at the application essays for the M.Div. program. Comparative research on other professional schools and seminaries would be a welcome complement to this study. But I believe that the results of my study can suggest to educators and readers some possibilities for the creation of an environment that will foster a sense of vocation among undergraduates and graduate students.

1. This article was possible only with the astute research and thoughtful editorial work of Jacqueline Hoffman-Blake, one of those called to ministry.

Group Demographics

My data for this study and its conclusions are based on the personal statements of the first one hundred students to be accepted and enrolled in the M.Div. program since its inception in 1989. Eighty-nine of these hundred students had graduated from the M.Div. program as of May 2003. Twenty-three are male and seventy-seven are female. They come from many walks of life[2] and are of various ages.[3]

Use of the Vocabulary and Concept of Call

Eighty-five of the personal statements used the word "call" or closely equivalent language, including "God revealed to me," "God telling me," "the Holy Spirit nudged me," "God leading me," "I felt drawn," and so on.[4] One person spoke of following the "telltale feathers of the Holy Spirit" at work through the books and poetry she was reading. Others wrote of hearing or no longer ignoring a voice, or of responding to an invitation. All of this language resonated with the meaning of call.

Male and female applicants seemed equally at home with the vocabulary of call. Not surprisingly, given the history of religious vocation, all applicants who belonged to religious congregations spoke

2. At the time of application, twenty females and fourteen males were married. Eighteen females and three males were members of religious congregations. Thirty-one females and five males were single, never married. Eight females and one male were no longer married.

3. At the time of application, twenty-four females and seven males were in their twenties. Fourteen females and seven males were in their thirties. Twenty-two females and seven males were in their forties. Fifteen females and two males were in their fifties. Two females and no males were in their sixties.

4. Eighty-six percent of the female and 83 percent of the male applicants used the term "call." With regard to life status, all applicants who were members of religious congregations used the term, although some of them used it only in reference to their call to religious life. Eighty percent of those who were married, 83 percent of those who were single and never married, and 78 percent of those who were no longer married also used the term. Hence the use of "call" crossed categories of gender and marital status.

of call. But the majority of married, single, and no longer married applicants also understood their applications to this academic program as a response to a call.

Fifteen persons, eleven of them women, did not use the term or the concept of call in their personal statements. About half of these described ministry as a career choice and a part of their life goals. The choice of ministry was described as a decision based on what the person wanted to do: "I developed dreams and goals for my life and started moving in a certain direction to attain them." "I decided to pursue a life in youth ministry." "I discerned a new career path." For these persons, the decision to move into ministry could be described as composing a life narrative out of their own experience.

For those who were making the transition from a business career into ministry, the integration of business skills with ministry surfaced. One was "preparing to apply the last twenty-six years of business experience and varied volunteer parish ministry to become a non-ordained parish administrator." Another planned to "integrate my business career with ministry work." In these cases, the understanding of ministry as a career reflected the world and vocabulary from which they were making the transition.

For others, ministry was the outgrowth of their intimate personal relationship with a partner God, which did not result in a call *per se* but rather in a desire to share this God relationship with others. Still others used the language of conversion. In one case the impetus for conversion came, in part, from two questions addressed to Mary of Magdala in the Gospel of John, chapter 20, namely, "Why do you weep?" and "Who are you seeking?" This experience of conversion began a "shift of center" that moved the applicant toward a life of ministry. A few applicants spoke of following and accepting "God's plan" or of a need in themselves to minister.

Applicants who did not use the vocabulary of call tended to prefer the language of career, or of relationship, or of theology. As noted, however, 85 percent of the personal essays did rely on the vocabulary and concept of call in narrating the life experiences and worldview that brought applicants to the threshold of an M.Div. program.

The Meaning of Call

What does call mean? What do people mean when they speak of hearing a call? The personal statements I studied suggest five areas of meaning, undergirded by the belief that a call to ministry means entering into a realm of mystery. These writers addressed the mystery of their choice of ministry in a number of ways. They fumbled for words to explain their call to ministry, both to others and even to themselves. They expressed surprise and delight that they were called to ministry. They acknowledged a call to ministry, but also an uncertainty about what exactly that meant. Often this uncertainty was accompanied by a conviction that God would continue to walk with them in this "holy process." For example, "God's sense of ideal [ministry] differs from my own. Therefore, I am open to what will come."

The first of the five areas of meaning expressed in the concept of call was the realization that this call included something beyond themselves and their own control of destiny. Sometimes this "other" was identified as God or divinity, or as the common good, or as the needs of the community. Some applicants insisted that they "did not seek" this calling. One person noted that "without any prompting from me, the call became more and more pronounced." Another wrote, "I would be lying if I said it was my idea." Some held that the call pursued them, in an image reflective of Francis Thompson's *Hound of Heaven.*

A second area of meaning of call embraced the belief that a life work comes from a place other than unchecked self-interest or mechanistic logic. Self-interest became service to others, contributing to the common good, making a better world, or building the City of God. One spoke of the call to ministry as making herself "available to something much larger than I thought—the unfolding of a whole new plan." Cold logic had little to do with the sense of call, which seemed to come from the heart or from intuition and which brought a deep sense of personal peace: "My heart had its reasons which reason did not know." The statements mentioned stirrings in the imagination and compelling visions. They identified the call with inner peace and feelings of rightness.

Third, applicants expressed their belief that following the call to religious ministry would break social conventions and conventional wisdom about career advancement and social status. Applicants were unable to ignore the call they felt to ministry, even though social convention holds that Roman Catholics do not do ministry and that women cannot have leadership roles in the church. For several women, embracing the call to leadership ministry came only after years of socially ingrained shame and embarrassment. Although prevailing social wisdom holds that people cannot make a living as a minister and that ministry confers low social status, for these writers listening to the call entailed "trusting a truth that doesn't make sense to the world or significant people in my life."

Fourth, the idea of call was used to articulate applicants' conviction that their life work was built on personal giftedness from creation and baptism. One writer, who served as a campus minister, wrote, "I began to realize that I had my own spark, my own gift of life which benefited the community." Another commented, "I was astonished to learn that I had something of meaning to share with the faith community." Here again the sense of call went against the grain of career wisdom ("do what you love and the money will follow"). Rather, it signaled integrity between the gift and the needs of the community, or, as Frederick Buechner put it: "The place God calls you is the place where your deep gladness and the world's deep hunger meet."[5]

Fifth, call was used to express a kind of divine sanction for applicants' sense of a life work. Many of the essays referred to the Spirit's work in their lives or to recurring signs from God or to guidance

---

5. Frederick Buechner, *Wishful Thinking: A Seeker's ABCs*, rev. and exp. ed. (San Francisco: Harper San Francisco, 1993), 119.

from God. This dimension of the concept of call contained an ambiguity. The meaning of call as divine legitimization can immunize the one who is called to criticism of others or even of the person him- or herself. But this divine affirmation is critical, especially for applicants who had no institutional or other external confirmation. Some applicants noted that their call helped them realize that they "didn't need ordination to be a priest" or to do ministry.[6] Others spoke of the M.Div. degree as a necessary credential in the absence of institutional rituals and confirmation for professional lay leaders.

The meanings attributed to call in these personal statements may suggest some helpful lenses through which educators can explore the sense of calling or vocation with both students and colleagues.[7] More immediately, these meanings provide a foundation from which to examine further what might be called the personal dimensions of call: first, the perceived relationship between God and a call; second, the perceived connection between self and a calling; and finally, a link between call and stages of personal development.

Relationship between God and Call

The applicants wrote readily about receiving a call from God. Sometimes this was experienced as an invitation to a direct encounter with God. For example, applicants spoke of God calling them by name in prayer, through illness, or in struggles. They wrote of a new experience or awareness of God's presence, of falling in love with God or of God calling them home to the practice of religion or to relational intimacy. For others the call to relationship with God was incarnated in the people and events of daily living: "I hear God's voice in those around me." For these respondents, then,

---

6. This statement occurs in the context of the priesthood of all believers.

7. These meanings are consistent with some of the traditional understandings of call, for example, entrance into mystery, beyond the self, and beyond self-interest. The use of call to express a break with social convention, giftedness for community, and divine legitimization extend more traditional notions of call as leaving the world, giftedness for personal salvation, and ecclesial confirmation in ordination.

God's call was an invitation to become beloved friends or trusted intimates.

Some were motivated to share this God relationship with others. One wrote that the "feeling of being loved had such an impact, I knew I wanted to share it with others." This "heartfelt understanding" of God's unconditional love has defined "my desire and purpose," namely, to "help others heal emotionally, spiritually, and physically through the Word that renews and transforms." "I was able to allow the Spirit to work through me and awaken new life in the people I serve." These persons encountered God and entered into a relationship with God that needed to be made public or expressed.

Through ministry the call could be given public expression. Typically, these persons experienced God's action and presence in their daily lives. Thus their life experiences, "touched by the finger of God," provided both preparation and confidence for ministry. These applicants understood their ministry as helping people connect life with faith to make meaning. These understandings may well challenge educators and readers to reflect on their own daily life experiences in light of their religious traditions, so as to recognize the hand of God in the lives of students and colleagues.

A number of essays spoke more specifically of a call from God to ministry as a call to do something specific: God called them to be a prophet, or to proclaim God's word, or to serve the people of God, or to heal those who are sick and broken. Some wrote of Christ "inviting me to make a difference." God led or directed some applicants to experiences through which they sensed a call to ministry. Others moved easily between the "will or plan of God" and the "call of God." At times God's plan seemed to be the call, while in other instances the call was to carry out God's will. These statements associating God with ministry suggest a transcendent dimension to call.

For several applicants, the call to ministry was an experience of joint collaboration with God. "God would not call us to do something we do not enjoy. Ministry is where I can best put my talents to use." "God embraced my plans and guided things to work out."

"I wanted God to tell me what to do, but I learned that God works through my choices." "I was listening for direction, yet I felt a responsibility to be an active participant in my own decisions." "The voice of the Lord called me to IPS for personal growth through working out my true calling in ministry." These perspectives demonstrate a healthy personal agency connected with the call to ministry that enabled applicants to understand themselves as partners with a God who delights in human joys and giftedness.

Relationship between Self and Call

More than one-quarter of the personal statements located a call to ministry as emerging from deep within themselves. They commonly experienced this call in and through their desires and longings, as well as in the movements in their lives and spirits. For example, they spoke of a hunger for prayer, a desire to serve, a longing for community, a yearning for peace, or the movement toward justice. Some spoke of a sense of obligation to live out their baptismal covenant, or of a responsibility to lead faith-sharing groups, or of a need to take over the RCIA (Rite of Christian Initiation of Adults) program. Many experienced such yearnings as the Spirit urging them to action. Educators and readers may well foster a heightened awareness of a calling by paying attention to and trusting in these desires and longings.

Others recognized the call in their deepest center or core. They noted, "at my deepest inner being, it was what I wanted to do." "I have come to a peaceful place inside that's gently moved me to embracing my vocation." A calling is "something felt in the deepest part of one's heart and soul. Once I felt the call to ministry in my life, I could no longer deny it." "It felt right deep within." One person described this depth within as "a place that wanted connection with the divine." Practices of meditation, centering, and silence may well provide a space for awareness of a personal center which can be home to a call.

Call and Stages of Personal Development

The final dimension of personal call looks at three patterns that emerge from the statements concerning the call to ministry and stages of personal development. For some, the call to ministry was a shock that invited an about-face and an abandonment of previously held values and beliefs. For others, the call to ministry had roots in childhood faith, but detours, losses, or disillusionment deferred the dream, which then returned later in adulthood. For the final group, the call to ministry was present from the earliest days or was experienced as simply the next step in a consistent and continuously evolving life journey.

For a small number, the call to ministry was a radical, discontinuous conversion from previous life and meaning. "God broke through into my life via a powerful way and I was aware of being called to some kind of service in the church." One applicant described the experience as a "loss of all familiar references" and the "loss of the old self to another way of life" through a "sudden, inexplicable, intangible understanding that the call was just and right." This pattern may be described as a reshaping of the self.

A larger number of applicants described childhood closeness with God, which changed during adolescence and young adulthood. The shift was occasioned by the press of social activities, pressures of relationships and career, or crises: death, chronic illness, divorce, or depression. At times, growth into adolescence or young adulthood occasioned disillusionment with church teachings and rituals as well as suppression of the call and faith of childhood.[8] Sooner or later, for this group, the call resurfaced. Some set out on a deliberate and intentional quest through multiple religious traditions and thinkers to discern the "God of their youth." Others seem to have fallen back into faith and relationship with God as quietly as they fell out. According to the personal statements, virtually all of

---

8. For at least one individual, the perceived call to ordained ministry in childhood was suppressed because family and friends scorned it.

the applicants encountered a God who called them into ministry at this mature point of their lives. This pattern may be described as remembering the self.

For the vast majority of applicants (80 percent), the call to ministry was a step along the way. These persons use the language of journey, of continuous conversion, ongoing process, a call within a call, and God's abiding action in their lives. "Continually, my experiences prepare me for the next experience." "God called me, even when I was young, and now in increasing and more tangible ways." Ministry is "what I had been growing toward all along." "Personal and spiritual growth led me to feel the confidence to follow my desire to do ministry." These journeys had roadblocks and potholes that led to deepening and transformation. The continuing process had "surprising encounters and unexpected questions" that opened up new paths and "roads less traveled." One statement insisted that the path to ministry was continuous but ever new because "God is always about something new." For a few, the transformation was not transition into ministry but consisted in giving the name "ministry" to their life work. This pattern might be called the progressive fulfillment of the self.

These three differing life patterns detected in the personal statements remind the reader and educator that "a calling" has its own dynamic and rhythm. A "call-friendly" environment must leave room for the personal rhythms of life. At this point, attention shifts from personal and interior dimensions of call to exterior dimensions—namely, local faith communities, circumstances or events that mediated the call, and, finally, the particular ministries to which these persons are called.

Local Communities and Call

The local faith community of the applicants played a significant role with regard to the call to ministry. The tradition and ritual surrounding ordination stresses that the call to ordained leadership comes from the community. This community dimension is also reflected in the statements of the applicants to the M.Div. program at Loyola. The roles attributed to the community are both rich and diverse. Some applicants understood a personal call as participation in a call issued to a larger group, such as a movement, the church, or the Reign of God. In the words of one, "My yearning for ministry fits into a bigger picture of a growing involvement of lay leaders in the renewal facing the church." For this writer, the church was called to ongoing renewal or conversion and her call to lay leadership was part of that call to renewal.

Other statements expressed an understanding of ministry as participation in establishing the Reign of God. Some wrote of "co-creation of the reign," of sharing in "Jesus' mission, namely to build up a just, peaceful and loving world," or of the "construction of the kingdom." Additional statements recognized that the realization of the Kingdom of God is the mission of the Church. For them, the personal call to form a community or create a just world is participation in the Church's call to bring forth the Kingdom. A living and practiced kingdom-directed ecclesiology prepares the way for students and colleagues to understand call as participation in the mission of Jesus the Christ.[9]

Some understand a personal call explicitly as participation in the Church's call as linked to the mission of Jesus. The Church is called to carry out the mission of Jesus; the minister's call to evangelize is a dimension of this mission of Jesus. The Church is called to complete the project of Jesus; thus, a minister's call to the healing ministries is a participation in the healing project of Jesus.

Local communities also issued a call to ministry by inviting specific individuals to paid or volunteer work in the local church. Being invited to minister in religious education, visitation of the sick, liturgical ministries, or faith formation came to be interpreted as a

9. James and Evelyn Whitehead, in *Christian Life Patterns: The Psychological Challenges and Religious Invitations of Adult Life* (New York: Crossroad, 1992), chap. 5, speak of the context of the Christian's dream as the Church's dream of the City of God. Individuals join their dreams to the collective dream; this is a moment of challenge and tension.

call to ministry. Some spoke of doing this service for the local community for years before they realized that what they were doing was ministry. This realization then served as an impetus, which moved them into formal educational programs.

The explicit personal call issued to a person, and the actual personal experience of ministry, both seem to provide a tangible invitation. Rituals of commissioning or authorization, however, were not mentioned as experiences of call or even as confirmation of the call to local church ministries. Perhaps such rituals did not take place in local churches and applicants had no opportunity to experience or witness such confirmations of ministry. This seems unfortunate in a sacramental church, whether the absence comes from neglect, fear of clericalizing ministries, or the deliberate decision not to highlight lay ministries. Thus a concrete, specific invitation extended to an individual can be understood as the locus of a calling. Perhaps the extension of invitations to take up a specific life work by educators and readers would contribute to an awareness of vocation in the world.

For others the call to ministry emerged from broad-based participation and involvement in parish life—for example, attending adult education classes or daily Mass, helping out with fund-raisers or parish events, or taking part in faith-sharing groups, marriage encounters, or sacramental preparation classes. These activities stirred up a hunger for more knowledge and formation in faith traditions as well as the willingness to share this knowledge and formation with others. More fundamentally, engagement in the life of the local church seemed to develop a sense of belonging and identity and a concomitant desire to contribute. Since awareness of self-identity and giftedness promotes a sense of calling, local communities—whether churches or other institutions—are opportune places to nurture hospitality and ministerial talents.[10]

---

10. Adair Lummis and Allison Stokes, "Catholic Feminist Spirituality and Social Justice Action," *Research in the Social Scientific Study of Religion* 9 (1994): 103–38, surveyed 3,746 women in the early 1990s. They concluded that "multiple group memberships and spending time in community outreach to the needy appear to facilitate and increase social activism" (103).

Some spoke of the support for an initial ministry from their parish community: "My parish supported me in the development of youth ministry." Support and encouragement to think about ministry as a life work also came from small groups to which they belonged. A ready word of thanks or affirmation for persons in service from educators and readers may well advance the sense of calling.

Some found a call to respond in the needs of the local church. One spoke about the need to deepen faith in adult members. When she talked to the pastor about the need, he suggested that she take steps to provide for adult faith formation in the parish. She did, and 150 adults joined faith-sharing groups that fall. Others named the needs of a Christian bookstore or homeless shelter, spiritual needs, and justice outreach. In the recognition of these needs in the local church, these applicants to the M.Div. program seemed to learn the wisdom of a story from the early desert writings. A pious believer prayed for a vision of all the suffering in the world. Upon being shown its extent, she cried out: "Oh God, how can you let all this suffering continue without doing anything?" God responded, "But I am doing something. I created you." For these persons, the experience of local need became the call to minister. When educators and readers identify local needs, students and colleagues may well experience a call to respond.

Finally, by virtue of their links to a larger religious tradition, local church communities provide a vocabulary, narratives, practices, and a tradition within which individual persons can name and interpret their experience of a calling. "Vocation" and "call" have long been associated with women and men religious, as well as with the leadership ministry of deacons, priests, and bishops. This understanding of call has been extended to the ministry of the laity. In the applications to the M.Div. program, Vatican II teachings—i.e., universal call to holiness, participation of the laity, and marriage as a vocation—opened the way for lay men and women to understand ministry as a calling.[11] In the words of one: "Response to this renewed

11. At least five applicants linked baptism to their ministerial call and a similar number linked their marriage with their call to ministry.

truth [ministry of the laity and the baptismal call] has created the opportunity and the challenge to seek appropriate training and education in order to become a credentialed and effective minister."

The personal statements also drew on scriptural call narratives to describe their own calls to ministry. "I was Lazarus, whom Jesus was calling from the tomb." "I was on the road to Damascus. I still could not see, for I had scales over my eyes." "Like Samuel, I was called in the night as a child." "I want to say like Moses I don't know how to speak or like Jonah I want to run away." Others looked to the tradition of the saints and heroes who responded to a call (for example, Ignatius of Loyola and Dorothy Day) for a narrative through which to interpret their call.

Still others mentioned active ministers who modeled the practice of lay professional leadership ministry. Women ministers on the staff of a university Catholic center or a parish pastoral associate offered exposure to ministerial roles. One person told the story of announcing to her minister, "I want to do what you are doing." These ministers provided living proof that baptized believers could be called to ministry.

Some referred to the experience of liturgy, including proclamation of the Word, music, and ritual. The message of the gospel, as proclaimed or preached, gave them a story in which to locate their experience of call. Music and ritual provided a place of encounter with the God who called them. When educators and readers facilitate access to the stories, theology, practices, and rituals of a faith tradition, they are providing both the language for an experience of call and a validation for that call.

The Mediums of the Call

Against this backdrop, which examined call in connection with God, the self, and local communities, let me turn now to the more specific and concrete circumstances that evoked these applicants' call to ministry. Between forty and fifty personal statements explicitly linked personal gifts with the call to ministry. Although some references were quite general, gifts tended to be understood as God-given, "for the church," or "for the people." Some of the gifts emerged from previous life experience (for example, addiction recovery programs, business, musical training, or teaching). Some gifts were personal talents (for example, leadership, flexibility, creativity, or insight). Other gifts were learned skills (such as active listening, consensus decision making, shepherding, or public speaking). For some, the major gift needed in ministry was the ability to call forth the still dormant gifts of the community itself.

Two things stand out in the remarks on giftedness: an awareness of fit and a sense of stewardship. It seems, then, that the promotion of a sense of vocation must attend to the fit between personal gifts and life work. Furthermore, personal gifts are for others or for a better world or to build the City of God. Perhaps educators and readers must be more ready both to identify the giftedness of young people or students and to challenge students to use their gifts for the creation of a better world.

A significant number of applicants specifically mentioned role models who encouraged them to examine the call to ministry. In some cases the applicants had already felt the stirrings of a call, while others received the encouragement as a new invitation. "I would be told about this gift I had for ministry." The role models included other ministers, teachers, mentors, spiritual directors, religious superiors, parish members, family, and friends. Pastors were noticeably absent from the list, although one statement noted, "pastors ought to empower, mentor and call forth ministers." A few applicants did mention that their pastors offered them jobs in ministry, through which they discovered or confirmed their calling.

The experience of being a minister and doing ministry appeared to be as important as awareness of gifts needed in ministry and encouragement. The ministry could be volunteer or part-time, but in the words of one, ministry "opened my eyes, haunted and challenged me." According to another, ministry provided "life-giving energy." Applicants' ministry experiences included campus or university ministry, coordination of small faith-sharing groups, postcollegiate volunteer work, leadership of communion services, visiting the sick and aged, youth ministry, retreat work, teaching children, international missionary work, evangelization, working with underserved groups, and serving persons with AIDS. Experience of service as a young adult often mediates the calling to a life work.[12] This reality highlights the importance of immersion trips, volunteer work, and service learning opportunities in fostering a sense of vocation. Educators are invited to support and develop service learning courses or moderate community service projects through university clubs.

Dissatisfaction with the "way things were," both in church and world, was another significant dimension of the sense of calling: "I have a healthy dissatisfaction with several characteristics of the church." The role of baptized believers, decreasing numbers of clergy, exclusion of women from ministries, and the lack of attention to young people's issues were most often mentioned as sources of dissatisfaction with the church. Dissatisfaction with the world included the economy, the growing divide between rich and poor, homelessness, AIDS, racism, poverty, and inadequate medical care for the poor. At the same time, many of the applicants expressed the conviction that the church and believers were untapped sources for transformation.[13] Others specifically mentioned anger as a tool that could empower persons for change.[14] Perhaps educators and readers need to befriend and channel anger at injustice into a passion for a life's calling.

A vision of what the world or the church could be was another recurring factor. Inclusion, equality, justice, peace, and community were typical elements of this vision. Some felt empowered for a par-

---

12. Laurent A. Parks Daloz et al., *Common Fire: Leading Lives of Commitment in a Complex World* (Boston: Beacon Press, 1996), 53, outlines a list of common experiences shared by persons who live lives of commitment in our complex world. One of these is the experience of working with others for others as an adolescent.

13. This sense of outrage resembles the prophetic "crying out" described by Walter Brueggeman in *The Prophetic Imagination* (Philadelphia: Fortress Press, 1978), 19–23.

14. Daloz et al., *Common Fire*, 178–79, also addresses the transforming power of anger.

ticular ministry, such as working with young people, while for others the vision was only beginning to take shape. One spoke of ministry as her way to "fulfill a deep dream which possesses me." Perhaps this understanding of a dream as the source of a calling, even for a particular ministry, can help educators and readers both to revisit our own vision of a better world and to listen to the visions of our students.

The practice of reflective action was another crucial dimension of the awareness of being called. Some learned this practice through spiritual direction; some kept journals for years; others experienced a group process in reflecting on their volunteer experiences; and still others were innately gifted to ask deeper integrating questions. This discipline of reflective action gave birth to a call to ministry for some: "My passion for theological reflection led to the desire to be an effective minister." Others spoke of uncovering the links between their daily experiences and their beliefs. Educators are urged to promote the practice of reflective action through formation into critical thinking skills. Readers and educators are invited to foster the discipline of reflective action through connections between actions and personal identity or between experiences and meaning in literature or media.

Finally, courses in theology, religious studies, or ministry taken in high school, undergraduate, or graduate programs were repeatedly mentioned as places that stirred a call. For some it was a specific course in peace or in prayer, while for others it was the larger desire to learn. Time and again, course material fanned a desire to proclaim this good news to others. The passion and conviction with which educators and readers teach and learn also contributes to the development of vocation.

A Call to Ministry

The writers of the statements experienced a call specifically to ministry. As in any profession, ministry has definable characteristics, which distinguish it from other activities. In his landmark work on ministry, Thomas O'Meara highlights six characteristics of ministry. "Ministry is: (1) doing something; (2) for the advent of the kingdom; (3) in public; (4) on behalf of the Christian community; (5) which is a gift received in faith, baptism and ordination; and which is (6) an activity with its own limits and identity within a diversity of ministerial actions."[15] O'Meara further distinguishes between the universal baptismal call to ministry and professional ministry, which requires more preparation, anticipates longer commitment, and is considered more central to the life of the church.[16] O'Meara's characteristics and distinctions provide a lens through which to survey the ministries to which the M.Div. applicants expressed a call. About one-quarter of the statements talked about a call to inner life and growth, which included deepened spirituality and conversion as well as basic human maturity and wholeness. They spoke of a call to "follow Jesus," to "put on Christ," and "to be more than a dim reflection of the One who created and blessed me." They wrote of a call to "grow into a deeper relationship with myself," to "wholeness" and to "maturity and self-definition." Although these statements reflect calls to personal transformation and a deepening identity, they do not meet O'Meara's first characteristic, namely, "doing something."

About one-third of the statements reflect the universal baptismal call to ministry. For example, they spoke of the call to be "grace for one another, to be church as best as we can," and "to be with people when they need God's grace." They wrote of a call to ministries of healing and reconciling, that is, to move beyond themselves and "toward supporting the healing journeys of others" or "to respond actively to the suffering in the world." The statements described a call to love: "to help people know they are loved," "to shape patterns of love," and to become "a skilled and talented lover." These examples express ministries of walking with, healing, and loving that flow from the baptismal call to all disciples and Christian believers. In

15. Thomas O'Meara, *Theology of Ministry* (New York: Paulist Press, 1983), 136–42.
16. Ibid., 148.

addition, the specification of the baptismal covenant as a call to vowed life in marriage or in religious congregations appeared in about 20 percent of the statements. These statements reflect foundational baptismal ministry. As such, however, they do not reflect a call to professional ministry as described by O'Meara.

Virtually all of the statements, however, describe a call to ministry that does reflect O'Meara's understanding of "professional ministry." Obviously, many of the statements spoke of calls to personal and spiritual growth and to baptismal ministry, as well as professional ministry. Furthermore, these comments included both general calls to service and specific calls—for example, to hospital chaplaincy. Drawing on Christian Scripture and tradition, I have grouped the ministries under the headings of service, leadership, prophecy (justice), ministries of the word, community building, and ordained ministry.[17]

Nearly half of the statements referred to a call to serve others. This ministry was frequently located "in the church," or sometimes in specific church communities, such as a Hispanic community or a rural parish. Other applicants desired to serve as a "resource in other's faith journey." Applicants also sought to serve by bringing people closer to God, facilitating spiritual growth, or helping people flourish. The sense of service in the statements reflected the characteristics of public activity for Christian communities.

A significant number of the statements named a specific call to leadership ministry, which was named as public leadership, parish administration, leading a parish or faith community, taking up a leadership role, and sharing leadership gifts with the church. One applicant sought to "influence the effectiveness of the institution's mission and values." Frequently, part of this ministry of leadership entailed calling other persons to their baptismal ministry. These ministers sought to call other people to discipleship, to develop

17. See ibid., 82–83. The early and later letters preserved in the Christian Scriptures record the ministries of service *(diakonia)*, apostles (evangelists), prophets, teachers, and administrators. Terms for these administrative functions included overseers *(episcopos)* or elders *(presbyteros)*.

their giftedness, to realize their potential as God's people, to recognize their greatness as God's children, to leadership, to an active life of faith, and to teach others to serve. The link of leadership and calling others is consistent with the recognition reported earlier, namely, that other persons had called these believers to consider ministry. The overall sense of a call to leadership included the characteristics of identifiable public activity for the community, as well as a sense of gift from creation and experience.

Fewer statements referred to justice ministries within church and society. They wrote about a call to renew or work actively within the church for change. They also noted a call to challenge prevailing culture, to work for justice, and to resolve injustice nonviolently. They sought to be a catalyst for change or a countercultural witness. Although the applicants did not explicitly say so, the professional lay ministry they sought was to change the church. These ministries of justice seem to be more obviously directed to the advent of the kingdom, but O'Meara's characteristics of a circumscribed public activity on behalf of a Christian community are also present.

A similar number mentioned ministries of the word—including teaching, preaching, and proclaiming the word of God. A smaller number expressed a call to build up both local faith communities and society. One person spoke of the Spirit as the One who called the community together; she felt called to build up the community. Others spoke of a call to build bridges and live in solidarity with persons who experienced discrimination or lived on the fringes of society. These ministries of Word and community are identifiable public activities for the Christian community.

These ministries reflect the broad strokes of recurring ministries in Scripture and church practice throughout the ages. Nearly half of the personal statements also mentioned specific ministry positions and areas. Both men and women expressed their call to ordained ministry, whether as deacon or priest. In the words of one woman: "I am called to be an ordained Roman Catholic priest, to ordination from the community as an equal opportunity empowerer."

Other specific ministry positions included hospital chaplain, spiritual director, parish life coordinator, parish minister, pastor, youth minister, campus minister, and pastoral counselor. Specific groups of persons to whom the applicants experienced a call to minister included women, survivors of abuse, persons with AIDS, Hispanic people, rural parishes, the homeless, elderly, sick, or imprisoned. Still others spoke of calls to financial, ecumenical, nursing, and writing ministries.

Taken together, these statements do reflect the six characteristics of professional ministry noted by O'Meara. Explicit awareness of ministry as leading to "the advent of the kingdom" and "on behalf of the Christian community" was infrequently expressed.[18] The applicants, however, were quite articulate about their understanding of ministry as service to others rather than to self. Although a few wrote of ministry as presence, most statements understood ministry as doing something that has a public dimension. The personal statements readily described ministry as linked to gifts, talents, and abilities received in baptism and creation. Volunteer and paid opportunities gave these applicants some sense of ministry as an identifiable and circumscribed activity. Still, the professional ministry for which they were preparing was not always distinguished from baptismal ministry or a deepening Christian identity. These distinctions are also part of ongoing discussion and reflection in the theological and hierarchical communities of the Roman Catholic Church.

Although the statements focused on the ministries to which the applicants experienced a call, they occasionally contained glimpses of what the applicants were leaving behind. Careers in business, teaching, coaching, social work, and former career goals were mentioned. More often, personal and socially approved attitudes, roles, and beliefs were noted as what had to be left behind in order to re-

---

18. A discussion of the social, ecclesial context that diminishes awareness of these characteristics is beyond the scope of this essay. As a beginning hypothesis, I would suggest that (1) a practiced ecclesiology that understands the institutional church as an end rather than in service of the Reign of God, and (2) the diminished role for women in the church both contribute to a weakened sense of ministry as hastening the end times and as representative of the Christian community, when the authors are predominately lay and women.

spond to the call to ministry. The statements indicated the need to leave behind the expectations of other people, an inadequate self-concept, and an old self. One statement spoke of leaving behind her self-understanding as a "task-driven, achievement-oriented bright girl." Applicants also spoke of letting go of such worldly goals as prestige. A couple of applicants mentioned leaving behind familiar places, worldviews, and certainty about their futures. Men and women spoke of leaving a religious congregation or the dream of or-dination to the Roman Catholic priesthood. As the majority of ap-plicants were women, the emphasis was usually on the roles, atti-tudes, and beliefs—rather than the lucrative careers—that were being left behind.

The calling to a life work involves doing something for others on the basis of God-given gifts. A vocation usually entails a public and a leadership dimension. The exploration of these dimensions with students or colleagues can be a helpful means of discernment. Not all students considering a vocation are interested in a calling with these characteristics. Some may be neither drawn nor suited to posi-tions of leadership or public life. Others may have to struggle to find a fit between their gifts and an appropriate calling. For these reasons, it is important to think closely about identifying whether one feels genuinely called, and if so, to what particular vocation.

What's an Educator to Do?

How can educators and readers learn from the M.Div. applica-tions to create an environment that fosters an understanding of a life work as a calling? Let me suggest four ways to contribute to such an environment, with the understanding that one or another may fit more authentically with the life work of various readers.

First, as educators, we are invited and challenged to facilitate ac-cess for students and colleagues to the stories of people who under-stand their life work as a vocation. This can include the stories from the Christian tradition, or from others in a particular profession or recent alumni. This goal could be pursued through biographies or articles or narratives from religious writings that describe the call and individual responses to it. Panels or newsletters highlighting the life work of alumni offer contemporary understandings of living with and responding to call. Access to the narratives of others provides awareness, vocabulary, and encouragement for those who may feel themselves called.

Second, we are asked and challenged to recognize gifts and to invite students to consider a life work as a calling. Some gifts that may signal a calling to a life work include a sense of the dignity of the human person, leadership skills, willingness to engage in activities, altruism or service for the common good, and awareness of human needs. The recognition of such gifts urges educators to read between the lines, to listen in the pauses, and to notice student interactions. This focus on gifts may enable educators to invite a rich diversity of students to their life works.

Third, we are invited and challenged to support, encourage, and initiate possibilities for service in areas that address human needs or promote the common good. Volunteer opportunities, immersion experiences, and involvement in the larger community provide occasions for students to learn about a specific life work and to experience the fit between personal gifts and community needs. Required or optional service learning opportunities can be connected to a wide variety of courses in ways that enrich classroom work and student awareness of human needs and the common good.

Finally, we are invited and challenged to foster and provide tools for reflection on experiences and activities. As educators, we have the opportunity to develop skills for critical and reflective thinking. In some settings, explicit space for silence may be appropriate. Attention to the longings and the outrage at injustice in students may provide an opening for discernment of a vocation.

After Words

We, the authors of this volume, did not want to bring our volume to a close without recording our collective state of mind about the subject of calling at the end of the project. Naturally, being faculty, we were not of one mind. But, by the same token, we did not find ourselves deeply divided. What follows is my own rendering of the conversation that took place after we had completed our individual contributions and had read and discussed one another's work.

This epilogue is meant to hint at the depth of the contributors to this volume and the breadth of their understandings. It should also convey our collective sense of the significance of the subject matter as we have come to understand it in the course of research and discussion with one another.

Eddie Breuer, our Jewish scholar, set the conversation in motion when he wondered whether our use of the term *calling* might be obscuring much more diversity than we realized. Might there even be a discontinuity between our various uses of the term? Although our essays represented three different faiths, as well as multiple religious traditions and historical periods of the Christian faith, the general consensus seemed to be that we have not equivocated in our use of the language of call. We did not take his question lightly, as the phrase "personal call" did not have much currency before the Renaissance. Breuer's essay, "Vocation and Call as Individual and

Communal Imperatives: Some Reflections on Judaism," is a good reminder of how collectivist anthropology had been when the idea of the call first surfaced, at least in Western civilization. Israel was called as a people to respond to the covenant Yahweh had extended to them. The personal calls to Abraham, Moses, the prophets, and others were given and heard in terms of the formation of a people's response to its call.

The conversation quickly gathered steam. What, in fact, had modernism and postmodernism done to the idea of call? Had the modern period privatized the concept, severing it from its connection with the past? Had the concept of calling been secularized; had it lost its connection with God? Had it become individualistic; could a notion so quaint as "the common good" as the purpose of personal calling be spoken of without irony? Had the whole concept of vocation been professionalized, its earlier meaning displaced by considerations of career that put the individual at the center of the universe? If the answer to any of these questions was yes, then we might indeed be guilty of linguistic equivocation, and there might well be disjunctions between the ways each of used the term "call."

But each of the essays in this volume seems to bear witness to the persistence, even today, of the early meaning of calling. We are all theologians, of course, and are paid to see something different from what our colleagues in the social sciences tend to see. I then floated the idea, elaborated in the introduction to this volume, that before "call" can have a meaningful content, it must be seen as a preconceptual notion. The notion of "call" as a notion is primary, even primal—that is, it is something we are all scripted with, something that orients our intentionality, so that by responding we can transcend the solipsism and subjectivity to which we are naturally prone. Human beings are called to go beyond themselves in order to understand, to be about what is of value, to be worthwhile. Camilla Burns's essay, "The Call of Creation," suggests this line of thinking.

Every human being is born into a particular generation and family and culture and community of memory with a particular history and language. These move the intender from notion to concept, to a particular understanding about what one's humanity is calling one to be and do. At some point, therefore, call takes on a specific content and specific conceptualizations of the possibilities embodied in one's circumstances. In other words, there is a universal anthropology to the idea of calling that goes along with being a conscious person. This movement from notion to concept explains the almost bewildering diversity there is in the idea of call, yet at the same time the universal character of the experience. Granted, the cultures of modernity may have made deep inroads into the ways we construe being called, but the dynamism has been there all along.

Another question we wrestled with was the difference between an understanding of calling that focuses on being or becoming a particular kind of person and one that focuses on being called to perform a particular task or role in society. If the second way of looking at calling is truer, does that mean that one's calling is one's work and that one loses one's vocation when one is no longer productive or can no longer perform a particular task or take on a particular role? As that didn't seem right to us, someone suggested that taking a long, evolutionary view of the subject might help. Ever since the big bang, there has been an ever increasing differentiation of the manifestations of God's creative power. This has been even truer of humans, whose differentiations from one another are more and more marked. But these differentiations occur not so much in the area of work as in the attitudes, intentions, virtues, and characters of each person. Each person is a potentially distinct manifestation of God's creative presence, empowered to unique activity but also to unique personhood. My essay, "The Three Conversions Embedded in Personal Calling," unpacks this idea. In general, we distrusted an understanding of calling that would suggest that "I am what I do."

Marcia Hermansen, our Islamist, raised a question that she had been mulling since we first began discussing our project, though she did not address it in her fine essay, "Islamic Concepts of Vocation." She raised her question in terms of the new-age word "bliss"; is it accurate to connect "following one's bliss" with pursuing one's vocation? Since a number of us in the room were versed in Ignatian discernment terminology, it was suggested that the possible meaning of bliss in this context could might be made clearer in light of the more classical notion of consolation. If bliss could be seen as akin to consolation, then Paul Harman's essay, "Vocation and the *Spiritual Exercises* of St. Ignatius of Loyola," could flesh out this connection. Someone else reminded us of the wonderful description of vocation ascribed to Frederick Beuchner—that one's vocation is found at the point where the world's deep hunger and the person's deep gladness meet. While bliss alone can seem pretty self-centered, bliss connected to meeting the world's deep need takes on a much richer meaning. We also acknowledged the paradoxical truth that only when one transcends oneself can one truly find self-fulfillment.

Connected to this theme is the contribution of Mary Elsbernd, the director of Loyola's Institute of Pastoral Services. In "Listening for a Life's Work: Contemporary Callings to Ministry," she studied student applications to the institute's M.Div. program. The students whose applications she read were all adults seeking degrees that would enable them to respond to what they take to be a call from God to serve their churches and society in some form. What is remarkable about these students is the amount of risk they are willing to take and the amount of money they are willing to spend in order to be faithful to lay ministries that churches often devalue in comparison with ordained ministry or vowed religious life.

We eventually got around to an even more difficult question. When obvious injustice is present in someone's purview and the person feels no "call" to deal with it, what are we to make of this seeming pusillanimity? I am not sure we answered the question, but I will relate some of the responses it received. We are all called to be responsible, but we are not called to be responsible to the same thing, or in the same way. Following one's call will invariably involve difficulty and hardship. To move always in the direction that makes one feel more comfortable will hardly win plaudits for the courage or generosity that are always necessary for following through with one's calling. Someone even raised the question of whether a person can lose a sense of one's vocation through a lack of certain virtues. Of course, we acknowledged the possibility that circumstances might prevent a person from intervening in an unjust situation. But we did not want to subscribe to an idea of a call that fails to face its more difficult aspects by being overly selective about what is entailed in following a call fully. It would surely be an abuse of the concept of calling to term something a calling that allowed one to neglect the work of God, which we all agreed includes doing justice to and by one another.

As he had done in his essay "Protestantism and the Vocation of Higher Education," Dan Williams continued to get us to look at the educational environment that fosters or jeopardizes personal vocations. He wondered about two kinds of educational reductionism, one of which operates on a bottom-line mentality that assigns value on the basis of what sells or what the students think will bring them high salaries. The other form of reductionism comes from a poverty of vision in educators themselves about what liberates a self to respond openly to the needs of others. In particular, he warned us that the educational culture in which we function—even at our own university—is able to forget the genius of the liberal arts in Western civilization, which sought to provide the conditions for the experience of self-transcendence in students that makes discerning and responding to call more likely.

Another important moment in our conversation came when someone wondered whether the fact that we are all theologians made our essays, and therefore our volume, unusable by those without religious faith. Do we consider nonbelievers incapable of being called? I and the members of the EVOKE project at Loyola have been sensitive to this issue and concerned that we exclude no one by how we understand vocation, knowing full well that many will excuse themselves because the concept of call implies a Caller. Not everyone has grown up in a faith environment, but we have all inherited some account of the good that we in turn have made our own—one way or another. The calling of nonreligious people is to be responsible to the good, as they have come to understand it.

But there was a tension among us about this virtual universalizing of the idea of calling. One person had serious misgivings about whether, in our sensitivity and determination to be ecumenical, we might be prostituting the very notion of call. By our throwing the net so wide that no one was left out, this person asked, might we dilute the idea of call so radically that it would end up being meaningless? A fair enough question. Let me recommend John Neafsey's piece on theology and psychology, "Psychological Dimensions of the Discernment of Vocation," which shows how personal distinctiveness is universal and how the idea of call can be interpreted in different ways yet still retain its fundamental character. Neafsey sees everyone as summoned beyond themselves toward a uniqueness, whether they sense this summons as divine in origin or as something archetypally embedded. In either case, personal fulfillment is contingent on a right reading of this summons.

Clearly, we all believed that calling is an analogous thing. Analogies have greater coherence and intelligibility if they have an analogate. Urban von Wahlde develops a creative way of seeing call in Christian terms in his essay on Jesus as a model of vocation in the Gospel of John. Because Jesus was called by God, he can be seen as the prime analogate for call, as Christians understand it. And Mark McIntosh's essay on vocation and discernment in Bunyan's *Pilgrim's Progress* spells out in very concrete ways a seventeenth-century understanding of the stages of a person's response as a pilgrimage.

None of us could deny that one of the ways we have come to understand our own callings is through the phenomenon of door slamming. A call is something that has both an interior and an exterior side. Some of our undergraduates, for example, feel called to be doctors, but the door slams for many of them when they get their undergraduate biology grades. In other words, a call needs the affirmation of the external authorities or institutions. Like it or not, there are gatekeepers who pass their verdicts on what individuals think they are meant to be or do in life. There was a general nodding of assent when one of us remarked that suffering is often the cauldron in which personal call is best tested and followed.

Finally, and naturally, as in nearly every academic discussion, there was a strain of postmodernism in our conversation. Here it entered the room when someone wondered about the connection between language and call. The questions were several. Does the language we imbibe from our culture generate the awareness of call, or does the experience of being called generate the language for our cultures? Can it be that the language of career has become so ubiquitous that call has lost any cultural currency? Both Camilla Burns and Dan Williams have important insights into these questions in their essays. Theological anthropology can give the impression of being dualistic, in this case by making call seem adventitious. Or it can be embedded in the human, conveying the idea that call is endemic to human experience, yet without denying a supernatural understanding of it. Most of us, I believe, took the latter view.

In general, participating in this project brought the idea of call, which usually hovers somewhere on the margins of our work as professors, much closer to the center of our attention. We hope that this will be one of the effects our volume has on readers.

Contributors

John C. Haughey, S.J.

John C. Haughey, S.J. has been a professor of Christian ethics at Loyola University Chicago's graduate program since 1991. He has also been an adjunct professor in Loyola's School of Law and its School of Social Work. Before coming to Loyola, Father Haughey was associate editor of *America;* pastor at St. Peter's Church in Charlotte, North Carolina; senior research fellow at the Woodstock Theological Center at Georgetown University; and visiting professor at the Weston School of Theology in Massachusetts and at Seton Hall University, New Jersey. He was a member of the Vatican Council on Christian Unity's dialogue with World Pentecostalism from 1985 to 1998; in 1999 he was appointed by that council to the dialogue with the World Evangelical Alliance. He has published numerous articles and ten books, most recently *Housing Heaven's Fire: The Challenge of Holiness* (Loyola University Press, 2003).

Edward Breuer

Edward Breuer is associate professor of Jewish Studies in the Department of Theology, Loyola University Chicago. His primary field of research is the eighteenth-century Jewish Enlightenment and nineteenth-century traditionalist responses to modernity. He is the author of *The Limits of Enlightenment*, a study of the Jewish Enlightenment and its interest in Scripture. He is also the author of a dozen articles and is currently translating the Hebrew writings of Moses Mendelssohn.

Camilla Burns

Camilla Burns is the Superior General of the Sisters of Notre Dame de Namur. She resides in Rome. She was formerly the director of the Institute of Pastoral Studies at Loyola University Chicago. She did her doctoral studies in Scripture at the Graduate Theological Union, Berkeley.

Mary Elsbernd

Mary Elsbernd, O.S.F., is the director of the Institute of Pastoral Studies, Loyola University Chicago, and an associate professor of pastoral studies and social ethics. She received her doctorate at the Katholieke Universiteit Leuven (Belgium) and has published in the area of Catholic social teachings, theology of peace, justice, and women's leadership ministry. Her most recent publication is *When Love Is Not Enough: A Theo-ethic of Justice* (2002).

Paul F. Harman, S.J.

Paul F. Harman, S.J., is a priest in the Society of Jesus (Jesuits). He holds degrees from Boston College, Weston Jesuit School of Theology (Cambridge, Mass.), and Columbia University. He has been a teacher, academic administrator, religious superior, and spiritual director. He has also had experience in directing men and women in the *Spiritual Exercises*.

Marcia Hermansen

Marcia Hermansen is professor of theology at Loyola University Chicago, where she teaches courses in Islamic Studies and World Religions. She received her Ph.D. from the University of Chicago in Arabic and Islamic Studies and is herself Muslim. Her book *The Conclusive Argument from God* was published in 1996. She has also contributed numerous academic articles in the fields of Islamic thought, Sufism, Islam and Muslims in South Asia, Muslims in America, and women in Islam.

Mark A. McIntosh

Rev. Mark McIntosh is an associate professor of theology at Loyola University Chicago and the author of *Mystical Theology: The Integrity of Spirituality and Theology* and two other volumes. An Episcopal priest, he currently serves as chaplain to the House of Bishops of the Episcopal Church of the United States.

John P. Neafsey

John P. Neafsey is a licensed clinical psychologist and a senior lecturer in the Department of Theology at Loyola University Chicago, where he teaches in the area of religion and psychology. He also teaches a course he developed on the theology and psychology of vocation and serves as a consultant on a variety of projects for Loyola's Project EVOKE. In his work as a psychologist, he has a private psychotherapy practice in Chicago and serves as a consultant for the Child Abuse Unit for Studies, Education & Services at Illinois Masonic Medical Center. He also volunteers as a therapist for the Marjorie Kovler Center for the Treatment of Survivors of Torture in Chicago.

Urban C. von Wahlde

Urban C. von Wahlde holds a Ph.D. in New Testament Studies from Marquette University. He is professor of New Testament at Loyola, where he also served as chair of the department from 1987 to 1993. He has written two books and more than thirty articles on various aspects of the Gospel and Letters of John. He is currently at work on a three-volume commentary on both the Gospel and the Letters.

D. H. Williams

Rev. D. H. Williams is professor of Patristic and Historical Theology in the Department of Religion at Baylor University. From 1994 to 2001 he was an associate professor in the Department of Theology, Loyola University Chicago. He has published four books and numerous articles, focused primarily on the thought and historiography of early Christianity and on the contemporary movement of Protestant reappropriation of the early Fathers. Williams is currently preparing the first English translation of Hilary of Poitiers's fourth-century commentary on the gospel of Matthew for *Fathers of the Church*. He also is a volume editor for *The Church's Bible* series (Eerdmans Publishing) and a general editor and contributor for a new series of monographs, *Evangelical Resourcement: Ancient Sources for the Church's Future* (Baker Academic Books).

Scriptural Index

General Index

AAUP (American Association of University Professors), 145, 145n, 153, 153n, 154, 155
abilities, 38, 80, 81, 107, 120, 217
ability, 37, 38, 39, 46, 47, 55n, 59, 99, 124, 132, 135, 184, 211
Abraham, 25, 42, 78, 221
absolute/absolutism, 147, 148, 149, 192
academia, 142, 149
academic: administrator, 228; articles, 229; atmosphere, 141; circles, xiii; context, 146; discussion, 225; freedom, 145, 153, 154, 154n, 155, 161; guilds, 152; ideals, 154; inquiry, 153; institutions, 151; interest, ix; life, 31, 150; opinion, 162; program, 199; pursuits, 38; research, 154, 155; respectability, 149; stature, 151; vocation, 159
academics, 160; liberal Protestant, 153
acceptance/accept, xiv, 17, 54, 65, 69, 80, 89, 98, 108, 110, 112, 115, 153, 170, 180n, 185, 197, 198, 199
Achtemeier, Elizabeth, 31
action(s), xi, 10, 12, 13, 30, 32, 64n, 66, 82, 84, 85, 85n, 86, 88n, 102, 180, 192, 204, 208n, 213, 214; God's action, 25, 106, 107, 108, 116, 193, 203, 206; Jesus'

action, 58, 61, 63, 68, 72; the Spirit's action, 19, 169
activity, 10, 30, 48, 80, 81, 82, 83, 85, 93, 95, 101, 109, 154, 205, 208, 213; divine, 27, 30, 35, 66, 136; public, 215, 216
Adam, 79, 117
administrator, x, 38, 92, 197, 199, 215n, 228
Advent/adventitious, 19, 57, 60, 214, 216, 217, 226
affect/affections/affective component of discernment, 107, 113, 113n, 138, 169, 170, 171, 173, 175, 179, 180, 193, 195
al-Ash'ari, 86, 90
al-Asna, 90n
al-Bukhari, 84n
al-Dawwani, 81n, 87
al-Din, 86n
Al-fada'il al-khuluqiyya fi-l islam, 94
al-Farabi, 87
al-Fatiha, 93
al-Ghazzali, 86, 86n, 87, 88, 88n, 90, 90n, 94n
Allah, 80, 81, 82n, 83, 84, 85, 86, 90, 92, 94
Al-Muhasibi, 82n, 84n, 84n,
al-Mustafa (Muhammad=the Elected One), 78

161, 162, 171, 172, 176, 208, 213, 214, 217

ideology, 4, 144, 148, 151, 152, 161n, 162

Ignatian, 4, 163–95, 222

Ignatius of Loyola, Saint, xii, xiv, 97–118, 163–95, 210, 223

illness, 170, 174n, 177, 202, 205

illusion, xiii, 107, 114, 119, 120, 121, 125–28, 146, 153

image/imagery, 13, 28, 35, 46, 59, 60, 82, 109, 120, 134, 146, 168, 185n, 200

image of God/ *imago Dei,* 24, 25, 28–29, 39, 172, 174n

imagine/imagination, 19, 31, 31n, 107, 114, 118, 122n, 123, 125, 128, 131, 169, 185n, 201, 212n

imbalance, 162. *See also* balance

imitate, 29, 74, 75, 99, 100

immanence, ix, 2, 4, 144, 152

imperatives, divine, 17, 41–52, 141, 142, 162, 221

inauthentic/inauthenticity, 3, 7, 121, 185, 188

Incarnation/ the Incarnate, 103, 110, 117, 156n, 158; incarnated, 203

inclination(s), 81, 167, 179, 181, 183, 186, 187, 194

individual(ism)/individualistic(ally), 19, 49, 142, 143, 150, 157, 159, 221

influence(d)/influential, 5, 19, 90, 95, 99, 122, 129, 153, 157, 164, 165n, 170, 171, 172n, 180, 181, 186, 194, 215

injustice, 170, 212, 216, 219, 223

inner critic, 188, 189, 189n, 190

insight, xii, xiii, 3, 8, 23, 24, 29n, 37, 40, 54, 55, 57, 88, 97, 100, 123, 165, 167, 168, 169, 171, 174n, 176, 177, 177, 184, 188, 211, 226

Institute of Pastoral Studies, ix, xiv, 196–219

institution(s)/institutional(ism), 17, 91, 92, 144, 156, 196, 202, 208, 215, 217n, 225

institution(s) of higher learning/education, xiii, 141–62

instruct/instruction, 39, 40, 56, 76, 90, 98, 124, 136, 147

integrity, 26, 154, 165, 195, 201, 229

integrate/integration, 91, 147, 171, 199, 213

intellect/intellectual, 46, 47, 94, 107, 113, 141–62

intellectual conversion, 1–23

intelligence, 3, 142, 165

intend, x, 4, 12, 19, 43, 45, 47, 51, 61n, 105, 107n, 110, 112, 146n, 161, 164, 176, 221

intention/intentionality, ix, 2, 55, 72, 78, 84–85, 85n, 101, 184, 193, 205, 221, 222

interior/interiority, x, 6, 102, 107n, 109, 114, 117, 133, 137, 206, 225; interior attitude/state of Jesus, 55, 56, 64

International Synod on the Laity (1987), 17

interpret(er)/interpretation, 1, 22, 24–40, 43, 46, 47, 48, 59, 71, 78n, 90, 93, 94, 121, 122, 123, 124, 126, 131, 136, 139, 140, 143, 149, 158, 164, 165, 170, 175, 193, 194, 207, 209, 210, 225

intimacy, 75, 76, 112, 202

intimate(ly)/intimates, 29, 30, 37, 50, 51, 67, 98, 104, 116, 143, 199, 203

intuit(ive)/intuition(s), 3, 23, 136, 195, 201

invite/invitation, x, 2, 5, 20, 25, 38, 40, 53, 54, 104, 105, 106, 111, 112, 113, 115, 126, 137, 166n, 167, 198, 202, 203, 205, 207, 207n, 208, 211, 212, 213, 218, 219

IPS. *See* Institute of Pastoral Studies

Iqbal, Muhammad, 94, 95n

Israel/ Israelite(s), 29, 33, 33n, 34, 37, 38, 42, 43, 49, 70, 221

Jerusalem, 9, 56, 68, 60, 99

Jesus, xii, 8, 12, 14, 25, 53–76, 97–118, 137, 144, 175, 175n, 179, 181, 207, 210, 215, 225, 228

Jew(s)/ Jewish, xii, 40n, 41–52, 56, 56n, 57, 62n, 65n, 66, 172, 220, 227, 228

Mary of Magdala, 199

Masters of Divinity/ M.Div., xiv, 196–219, 223

mature/maturation(al)/maturity, 7, 23, 40, 109, 138, 140, 165n, 181, 206, 214

meal (Last Supper), 56, 61

meaning(s), 1, 2, 3, 4–6, 15, 16, 23, 24, 25, 30, 35, 37, 39, 59, 66, 67, 80, 93, 95, 103, 116, 121, 123, 124, 125, 136, 137, 153, 156, 157, 162, 165, 166n, 170, 171, 174n, 175, 177, 180, 193, 194, 198, 200–2, 202n, 203, 205, 213, 221, 223

meaningfully/meaningfulness, 1, 2, 5, 7, 44, 77, 147, 161, 170, 221

Mecca, 82, 84

medieval (Judaism), 44, 46, 47, 48, 49

Medina, 95

meditation/meditate, 38, 101, 104, 105, 106, 109, 110, 111, 136n, 137, 204

mentor, 170, 211

mercy/merciful, 40, 79, 81, 113, 127, 137

Merton, Thomas, 102, 102n

message, 18, 29n, 61, 95, 156, 193, 194, 210

messengers, 79, 80, 83, 85

metaphor, 12, 31n, 82, 93, 122–23, 166

Metcalf, Barbara, 89, 89n

method/methodology, 22, 23, 90, 93, 101, 126n, 149, 154, 155, 162, 163, 164

Method in Theology (Lonergan), 1n, 23,

Methodist, 151, 152n

mind/minded, 1, 2, 14, 15, 19, 39, 46, 63, 102, 103, 107, 112, 113, 116, 122, 123, 124, 125, 133, 135, 137, 147n, 148n, 150, 153, 157, 160, 161, 168, 170, 178n, 179, 180, 183, 186, 187, 191, 220; in mind, 1, 20, 51, 52, 105, 168; mind of Christ, 111; mind of God, 191, 192

minister/ministerial, 10, 11, 15, 51, 142n, 196–219

ministry, 10, 11, 12, 14, 32, 43, 53–76, 158n, 166n, 196–219, 223, 228

miracle, 56, 58, 59n, 60, 66, 68, 70, 89, 181

mission/missionary, 8, 9, 18, 19, 54n, 64, 72, 148, 154, 207, 212, 215

modern, xiii, 30, 46, 48–52, 59, 74, 91n, 94, 124, 136, 144, 145, 146, 150, 151, 153, 153n, 155, 156, 164, 168, 177, 180, 183, 221; period, 81

modernism/modernity, 48–52, 95, 121, 146, 152, 157, 159, 221, 222, 228

money, 85, 154, 194, 201, 223

Montserrat, Benedictine Monastery at, 100

moral(ity), xi, 1, 2, 4, 5, 6, 7, 20, 22, 38, 47, 81, 82, 85, 89, 89n, 94, 95, 96, 106, 124, 141–62, 186, 187, 188, 189n; moralistic, 188

Moses, 25, 38, 42, 78, 84, 139, 210, 221, 228

motivate/motivation, 23, 30, 61, 71, 72, 113, 127, 132, 149, 185, 203

Muhammad (The Prophet), xii, 78, 78n, 79, 82, 83, 84, 93

Muir, John, 20

Mulla Sadra Shirazi, 87

Murray, John Courtney, 21

music, 31, 38, 164n, 167n, 175n, 210, 211

Muslim, xii, 77–96, 229

mystery/mysterious, xiv, 8, 62, 113, 122, 134, 136n, 158, 164, 166, 167, 172, 173, 190, 200, 202n

mystic/mystical(ly)/mysticism, xii, 46, 47, 48, 50, 78, 80, 84, 87, 89, 89n, 90, 90n, 91, 143, 144n, 229

myth/mythic/mythologize/mythologist, 27, 47, 121, 156n, 159, 195, 195n

Nasirean Ethics (al-Tusi), 87, 87n

Nasr, Seyyid Hossein, 91, 91n

National Endowment for the Humanities, 156

Native Americans, 20

meighbor, 2, 19, 37

Neoplatonic tradition, 77

New Testament, xii, 8, 11, 16, 25, 31n, 55n, 56n, 65n, 72, 73, 74, 77, 100, 156, 157, 174n, 177, 181, 189n, 230

Revisiting the Idea of Vocation: Theological Explorations was designed and composed in Garamond with Colmcille display type by Kachergis Book Design, Pittsboro, North Carolina; and printed on 60-pound Glatfelter Natural and bound by Edwards Brothers, Lillington, North Carolina.